IN SEARCH OF
P. D. OUSPENSKY

IN SEARCH OF
P. D. OUSPENSKY

The Genius in the
Shadow of Gurdjieff

GARY LACHMAN

Quest Books
Theosophical Publishing House
Wheaton, Illinois ♦ Chennai (Madras), India

Quest Books
The Theosophical Publishing House
P.O. Box 270
Wheaton, IL 60189-0270

www.questbooks.net

Cover design, book design, and typesetting by Madonna Gauding

Photo credit: Hulton Archive/Getty Images
Every effort has been made to secure permission to reproduce photographic images for this book. Additional copyright holders are invited to contact the publisher so that proper credit can be given in future editions.

Library of Congress Cataloging-in-Publication Data

Lachman, Gary.
In search of P. D. Ouspensky: the genius in the shadow of Gurdjieff / Gary Lachman. — 2nd ed.
    p. cm.
Includes bibliographical references and index.
ISBN-13: 978-0-8356-0848-0
ISBN-10: 0-8356-0848-4
1. Uspenskii, P. D. (Petr Dem'ianovich), 1878–1947. 2. Gurdjieff, Georges Ivanovitch, 1872–1949. 3. Fourth Way (Occultism)—History.
I. Title.
BP605.G94U755 2004
197—dc22

                                                            2003069026

First Quest Hardcover Edition 2004
Quest Hardcover ISBN-13: 978-0-8356-0840-4
Quest Hardcover ISBN-10: 0-8356-0840-9

5   4   3   2   1   *   06   07   08   09   10

Printed in the United States of America

To Donald, Lisa and Xander, compatriots in the Metafour.

They went the whole hog, including postage.

One repays a teacher badly if one remains only a pupil.

—Friedrich Nietzsche, "Of the Bestowing Virtue,"
Thus Spoke Zarathustra

The most dangerous follower is he whose defection would destroy the whole party: that is to say, the best follower.

—Friedrich Nietzsche, *Human, All Too Human*

CONTENTS

ACKNOWLEDGMENTS

Many people helped make this book possible. I would like to especially thank John Algeo for putting me in touch with Quest Books, and for his thoughtful comments and suggestions during his time as editor of Quest magazine. I would also like to thank the Yale University Library for providing a copy of their brochure *Remembering Pyotr Demianovich Ouspensky*. J. Walter Driscoll and Gregory M. Loy of the *Gurdjieff International Review* were of inestimable assistance, as was William Patrick Patterson, whose book, *Struggle of the Magicians*, gave me the initial idea for my own work and whose journal *Telos* makes an important contribution to Fourth Way studies. James Hamilton's sage conversation opened many new avenues of thought, as did my correspondence with James Moore, whose writings on Gurdjieff remain exemplary. Bettina Gracias, Pedro Vasquez, Roger Aznar, and John Harrison supplied much support and friendship during a difficult time while writing the book, as did my two sons, Max and Joshua. My very special thanks, however, go to the individual or individuals who, on a brilliant September day in 2002, saw fit to steal Max's pushchair while the two of us were enjoying our morning stroll. Foolishly, I had put my bag underneath Max's seat, and within it were all my notes for this book, and for another I was working on at the same time. Pushchair, bag, and notes were never seen again, but because of this, my familiarity with the material became doubly intimate.

THE SEEKER AND THE SLY MAN

I N 1915 A MAN of uncertain origin appeared in Moscow and gathered a core of devoted followers, students of his strange and unsettling system of esoteric doctrine and psychological development. In his mid-forties, with his shaved head, Mongol-like mustache, piercing eyes, and unnerving composure, he exuded an atmosphere of mystery, power, and knowledge, and those who had accepted him as their teacher followed his instructions without question. Eager to expand his operations, he placed an advertisement in a Moscow newspaper announcing an unusual ballet entitled "The Struggle of the Magicians." The advertisement attracted the attention of a brilliant writer, who was himself a student of the occult, as well as a theoretician of the higher dimensions of consciousness. Recently the writer had returned from an extended journey to the East, where he had unsuccessfully sought out traces of forgotten knowledge and lost wisdom, and his lectures on his travels attracted thousands, eager for a taste of worlds beyond. Approached by a student of the mysterious teacher, after much solicitation, the writer agreed to meet with the master. Yet the earnest seeker of wisdom was dismayed to find that the place of his encounter was not one he might have expected. For it was not in an incense-filled ashram of a holy guru, but in a cheap back-street café, frequented by prostitutes and petty thieves, that the writer P. D. Ouspensky first met the remarkable man G. I. Gurdjieff. Thus was set in motion the long, complex, and fascinating history of the esoteric teaching known as the Fourth Way.

Along with Madame Blavatsky, Rudolf Steiner, and Aleister Crowley, Georges Ivanovich Gurdjieff and Peter Demian Ouspensky were leading figures in the revival of occult and esoteric ideas in the early part of the twentieth century. Yet though steeped in occult wisdom, Gurdjieff brought to the study of esotericism a new and brutally austere doctrine. Human beings, he told his followers, are asleep, mere machines manipulated by the forces around them. Although they believe they are conscious and have free will, these are only illusions. Humanity's only chance of freeing itself from this bondage is to awaken, a difficult and dangerous task requiring much work and tremendous efforts.

To students familiar with talk of astral bodies, third eyes, and reincarnation, Gurdjieff's message was cold, sobering, and provocative. Yet it had a ring of precision and practicality missing from the usual occult fare. Gurdjieff told his students that for people of the modern age, the original three "ways," those of the fakir, the monk, and the yogi, were obsolete. What was needed was a new approach to raising consciousness, what Gurdjieff called the Fourth Way, and which its practitioners soon referred to as the Work.[1] From 1915 until his death in 1949, Gurdjieff devoted himself to the often unrewarding task of waking up his fellow human beings, attracting as students some of the most brilliant men and women of the time. His methods involved various exercises designed to awaken the physical, emotional, and mental life of his followers, which he claimed he had learned in secret monasteries in Central Asia. Physical labor, psychological drama, demanding dance movements, and radically new techniques of focusing the mind were employed to help Gurdjieff's pupils arrive at the grim realization that *they did not exist*—at least not in any real sense. It was only after reaching this troubling insight, he told them, that they could begin to grasp what it meant to be conscious. Often the most persuasive means of arriving at this conclusion was Gurdjieff himself, whose powerful presence and extraordinary powers acted as both stimuli and goal.

Yet the student of Gurdjieff's work, or even the interested reader, soon discovers that the path to consciousness is not straight. Along with the many strange ideas he or she encounters, like "self-remembering," "the Ray of Creation," "the law of octaves," and "super efforts," a reader interested in the Fourth Way soon becomes entangled in a web of Byzantine politics and esoteric psychodrama, centered around the turbulent relationship between Gurdjieff and his most famous pupil, Ouspensky. Most books on Gurdjieff paint him as an infallible superman, whose every action was planned and conscious, and depict Ouspensky as a weak intellectual, unable to grasp the true meaning of the master's teaching. But there is another way to look at the complex relationship between these two men. Ouspensky was no stranger to the realms of higher consciousness, and to the readers of his early books, it's clear he already knew a great deal before his fateful meeting with Gurdjieff. His introduction to Gurdjieff was without doubt the central experience of Ouspensky's life. Yet some, like myself, may wonder if his meeting with his master wasn't perhaps the worst thing that ever happened to him.

After only a brief encounter with it, a question comes to most students of the Fourth Way: why did Ouspensky, the seeker of knowledge, break with Gurdjieff, the man who knew? Did he, as many have inferred, steal Gurdjieff's ideas in order to set himself up as a teacher? Or did he try to save them from ruin at the hands of a once formidable master who had to all appearances gone mad? John Pentland, to whom, just before his death, Gurdjieff had given the responsibility of overseeing the work in America, summed up the situation in a concise and exhaustive remark: "The break between the two men, teacher and pupil, each of whom had received much from the other, has never been satisfactorily explained." Nevertheless, there has been considerable speculation. To some, the split between the two formed the central act in a modern mystery play, and initiated a spiritual current the fulfillment of which would coincide with the inauguration of a new age. To others Ouspensky was an opportunist and renegade, a mere philosopher who appropriated Gurdjieff's teaching and established himself as his rival. "All that Ouspensky had of value he got from Gurdjieff, and that only with his mind," one student remarked.[2] "Ouspensky is a professional philosopher who studied with Gurdjieff and has now set up a sort of rival school," said another.[3] Gurdjieff's own assessment is none the less damning. "Ouspensky very nice man to talk to and drink vodka with, but he is weak man."[4]

Far from being the final mystery in the history of the Fourth Way, the split between Ouspensky and Gurdjieff is rather the tip of the iceberg, the first of many troubling reflections to emerge from a fascinating Pandora's box. Why, for instance, did a successful writer like Ouspensky abandon his career to devote himself to teaching the ideas of a man he had repudiated? Why did Gurdjieff draw Ouspensky into his circle in the first place? Was it simply to use him to advance his own designs? What had happened to turn the brilliant philosopher against his enigmatic teacher? Gurdjieff's past was mysterious. Did he really spend the years before his arrival in Moscow traveling through Central Asia as a member of an esoteric brotherhood called the Seekers of Truth, as he had claimed? Or was he, as some have suggested, really a spy, working for the Tsar during the years of the Great Game? Why did Gurdjieff antagonize and alienate his best pupils, Ouspensky included? Was it a tactic in the difficult business of waking up? Or were there other reasons? Was Gurdjieff the superman many of his followers believed he was? Or did he have a dark side? In this book

I address some of these questions and attempt to throw some light on what remains a fascinating and perplexing riddle.

For me, it's a riddle I've been occupied with for many years. I've been fascinated with the story of Gurdjieff and Ouspensky ever since I first read Ouspensky's account of his time with Gurdjieff, *In Search of the Miraculous,* in the late 1970s. My first impression was that I had come into contact with a system of ideas unlike any I had encountered before; some years later this belief led to my becoming involved in the Gurdjieff work itself. Along with other students, for several years I followed the teaching set out in Ouspensky's writings, as well as in Gurdjieff's own books. I count that time well spent; yet, eventually I found myself moving away from the work to explore other ideas. But as the years went by I returned to Ouspensky's books—not his writing on Gurdjieff but his early works: *Tertium Organum, Strange Life of Ivan Osokin, A New Model of the Universe.* Here I found a stimulating and exhilarating mind that is oddly lacking in books like *The Fourth Way,* a collection of questions and answers gleaned from the hundreds of meetings Ouspensky held during his years in London as a teacher of Gurdjieff's ideas. I wondered what had happened between 1912, when his early book, *Tertium Organum,* was published in Russia, and his later years as a teacher of the work to make the difference? What had turned the young poetic Ouspensky into an often stern and demanding taskmaster?

Although several books have been written on Gurdjieff, few have focused on Ouspensky, and most of those that have are no longer in print. One exception is William Patrick Patterson's *Struggle of the Magicians.* Patterson's fascinating book focuses on why Ouspensky left Gurdjieff, and when I discovered it I was excited to see that someone had finally decided to tackle this mystery. Yet in reading Patterson's book, I found myself questioning his premises. For Patterson, Ouspensky failed to grasp the import of Gurdjieff's mission and, when it came to it, couldn't abandon his own independence, self-will, and egoism in order to devote himself entirely to Gurdjieff's work. Ouspensky was not alone in this; according to Patterson, A. R. Orage and J. G. Bennett—Gurdjieff's other two right-hand men—also failed the test. But as I read on, I found myself cheering for the wrong team. It's true that Gurdjieff's treatment of these three men, as well as that of his other followers, could be seen as a form of spiritual "tough love," presenting a kind of esoteric version of the need to "be cruel to be kind." Yet I came away from Patterson's book wondering if the many instances of Gurdjieff's harsh treatment, bullying, incessant demands, and domineering presence, as well as his often seemingly irrational behavior, were at all times necessary steps in fulfilling his aim. Like Ouspensky, I found myself separating the man from the teaching and asking questions like: How much of this behavior is a real teaching strategy, and how much is it simply Gurdjieff's personality? How much did his followers read into his actions? And how much did he need to control, dominate, and master other people?

In this book I try to complement Patterson's approach and have attempted to tell the story of Gurdjieff and Ouspensky from Ouspensky's perspective. Many books have been written about Gurdjieff's ideas, and I have explicated his teaching where it seemed helpful, but for the most part I've tried to stick to the story. An interested reader could do no better than to go to Ouspensky's own account, *In Search of the Miraculous*, for a lucid presentation of Gurdjieff's system, unrivaled for clarity, eloquence, and rigor. He or she may also find, as I have, that beneath the crystalline surface there lies another, more elusive account and that the book is indeed a work of Ouspensky's and not, as many have claimed, merely a parroting of Gurdjieff. Ouspensky was a scrupulous writer, almost to his detriment; he was never happy with his account of his years with Gurdjieff and refused to let the book be published. It did not see printer's ink until after his death. Yet for all Ouspensky's efforts at objectivity, the book remains a highly personal work. Between the lines one can detect a forceful personality, as original and powerful as that of the character he so painstakingly portrays. It is also, like all of his work, a testament to Ouspensky's sheer skill as a writer; few who have written on esoteric ideas are as persuasive and captivating as he.

Gurdjieff's ideas, radical and unsettling as they are, are not as unique as many of his followers have claimed. To explore how they tally up next to the work of Rudolf Steiner or C. G. Jung would be fascinating but would take me too far away from my aim. (In a note further on I do, however, offer some comparisons between some of Gurdjieff's key ideas and some of Jung's.) But what strikes me is how some of Ouspensky's own ideas, arrived at independently before he met Gurdjieff, are similar to those he would receive from his master. Little has been written about the work Ouspensky did in the years prior to hitching his star to Gurdjieff's wagon, and in the opening chapters I go into some detail about his ideas on time, dreams, higher space, and mystical experience. That Ouspensky's ideas were instrumental in providing a theoretical framework for early Russian modernism is still too little known. The thousands of new readers who come to his books each year know little about Ouspensky's influence on the avant-garde movements of the early twentieth century, or about his importance for writers like Aldous Huxley, J. B. Priestley, and Malcolm Lowry.

But for the most part, this is a story of two men. It's a commonplace that opposites attract, and in Gurdjieff and Ouspensky's case, this seems obvious. But they often also repel, and at some point in their association, the magnetic energies of these two men began to push them apart. From Moscow to New York, via Central Asia and the dervishes of

Constantinople, here is the story of the intense and highly symbolic struggle acted out between Ouspensky and the man from whom he was never able to completely separate himself. Gurdjieff and Ouspensky's story is, I believe, one of the great mystical adventure tales of our time, on a par with encounters like that between Don Juan and Carlos Casteneda, or, perhaps more appropriate, Mephistopheles and Faust.

CHAPTER ONE

CHILDHOOD OF THE MAGICIAN

I N OUSPENSKY'S FAMILY there was a tradition that the names "Peter" and "Demian" were passed on from father to son alternately, one generation to the next. The Peters were life-affirming optimists who enjoyed good food and drink, companionship, and the pleasures of art. The Demians were world-rejecting ascetics, pessimistic critics who viewed life as a deceptive trap. Readers of Hermann Hesse's novel *Narcissus and Goldmund* will recognize the polarity immediately.

Peter Demianovich Ouspensky—the last of his line—was saddled with both character traits, an inheritance perhaps at the root of his paradoxical personality. Ouspensky once remarked that he had the smells of the tavern in his blood, and in his later years he would often reminisce in late-night drinking sessions about his wild days in Moscow and St. Petersburg when he knew "everyone" and would hold court at the infamous Stray Dog Café. This same Ouspensky, however, never got over his feeling that life—our ordinary, everyday life—is a trap. *Byt* was the strange Russian word he used to describe this feeling of a "deeply rooted, petrified routine life." It was, in essence, to escape the deadening monotony of *byt* that he set off on his search for the miraculous, the strange inner and outer journeys that led him to Gurdjieff. A central part of Gurdjieff's work is the notion that anything of value must be gained through one's struggle with oneself, with the "yes and no" within. If this is the case, then fate seemed at work well before Ouspensky ever thought of his search. The Peter and Demian within him predisposed him to a lifelong "yes and no." If in the end it was Demian who won, it was not an easy struggle, nor a lightly held victory. Beneath the formidable exterior of the stern taskmaster of the work, the warm, friendly, and poetic Peter still lived, and when relaxed and in congenial company, he would make occasional and sometimes surprising appearances.

The source of this coincidence of opposites—the basic formula for the alchemical Great Work—can be found in Ouspensky's parents. His mother was a painter and was well-read in Russian and French literature; more than likely it was her influence that had the young Peter reading books like Lermontoff's *A Hero of Our Time* and Turgenev's *A Sportsman's Sketches* at the age of six. Later he would tell his more intimate pupils that Lermontoff was his favorite poet. His father, an official in the land survey office, was also a painter as well as a lover of music, a trait that apparently he did not pass on to his son. Another of his interests, however, would become a central symbol for his son's life work. Ouspensky's father was a good amateur mathematician whose special pastime was the fourth dimension, a topic that held widespread interest among mathematical professionals and hobbyists in the late nineteenth century. Although Ouspensky later wrote on higher mathematics and adopted the imperturbable demeanor of a demanding tutor, he was never a professional mathematician, despite the descriptions of him that still appear on the covers of his books. In fact, he never completed his university education and was, in effect, a dropout. He did, however, absorb his father's interest in the mysterious fourth dimension, which became for him a kind of metaphysical magic bag into and out of which emerged everything that the dreary, pedantic, and severely limited positivism of his youth rejected—that is, everything that was "miraculous." It is this combination of the artistic and the scientific, the poet and the mathematician, that gives Ouspensky's early writings their particular zest and attraction.

Peter Demianovich Ouspensky was born in Moscow on March 5, 1878. He later told his students that his earliest memories were of his maternal grandmother's house on Pimenovskaia Street and of the stories of old Moscow she would tell him and his sister. For someone for whom self-remembering became a nearly lifelong obsession, it shouldn't seem surprising that memory, the clear evocation of the past, was of central interest. Like his contemporary the French novelist Marcel Proust—his elder by only seven years—Ouspensky had an uncanny ability to recreate the past, to recapture "other times and places," in Colin Wilson's useful phrase. He claimed to remember himself at an early age, with clear recollections of events before the age of two. By the time he was three, he remembered events and his surroundings with a poignant vividness. He spoke of a trip down the Moscow River—the boats gliding down the water, the smell of tar, the hills covered in deep forests, an old monastery. The exhibition of 1882 and the coronation of Alexander III in 1883 stood out particularly, with their fireworks and celebrations. Years later, Ouspensky would tell his most important student, Maurice Nicoll, that he didn't have the same interests as other children, that the usual toys and games held no attraction for him. "At a very early stage," he said, "I saw what life was like." Ouspensky believed this was so because as a child he could still recall his past life, his last time around on the wheel of recurrence. Nicoll, who had been a more normal child, was a "young soul," still fresh to things, and so could not. Ouspensky believed he had already been around many times. "The study of recurrence must begin with the study of children's minds, and particularly before they begin to speak," he told his students. "If they could remember this time they could remember very interesting things."[1] Whether Ouspensky's vivid early recollections were the product of recurrence or of a peculiarly strong but normal memory is an open question, as is the notion that as a child he remembered his past life. What is clear is that remembering is something he would spend all of his life trying to do.

Although Ouspensky tells us that his family didn't belong to any particular class and that his grandmother's house was a meeting place for people from a variety of social strata, in the Russia of his youth the social world was strictly divided. Either one was part of the peasantry or one was a gentleman. Given its cultured background, Ouspensky's family belonged to the intelligentsia. They were decidedly not peasants. Young Peter grew up in a milieu of writers, artists, and poets. Ouspensky's grandfather was a painter, adding to the artistic influence of his parents, and although he died when Peter was only four, it's clear he had a powerful influence on the young boy. A portrait painter at first, Ouspensky's grandfather later worked for the church, which provided him with his own studio where he worked on his religious paintings. Church painting at that time was a special industry, a particular artistic guild with its own unique importance. Although the later Ouspensky showed little interest in religion—when the journalist Rom Landau asked if he believed in God, Ouspensky said, "I don't believe in anything"[2]—it would be surprising if seeing the images in his grandfather's work had no effect on the imaginative young boy. Along with art—and later, science—the atmosphere of the holy and sacred must have given the precocious child an early sense of the transcendent. He surely inherited a love of painting, and from an early age began to sketch, an interest that in later life would express itself in his fondness for old prints and for photography. This last interest shows Ouspensky in an unusual light, revealing a keen awareness of new developments in culture. Although his tastes ran to traditional modes he was also aware of the influence a burgeoning technology was having on the sensibilities of his day. His first novel,

Kinemadrama—later published as *Strange Life of Ivan Osokin* but written in 1905, when he was twenty-seven—was originally conceived as a film script. The man who sought out hidden knowledge and the ancient wisdom of the past was also very aware of how new developments in mass culture were affecting the consciousness of his time.

Along with his vivid childhood memories, Ouspensky relates some early experiences of what he later called the "miraculous," that "other world" of magic and mystery that attracted him his entire life. When his mother took him to school for the first time, she became lost in a long corridor and did not know which way to turn. Peter then told her the way, although it was the first time either of them had ever been in the building. He described a passage at the end of which were two steps, and a window through which they would see the headmaster's garden. There they would find the door to the headmaster's study. This turned out to be true. He also related an experience at an even younger age, when on an outing to a town outside Moscow, he remarked that it wasn't as he had remembered it from a previous visit, some years before. As with the school, he had never been to the place before. He later realized that in fact he hadn't visited the place, but had *dreamt* of being there. The notion that in dreams we sometimes have a vision of the future would become a central theme of another time-theorist with whom Ouspensky's name would later be linked, the aeronautical engineer J. W. Dunne. As we will see, in the 1920s and 30s, Dunne's ideas, like Ouspensky's, would influence some of the leading writers of the time.[3]

Ouspensky would soon become interested in dreams. "Possibly the most interesting first impressions of my life came from the world of dreams" he would later write. But unlike Dunne, he didn't relate his dreaming mind to his precognitive experiences. For him, the feeling of déjà vu was linked with the idea of "eternal recurrence," the strange belief, which he later found in the philosopher Nietzsche and other writers, that we live our lives in exactly the same way, over and over again in an endless series of repetitions. It was an experience he seems to have shared with his sister, with whom he was exceptionally close. He tells how they used to sit at their nursery window and predict how people passing in the street below would act. Their predictions were usually accurate. But they would never mention this to the adults, who would simply not believe them. Ouspensky believed that in their early years, children were much more open to the miraculous, and it is only when they begin to imitate the adults around them that they lose touch with it. Ouspensky clearly belonged to that small group of human beings who are determined not to lose this sensitivity, and for him it emerged as a haunting, almost painful sense of the mystery of time.

But the forces working against him were considerable. Another pastime brother and sister shared was enjoying a strange little children's book called *Obvious Absurdities,* which showed odd pictures, like a man carrying a house on his back, or a cart with square wheels. To the prescient young children the oddest thing was that the pictures didn't seem absurd at all. "I could not understand what was absurd in them," Ouspensky wrote. "They looked exactly like ordinary things in life." As he got older Ouspensky became "more and more convinced that all life consisted of 'obvious absurdities.'" Later experience, he said, "only strengthened this conviction."[4]

By the time Ouspensky was eight, he had developed a passion for natural science. Everything to do with plant and animal life fascinated him. His appetite for knowledge met with little satisfaction in the humdrum schools he was forced to attend. Like many brilliant but easily bored children, Ouspensky found school dull. But while his fellows, equally bored yet not so brilliant, occupied themselves during their Latin lesson with forbidden novels by Dumas or other romantic authors, Ouspensky read a textbook on physics. While his classmates may have been daydreaming of some adventure story or indulging in fantasies about the girl next door, Ouspensky was "greedily and enthusiastically" overcome by "rapture" and "terror," awed by the mysteries that were opening around him. Reading a chapter on levers, he found that all around him "walls are crumbling, and horizons infinitely remote and incredibly beautiful stand revealed."[5] For the first time in his life, his world emerged out of chaos. Between the disparate phenomena of experience his young mind began to forge links, connecting, ordering, unifying, and presenting to his consciousness an "orderly and harmonious whole."[6]

This is the archetypal appeal of science—the tremendous impact, on a sensitive mind, of its own ability to make sense of its experience. It shows that fundamentally Ouspensky was not, as he is often called, a mystic, nor even an occultist. The impersonality of his later years had its roots in the philosopher's attraction to a truth and order *beyond* the personal, beyond the self—something, as Ivan Osokin recognizes at the end of Ouspensky's novel, that would exist even "if he were not there." Some people find their greatest happiness in *objective* things, things having no immediate relation to their personal lives. Ouspensky was one of these people, and his early encounter with the liberating vision of science was his first introduction to the vast world beyond himself, a world of meaning and order.

But no one, not even Ouspensky, is wholly impersonal. And a boy of ten, even one who has just had his first vision of the fascinating universe beyond himself, has a great deal of the personal to contend with. In Ouspensky's case, there was more than the usual amount of chaos, not only in the world, but in his own life.

Before Peter reached his fourth birthday, his father died. Not long after, while he was living with his grandmother on

Pimenovskaia Street, his grandfather died as well. In effect, Peter became the sole man of his family, and no doubt his mother placed high hopes on her precociously brilliant son. The loss of two strong and influential father figures may well have primed Ouspensky for later events.

In other circumstances, given his family's status in the intelligentsia, expectations for Peter's future career would have been high. But personal shock and disruption were not the only elements at play. The Holy Russia that Ouspensky was growing up in was a society heading for a crash.

Russia in the late nineteenth century, like its counterpart and soon-to-be opponent, the Austro-Hungarian Empire, was a powerful old giant, tottering under its own weight and entering a cycle of bad government and neglect that would lead to the Bolshevik Revolution of 1917. In the year Ouspensky was born, the cry for a constitution went up among the liberal intelligentsia. Other, more extreme groups, like the political secret society The People's Will, openly espoused terror and revolution as a means of toppling the three-hundred-year-old Romanov regime. Just before Ouspensky's third birthday, Tsar Alexander II was blown to bits by an anarchist's bomb. Alexander III, his successor, who ruled for thirteen years, tried to clamp down with a policy of repression and "zero tolerance," but after thirteen years he died, exhausted by the effort. Nicholas II, the last of the Tsars, whose name, with that of his wife, Alexandra, will forever be linked to the strange "holy sinner" Rasputin, was a kindly, ineffectual dreamer, absolutely unsuited to deal with the crisis. He tried to reach a compromise between his unrealistic belief in his own absolute rule and the people's clamor for a constitution. But his actions were too little too late, and the momentum of radical change could not be stopped.

It was against this backdrop that young Ouspensky began to question authority as well. Not political authority; he was still a boy and in any case he felt little solidarity with the revolutionary cliques that made up the youth culture of his time. (He would later speak of political gatherings where everyone just "talked and talked.") The authority Ouspensky railed against was that of the science he had only recently discovered. After his initial enthusiasm, he slowly came to see that the vision of "horizons infinitely remote and incredibly beautiful" that had so powerfully affected him had little to do with the plodding conservatism of the professional scientist. "There was a dead wall everywhere," he said, and he soon found himself banging his head against it. Scientists, he said, were killing science just as priests had killed religion. He became very "anarchistically inclined." Not that he took to throwing bombs: like most creative thinkers, Ouspensky had a deep trust and confidence in his own insights and was inclined to favor them over the official, received opinions. Mentally, morally, and emotionally he was coming of age in a time that encouraged this kind of independence.

He made a vow never to accept any academic honors. "I particularly distrusted all forms of academic science," he wrote, "and took a firm decision never to pass any examinations and never to take any degrees."[7] Given what we know of Ouspensky's school days, this smacks uncomfortably of sour grapes. From what we can gather from *Strange Life of Ivan Osokin*—which, although Ouspensky denied it, is clearly autobiographical—Ouspensky, for all his brilliance, was not a model student. At least one of his close friends would later argue that it was precisely Ouspensky's lack of rigorous academic training that made him susceptible to Gurdjieff. For Boris Mouravieff, who met Ouspensky in Constantinople in 1920, Ouspensky was not "protected internally by that precious armor which is the scientific method." This left him "open to exterior influences."[8] Perhaps. But Ouspensky himself seems not to have been troubled by leaving school. Soon after, he discovered the works of Nietzsche; later he enrolled as a "free listener" at Moscow University, supplementing his reading with a variety of lectures. First-time readers who come to Ouspensky's work expecting to find a mystic are surprised when they instead discover a philosophically demanding mind of the first order. What might also surprise them is that the formidable metaphysician of eternal recurrence and the fourth dimension was something of a juvenile delinquent.

Like other novels of the time, Ouspensky's early work can be read as a novel of education, depicting a boy's coming of age during his school years. Probably all of us at one time or another have said, "If only I could live my life again, I would certainly do things differently." Ivan Osokin, Ouspensky's alter ego, does just that.

It may be going too far to agree with Colin Wilson that the Ouspensky we find in *Strange Life of Ivan Osokin* is "basically an ineffectual dreamer and a weakling."[9] Then again, we should take with a grain of salt Ouspensky's remark that he was "never such a fool" as Osokin. The truth is probably somewhere between the two. An Ouspensky who was very anarchistically inclined would certainly be capable of the schoolboy pranks Osokin plays. Likewise, a bored but brilliant Ouspensky who read books on physics rather than preparing a tedious Latin lesson and whispered his discoveries to a classmate would be a likely target for disciplinary action. Other circumstantial evidence points to a close association between Ouspensky and Osokin. Both were students at the Second Moscow Gymnasium and both had a pedantic, oppressive teacher as a nemesis. Ouspensky later admitted that the girl Osokin has a tragic affair with, which leads him to thoughts of suicide, is based on a real person. Like Osokin, Ouspensky was expelled from school, and also like Osokin, his expulsion broke his mother's heart; she died two years later. Like Osokin, Ouspensky traveled, and Paris was a city he loved; in *The Harmonious Circle*,

James Webb speculates that the young Ouspensky may have attended some lectures at the Sorbonne. Both Ouspensky and his character Osokin spoke French well and knew French literature. In the novel Osokin considers immigrating to Australia; Ouspensky once thought of doing the same. If we add the fact that the names "Ivan Osokin" and "Peter Ouspensky" (or "P. D. Ouspensky") have the same syllabification, there is enough evidence, I think, to suggest that the "strange life" Ouspensky depicts in his early novel is not Ivan Osokin's alone.

On the face of it, that life isn't particularly strange at all. Osokin is a bright, intelligent teenager with a knack for being at the wrong place at the wrong time, a youth of promise who somehow never makes good. At the beginning of the novel, he is in his mid-twenties, crushed by the end of his affair with the beautiful Zinaida. Succumbing to despair, he loads his revolver and contemplates ending it all.[10] But instead of blowing his brains out, Ivan decides to visit a magician, one with a fine taste in brandy and cigars. (Even on the point of despair, life-loving Peter still seems to have his priorities in mind.) The magician's spacious room is "richly decorated in a half-Oriental way" with precious Persian, Bokhara, and Chinese carpets. On one table rests an hourglass. Ivan tells his tale of woe. "If only I could bring back a few years of this miserable time which does not even exist," he moans. "If only I could do things differently."[11] The magician assures him that this can be done. "Everything can be brought back." The hourglass can be turned over. But it will change nothing; he will only make the same mistakes. As the novel goes on, Ivan indeed revisits his earlier years, and we discover that this is not the first time he has had this conversation.

In Ouspensky's later thought on recurrence, he developed a very curious idea: the notion of reincarnation not into the future but into the past. A similar idea can be found in sci-fi films like *The Terminator*, where the killer android is sent into the past to prevent a future ruled by machines. The evil of the present, Ouspensky believed, could only be eradicated by going back into the past and destroying it at its root. If the source of evil remained, so would its effects, and a reincarnation that moved us into the future would not escape the consequences of the past.

This is a difficult idea to grasp. Reincarnating into the past with the intent of changing it could lead to a very different future—so different that we, who have come from the future, would not exist, and so could not alter the past . . . But putting such mind twisters aside, it tells us something about Ouspensky that an idea he first presented in 1905 still occupied him years later. Nearly a decade after writing *Strange Life of Ivan Osokin*, Ouspensky wrote that "We cannot leave behind us the sins of our past." "If the cause of the evil lies in the past, it is useless to look for it in the present. And a man must go back, seek for and destroy the causes of evil, however far back they may lie."[12] One of the last pieces of writing Ouspensky worked on before his death was the English translation of *Strange Life of Ivan Osokin*. Reports of his last days describe a weak, dying man returning to several sites from his past in order to imprint them on his consciousness so strongly that he would "remember" them *the next time*. It is clear, then, that from the beginning of his creative life until its end Ouspensky had a profound concern with the possibility of *changing the past*. "If we knew definitely what would be the result of our actions," Osokin asks the magician, "do you suppose we should do all that we do?"[13]

More than a decade later Ivan's creator would ask a real-life magician exactly the same question.

In his later years Ouspensky was known for his chivalrous manners toward women, a character trait lacking in the unromantic Gurdjieff. For one of his first female students he was known to make tea and to buy quantities of cream buns; another, later in Ouspensky's career, said that no one was ever kinder or respected her more as a person.[14] Ouspensky found women more interesting than men and believed they belonged to a "higher caste," an attitude again at odds with Gurdjieff's. Women, Ouspensky believed, have for the most part not participated in what he calls "the history of crime." "For thousands of years they have taken no active part in wars and have rarely had anything to do with politics or Government service. In this way they have avoided the most criminal and fraudulent sides of life."[15] Yet Ouspensky's views are anything but feminist. Women play an important role in the advance of life because to them is entrusted the responsibility of "selection"—not in a simple biological sense, but in matters of a higher order, in aesthetics and morals. The trouble, he tells us, is that women too often fail to discharge their duties properly. Because most women "content themselves with insignificant men," their chief sin is that they are not "sufficiently *exacting*."[16] Exacting about what? Not, to be sure, their own practical interests. If a woman demands things for herself, that is "merely vulgar," a form of selfishness that is already far too prevalent. What, then? "Woman," he tells us, "does not demand enough from a man for *his own sake*."[17]

Woman, in Ouspensky's view, is a kind of ideal, a poetic symbol, and it is her task to draw from man his highest purpose and most demanding efforts. She is, in Goethe's phrase, *Das Ewig-Weibliche/Zieht uns hinan,* the eternal feminine which draws us upwards. In our cool, cynical times, such sentiments seem absurdly old-fashioned; most women reject the pedestal and want to be seen as equal to men. But like many of our "unromantic" modern ideas, what this gains in social equity it loses on a wider, metaphysical level. As Ouspensky argues, the erotic and sexual experience is closely tied to the aesthetic and mystical. He makes the point with almost clinical exactness. "In a man (or woman) of strong feeling," he writes, "sex sensations

awaken certain new states of consciousness, new emotions . . .
Mystical sensations undoubtedly and incontestably have a taste
of sex . . . Of all ordinary human experiences only sex sensations approach those which we may call mystical . . . only in
love is there a taste of the mystical, a taste of ecstasy."[18] Far
from the simple satisfaction of a natural appetite, relations
between the sexes are, or at least can be, a kind of springboard
into what the psychologist Abraham Maslow called "the farther
reaches of human nature." The reason should be obvious. Like
the mystical and aesthetic experience, the erotic takes us out
of ourselves, dissolves the barriers of the ego, and opens our
being to a wider, impersonal world. The attraction between a
man and a woman can lead to a banal one-night stand; it can
also, as in the case of a Dante and a Beatrice, lead to a beatific
vision. In the erotic grip we become aware of the strange "difference" between men and women. This seems so banal it is
hardly worth saying, yet the very difference between the sexes
is something we often take for granted. It is this "difference"
that causes men to see in women some infinitely alluring
ideal.

Ivan Osokin has a taste of the mystical power of eroticism
when, after his expulsion from school and the death of his
mother, he goes to live with his uncle in the country and meets
the beautiful and apparently more experienced Tanechka. In
their first embrace "thousands of electric sparks run through
Osokin's body."[19] Soon after, Osokin rides to town on a
favorite horse. "The strong, resilient movement of the horse
under him, the warm wind smelling of flowering limes and the
sensation of Tanechka in his whole body carry Osokin away
from any thoughts."[20] "Tanechka is part of nature, like this
field, or the wood, or the river. I never imagined that the feeling of woman was so much like the feeling of nature."[21] Later,
when they are out picking mushrooms, Tanechka decides to
bathe in a stream. Osokin, the gentleman, retreats and sits

alone, smoking. Then he hears her calling him. When he reaches the banks, he sees her standing naked, knee-deep in the water. To Osokin it is "all like a dream. Wild pigeons are cooing in the distance. A large spider drops slowly down from a fir tree on a shining thread."[22] But something has changed between them. Their childlike, almost animal playfulness has become something else. Osokin feels "an enormous mystery in her" which "frightens and troubles him, and puts a magic ring around her over which he cannot step."[23] That night, when she sleeps with him, it is clear that she is the seducer. Whether such an experience happened to Ouspensky is unclear. But given the vividness of the writing, and Osokin's passionate response to their lovemaking, one is justified, I think, in assuming that it did.

Yet all the romance in *Strange Life of Ivan Osokin* is not simply a prelude to philosophy. Some of it is sheer adolescent fun. And many of Ouspensky's reflections on women seem less an appreciation of their superiority than a frank appraisal of their charms. At a casino while in military school, Osokin is attracted to a "strangely thoughtful-looking fair girl" whose square-cut black dress reveals the curve of her breasts. Her white arms display "small blue veins," and he is strongly aware of the "woman in her."[24] In Paris, he meets Valerie, "a tall blonde girl with hair the color of autumn leaves." He admires her feet in "trim Paris shoes with high heels" but is also attracted to her mind: she reads Pushkin and is studying the history of the Gothic cathedrals. But there he has also met Loulou, who is "absurdity incarnate." Loulou is "the most enchanting absurdity possible. One never knows what to expect from her." Sometimes Osokin wants "to whip her," but she is, after all, "a real woman." In large doses they get on each other's nerves, because Loulou is "too primitive to spend whole days with." Yet he is beginning to find his Paris life too settled, and so fate intervenes. During an evening at the roulette table Osokin loses all of his inheritance in less than hour. His smooth, easy-going life is painfully disrupted.[25]

And so it is with most of the novel. Time and again, Osokin/ Ouspensky finds himself at the junctures of his life when, if he had acted differently, the outcome would have been otherwise. Yet at each intersection of the past and the present he is unable to act differently, and it is only after the fact that he realizes he has yet again made the same mistake. Each time he regrets his foolishness and resolves to mend his ways, yet each time he fails to alter the past. He goes on, compelled to continue, even though ahead lies the future, the revolver, and the magician. "At the same time, in the mysterious tomorrow, something flickers, something beckons, something inevitable and alluring is felt."[26] Recurrence may be eternal, but so is the attraction of the unknown, and it is the latter, more than anything else, that draws the young poet on. Ouspensky may not have realized it as he wrote the story of Ivan Osokin, but as his own life unfolded, he would come to know that attraction quite well.

CHAPTER TWO

DREAMS OF HIDDEN KNOWLEDGE

ASIDE FROM WHAT we can glean from *Strange Life of Ivan Osokin,* we have very little information about what Ouspensky did between his expulsion from school and the year 1905, when he wrote his novel and began to work for several Moscow papers as a freelance journalist. If Ouspensky was expelled when he was sixteen, the time lapse is about ten years, a considerable period in anyone's life and certainly a crucial time in a young man's development. If his alter ego Osokin's exploits are anything to go by, during this time Ouspensky received some kind of inheritance and used it to travel. He went to Paris, where he may have attended classes. From what we can gather from his remarks to Rom Landau, he may have attended lectures in Moscow and St. Petersburg too. He also visited some remote areas of Russia, and years later he told Maurice Nicoll how he repaid the generosity of the Caucasian chieftains he visited. He would admire some small object of no value, which his host was then obliged to offer him; in return, Ouspensky would present his host with one of the cheap revolvers he kept on hand. He undoubtedly did a great deal of reading and also allowed the Peter side of his character plenty of leeway. Years later, in 1919, trapped in the bleak backwater of Rostov-on-Don by the Russian Civil War, Ouspensky met the journalist Carl Bechhofer-Roberts and, under the influence of some homemade vodka, regaled him with stories of his early days. "People have been drinking since the beginning of the world," Ouspensky announced solemnly. "But they have never found anything better to go with vodka than a salted cucumber." Unfortunately, on that occasion no cucumber could be found, and the vodka itself arrived courtesy of Ouspensky's ingenuity with a bottle of spirits and some orange peel.

Given such constrained circumstances, Bechhofer-Roberts' account is almost festive. Ouspensky related how, in the old days before the revolution, he was known by "everyone," especially the police, who called him by his Christian name and asked him to help break up fights; unlike many drinkers, under the influence Ouspensky never became rowdy but instead acted as a peacemaker. He was also familiar with the porters in all the restaurants and was known to be a big tipper. He also seems to have been involved in some peculiar situations; on one occasion, he arrived home and discovered he had somehow lost the left sleeve of his overcoat. "How I lost it, and where, I have never discovered," he explained, but the incident piqued his fancy, and he thought he would even write a book about it.[1] The idea would have appealed to the sensibility of the time.

In 1905 Ouspensky began a study of dreams, something he had been fascinated with since his childhood.[2] By 1900, at the age of twenty-two, he had already read all he could find about dreams in the psychological literature. By "psychological literature" Ouspensky doesn't mean Freud and Jung. Ouspensky would later have nothing but contempt for Freud, and would in fact tell an early student that Jung's ideas about complexes had done her much harm. But in 1900, Freud and Jung were unknown; Freud's first major work, *The Interpretation of Dreams*, was published that year, and Jung was just starting his professional life at the Burgholzli Clinic in Switzerland. The literature Ouspensky speaks of predates psychoanalysis and was less concerned with interpreting dreams than with understanding how they form. One of the writers Ouspensky read was L. F. Alfred Maury, who coined the term "hypnagogic" to describe the curious half-dream states we enter as we fall asleep. Ouspensky's observations on dreams, collected in his essay "On the Study of Dreams and on Hypnotism," is one of the earliest accounts of this strange "twilight" state of consciousness.[3]

Ouspensky's fascination with dreams began with what he calls a "fantastic idea" that first came to him in his childhood: *"Was it not possible to preserve consciousness in dreams."*[4] Could he know, while dreaming, that he was asleep yet think consciously, as he did while awake?

Since Ouspensky began his study nearly a century ago, the phenomenon of "lucid dreaming," as it was named by early twentieth-century dream investigator Fredrick Van Eeden, has received much attention. But in 1905 little was known about it, and the twenty-seven-year-old Ouspensky was clearly a pioneer. Oddly enough, another writer who would become involved with Gurdjieff, the French poet René Daumal, also began his fascination with other states of consciousness through an attempt to remain conscious while dreaming. Daumal also employed the more hazardous method of drugs, something, as we shall see further on, Ouspensky resorted to as well.[5]

Ouspensky was interested in discovering the mechanism of dream formation, and as is usually recommended, he began his study by writing down his dreams upon awakening. He soon discovered, however, that this method had its drawbacks. For one thing, it quickly became clear that his very attempts to remember his dreams altered them. Writing down his dreams *changed* them; the very attention he was paying them transformed his dreams, and created new ones. Ouspensky realized a different method was needed, and he developed the knack of retaining consciousness while falling asleep. At first he did this at night, but he soon discovered that, as might be expected, this interfered with his sleep. He then transferred his attention to the morning, staying in bed and drifting back into what he called "half-dream states." This in itself tells us something about Ouspensky's life at this period: the fact that he could stay in bed suggests that the young novelist had a good deal of free time on his hands.

In half-dream states Ouspensky "slept and did not sleep at the same time" and their first effect on him was astonishment and a feeling of extraordinary joy. But they also brought on a strange sense of fear and a concern that he might become lost in them. His half-dream states both attracted and frightened him, offering enormous possibilities but also great danger. Nevertheless, he became convinced that without his "half-dream states" no study of dreams was possible. He now possessed a "key to the world of dreams," and like his youthful experience with physics, this insight turned what had been "vague and incomprehensible" into the "comprehensible and visible."[6]

Ouspensky's initial concern eventually gave way to a clear understanding of how most dreams are formed. For readers familiar with his "search for the miraculous," Ouspensky's conclusions may be disappointing. Ouspensky rejected the idea that our everyday dreams tell us anything about our true selves, our destiny, or have any message at all. They are, he says, meaningless, "entirely accidental, entirely chaotic, unconnected with anything";[7] rather, he argues, most dreams are the product of our physical condition or physiological state. Since his childhood he had had a recurring dream of being caught in a bog. Try as he might to avoid it, in the dream he invariably found himself sinking into deep, seemingly bottomless mud. Although for years he felt that something important was being revealed in this dream, in his half-dream state Ouspensky discovered that in fact the bog was the dream representation of his feet getting caught in the blankets.

Similarly, a persistent dream of becoming blind turned out to be caused by his efforts to open his eyes while asleep. His hand getting caught beneath his knee produced a dream in which a dog was biting his hand. A recurring dream in which he found himself crippled was the result of the muscles of his legs becoming torpid.

If we are disappointed in Ouspensky's treatment of dreams, it may help to understand when exactly in his career he started investigating them. By his own account, in 1905 Ouspensky had not yet encountered Theosophy. He speaks of a time when he kept himself within artificial "scientific" bounds and, frightened by some experience—exactly what is unclear—had "fled to the bare and arid desert of 'materialism.'"[8] The Ouspensky who began his study of dreams lived, it seems, in a "desiccated and sterilized world, with an infinite number of taboos" imposed on his thought. His discovery of Theosophical and occult literature, however, "broke down all the walls" around him and opened him to a world of new possibilities.

Whatever we may think of Ouspensky's conclusions about dreams, his account of how he watched them form is fascinating. "I am falling asleep," he writes:

> Golden dots, sparks and tiny stars appear and disappear before my eyes. These sparks and stars gradually merge into a golden net with diagonal meshes which moves slowly and regularly in rhythm with the beating of my heart . . . The next moment the golden net is transformed into rows of brass helmets belonging to Roman soldiers marching along the street below. I hear their measured tread and watch them from the window of a high house in . . . Constantinople . . . I see the sun shining on their helmets. Then suddenly I detach myself from

the windowsill . . . and . . . fly slowly over the lane, over the houses, and then over the Golden Horn.[9]

Categorizing dreams was important for Ouspensky, and he ascribes this dream to his first category: dreams that depend on accidental associations.[10] The sensation of flying in dreams was a favorite of his, and accounts of it appear in his writing. The morning after his night with Tanechka, Ivan Osokin walks by a lake and exclaims, "How incredibly beautiful it all is." Some deep insight into life makes him want to fly over the lake "as I fly in my dreams." And in a later story, "The Benevolent Devil," Ouspensky describes a half-dream state in which his character is flying over an exotic landscape filled with strange temples and stone pagodas. Interestingly, the story also speaks of the difficulty Ouspensky must have experienced when he did not enter his half-dream state: "When sleep is impossible," he writes, "one is overcome by a feeling of disintegration and one's normal self is transformed into a tired, capricious, irritable and listless creature."[11] That Ouspensky enjoyed dreaming throughout his life is clear from his remark to Maurice Nicoll years later that his cat, Vashka, scratched him in the morning and interfered with his "waking dreams."

Although Ouspensky seems to debunk the notion that dreams are meaningful, he did believe that some dreams convey a deep and profound message. These, he argues, are much more rare than people believe. Like our waking experiences, dreams vary in significance and importance. To speak of dreams as if they were all the same is a mistake. He also shows a preference for dreams that must have had a powerful effect on him—dreams of stairs, for example. He speaks of "a certain mystical significance which stairs have in the life of every man."[12] Later, in his time as a teacher of the work, the notion of the staircase would return in a different and more practical form: in the idea that, for older students of "the system" to advance, they had to bring in new students to take their place.

Other aspects of Ouspensky's study of dreams relate to his experiences as a student and teacher of Gurdjieff's work. Clearly, his observation that "we have dreams continuously, *both in sleep and in a waking state,*" is identical with Gurdjieff's doctrine, as is his conclusion that "when we awake sleep does not disappear, but to the state of sleep *there is added* the waking state."[13] Likewise, the struggle to "stay awake" and to "remember"—already important for Ouspensky—is found in his later work. While becoming more and more fascinated with observing how his dreams form, Ouspensky realized that if he let himself go, he would "forget the most important thing that I have to remember, namely, *that I am asleep and am conscious of myself*"—in other words, that he is "in the state for which I have long wished and which I have been trying to attain."

But perhaps the strangest thing Ouspensky discovered in his investigations was a kind of "dream artist" who possessed creative talents that he, in waking life, could never display. This dream artist was a playwright, a producer, a scene-painter, and a remarkable actor-impersonator. Ouspensky found this last capacity the most astonishing: in waking life he utterly lacked this ability. Ouspensky could imitate no one, not even his closest friends, and was incapable of remembering their most characteristic gestures, phrases, or movements; his "dream-impersonator," however, could do all this with consummate ease. Ouspensky remarks that dreams in which we see dead relatives or friends have a powerful effect precisely because of this strange talent. And he makes the curious comment that this capacity can "sometimes function in a waking state when man is absorbed in himself or separates himself from the immediate influences of life."[14] Ouspensky relates that most spiritualist phenomena, such as hearing voices of the dead, can be explained through this remarkable power of the dream-impersonator. He speaks of his friend Sherbakov, with whom he had traveled to Egypt and who died just before he was to accompany Ouspensky on his second voyage, this time to India. Two times during this second trip, Ouspensky "distinctly heard his voice, as though he was entering my mental conversation with myself." He spoke "in the manner in which he alone could speak and said what he alone could say."[15] Ouspensky did not consider this a visitation from the dead. "Obviously," he wrote, "he was in me, in my memory of him, and something within me reproduced him." Ouspensky comments that this kind of "mental conversation" sometimes occurs with absent friends, and when it takes place with living people, it is called telepathy.

As we shall see, the phenomenon of hearing remarkably accurate voices—or at least one remarkably accurate voice—would play a tremendous part in Ouspensky's later search for the miraculous.

Along with his own dreams, Ouspensky mentions those of a young girl, a "political prisoner who spent a long time in the Boutirsky prison in Moscow." During his visits, she told him of her dreams and how they often seemed to confuse her earlier experiences at "the institute," a privileged government school for girls, with her present predicament. Ouspensky surmised that the connecting link between her past and present situation was undoubtedly boredom, the sense of constraint, and "the general absurdity of all the surroundings."[16]

The political prisoner in question was Ouspensky's sister, whose name has not come down to us. The absurdity of her surroundings must have been desperately obvious to both of them. Exactly why Ouspensky's sister was arrested is unclear, but in 1905 in Russia, this hardly mattered. On Sunday, January 9 of that year, Ouspensky's sister was among the thousands of peaceful demonstrators who marched to the Winter Palace to present the Tsar with a list of their economic complaints. Led by a priest, the demonstration moved on and on, and the guards, unable to stop the flood of people, panicked and fired into the crowd. At least one hundred people were killed, and hundreds more were wounded. Strikes and protests broke out throughout the country. The Tsar sought to still the unrest by agreeing to the establishment of an elected Duma, although he still tried to keep real power in his own hands. It was again too little too late. The road to the Bolsheviks lay open.

Ouspensky's sister died in prison in 1908, from what, we do not know. With her death, Ouspensky became a man without a family. At thirty he was, in effect, alone. He had no interest in revolution. Clearly the death of his sister didn't endear the Tsar to him. Although his Peter side had much to recall, no doubt the Demian in him became very present. In 1906 Ouspensky began to work as a journalist. The work, however, seemed to have put him into even closer contact with the world of "obvious absurdities." At the editorial offices of a leading Moscow daily, *The Morning*, he sat at his desk reading the foreign papers; his abilities as a linguist made him a natural for international news. He was supposed to be writing an article on The Hague Conference.[17] Yet the French, German, English, and Italian newspapers all presented the same message. He read the same automatic phrases, the same pompous rhetoric, the same blatant lies, and the same tedious gesturing. Ouspensky the dreamer was supposed to assimilate these empty words and write something about them. Instead, he opened a drawer in his desk. Inside was an assortment of books that offered a world more real to him than a hundred international conferences and conventions.

The Occult World, Life after Death, Atlantis and Lemuria, Dogme et Rituel de la Haute Magie, Le Temple de Satan, The Sincere Narrations of a Pilgrim—from these and, we can assume, many other books Ouspensky had not been separated for months.

He had begun a very thorough study of occultism, and from his writing it's clear he was familiar with most of the authorities on the subject. Although he admits that much in these books was naïve, they also had a flavor of truth, and he felt that in some way they could lead *somewhere*. In any case, he was convinced that The Hague Conference and its like could, and would, lead nowhere.

With so many of his loved ones gone, and with his last link to his past about to be lost, is it any wonder that a sensitive character like Ouspensky would reject the world of politics and instead find some kind of comfort in *the unknown,* perhaps even in the possibility of finding those loved ones again? In these naïve books he found that "the thought became possible that death might not exist, that those who have gone might not have vanished altogether, and that perhaps I might see them again." This remark speaks volumes about Ouspensky's motivation, as he himself admits. Accustomed to thinking "scientifically" for so long, Ouspensky had forgotten that beyond the outer covering of life there may exist *something else.* What that something else may be, and how he might get to it, were unclear. The Russia of 1906, however, was certainly a good time and place to try.

Although for years officially banned, by 1907 Theosophical literature had flowered in Russia. This was in many ways the result of the work of another hugely influential esoteric teacher, the spiritual scientist and founder of Anthroposophy, Rudolf Steiner. A Goethe and Nietzsche scholar with a firm grounding in German Idealist philosophy, Steiner became the head of the German Branch of the Theosophical Society in 1902, and within a few years his influence in Europe and Russia had become astounding. Marie von Sivers, Steiner's second wife, was a Baltic Russian, and it was chiefly through her influence that Steiner's Christianized version of Theosophy spread to the Russian intelligentsia. The 1905 revolution prevented Steiner from giving a series of lectures he had planned for Russia. Many of the intelligentsia, however, fleeing the Tsarist regime, had crossed the frontier and it was arranged for Steiner to speak in the exile capital of Europe, Paris. In 1906 Steiner lectured to an audience among whom were some of the most influential figures in the Russian cultural renaissance: Dimitri Merzhkovsky, Zinaida Hippius, Konstantin Balmont, and Nicolai Minsky. By 1913, when Steiner gave a series of lectures at Helsingfors (Helsinki) Finland specifically for his Russian followers, there were already several Anthroposophical discussion groups and workshops in St. Petersburg and Moscow. Some of the most influential cultural figures became devoted followers of Steiner's teaching, among them the novelist Andrei Bely, one of the giants of modernism. Like Steiner, Ouspensky also had an influence on modern culture that is rarely recognized.

The Silver Age in Russian history—from 1890 to 1914—saw a tremendous surge of interest in various forms of mysticism and the occult. This should not be surprising. Holy Russia herself produced several of the most celebrated occult figures of the late nineteenth and early twentieth centuries. Along with Gurdjieff and Ouspensky there were Madame Blavatsky, co-founder of the Theosophical Society; Rasputin, "the holy devil"; and the artist Nicolai Roerich, who painted the backdrops to Igor Stravinsky's revolutionary ballet *The Rite of Spring* and later developed a spiritual teaching called Agni Yoga. In the atmosphere of "frenzied eschatological doom"[18] that pervaded Russia at the start of the last century, Theosophical ideas about a coming "new age" blended with revolutionary politics to create a heady mélange of spiritual libertarianism and hedonistic asceticism. Many of the most important literary and artistic figures of the time were touched in some way by the occult. Along with Bely, the novelist Valery Briussov, the composer Alexandre Scriabin, the philosopher

Nicolai Berdyaev, and many others were deep into the study of magic, mysticism, and Theosophy. At the cafés serious investigation of paranormal phenomena was as much the topic of conversation as were some of the more lurid manifestations of the time, like suicide clubs, satanism, and the almost obligatory black masses. Imported via French Symbolism, which reached the Russian steppes by the early 1890s, various forms of satanism and satanic worship became the central obsession of a host of Russian littérateurs, artists, and musicians. Through drugs, wild dress, overcharged eroticism, and other outré behavior, a variety of diabolical themes fascinated the intelligentsia. Philosophers like Vladimir Soloviev, writers like Vasily Rozanov, poets like Alexander Blok, and artists like Mikhail Vrubel all incorporated demonic and satanic themes into their work. Satanic erotica became a familiar part of mainstream journalism, with images of passive, half-naked women preyed upon by demonic incubi. On stage, the actor Fedor Chaliapin made a career portraying satanic figures, most famously Mephistopheles from Gounod's *Faust*. The artist Nicolai Riabushinsky, who hosted a suicide club called the Black Swan, published an advertisement in his journal, *The Golden Fleece*, asking for contributions for a special edition dedicated to the Devil; he received ninety-two replies.[19]

Ouspensky was very much a man of his time and place, as his collection of stories *Talks with a Devil* shows. Yet even here he cut his own path. While influential writers like Valery Briussov were portraying the Devil as a powerfully attractive rebel "beyond good and evil," Ouspensky rejected this adolescent romanticism and argued instead that the Devil is really "vulgarity and triviality embodied."[20] Ouspensky had his own share of the Nietzschean ethic, but he could not bear to see it falsified. The names of other figures from the Russian spiritual renaissance turn up in Ouspensky's books as well, placing him squarely in this milieu. He speaks, for instance, of

Alexander Dobrolyubov, a poet who, after a religious conversion, gave away his possessions and wandered throughout Russia, his body encased in iron hoops after the fashion of Orthodox holy men.

Ouspensky came to Theosophy in 1907, when he was just beginning his exploration of mysticism. Although he was to leave the Theosophical Society in 1914, the influence of Theosophical ideas remained with him throughout his life. He remarked that early on he had recognized Theosophy's "weakness." It had, he said, "no continuation," meaning that it had already hardened into an ideology, a hazard for any form of teaching. "Beginning with a bold, revolutionary search for the wondrous," he wrote, "Theosophy soon started to fall away from that and to stop at some 'found' truths." Yet he remained associated with the Theosophical Society and movement for many years and in later life was always proud of the fact that on one of his journeys to India he visited the society's headquarters in Adyar and was treated like royalty. The headquarters was a three-tiered building: the ground floor was accessible to the rank and file, the second floor was reserved for important financial donors, and the top floor was solely for visitors of the highest Theosophical rank. Ouspensky recalled with some satisfaction that he had been admitted to the highest group immediately.

He may have rejected some of the more naïve elements in Theosophy, as did another follower of Gurdjieff, the literary critic A. R. Orage. As the result of his drug experiments—discussed shortly—Ouspensky concluded that reports of the "astral plane" or "Akashic record" by prominent Theosophical figures like Rudolf Steiner and C. W. Leadbeater were at best questionable. Nevertheless, Ouspensky's Theosophical inheritance remains clear. Theosophy's moral and ethical values appealed to the Demian in him; he agreed with its emphasis on the study of comparative religion; and the idea that science, art, religion, and philosophy all stemmed from a common source was fundamental to his own vision. Years later he told Rom Landau that when he first began to read Theosophical material, the authors were in touch with a profound truth and hadn't yet begun to "repeat themselves." And in the last decade of his life, Ouspensky hoped to communicate the ideas of the work to a larger audience by forming what he called the Historico-Psychological Society. Although World War II smashed his plans for the society, the prospectus Ouspensky drew up suggested that the Theosophical concerns of his early days were still active.

Theosophy, Ouspensky remarked, "opened doors . . . into a new and bigger world." One of the central ideas in that new and bigger world was esotericism, the notion of a hidden or secret knowledge. Though obscured to the ordinary mind, this hidden knowledge could be discovered through a careful study of the literature and artifacts of the past. Through his reading Ouspensky believed he had discovered "an unbroken line of thought and knowledge which passes from century to century, from age to age, from country to country." This thought is "hidden beneath layers of religions and philosophies which are, in fact, only distortions and perversions of the ideas belonging to the line." "An extensive literature" that is "quite unknown" nevertheless "feeds the philosophy we know, although it is scarcely mentioned in the text-books."[21]

The idea of a secret or sacred knowledge has, of course, existed from the earliest times on; the ancient Greek mysteries suggest it, and the alchemical writings of the fifteenth and sixteenth centuries are clear examples. In Ouspensky's time, the most prominent advocate of this idea was Madame Blavatsky. Her book *The Secret Doctrine* argues that for all his scientific progress, modern man has lost the key to a deep, ancient wisdom. Ouspensky's particular talent was to link this idea to other equally stimulating notions bubbling in the collective consciousness: the notions of the God-Man promoted by thinkers like Vladimir Soloviev, Nietzsche's vision of the superman, and what Ouspensky and others would call "cosmic consciousness."

Not surprisingly, Ouspensky gave the idea of cosmic consciousness his own particular twist. Heavily influenced by Nietzsche, he rejected the Theosophical idea that the entire human race is slowly evolving into a higher form of consciousness. He argued instead that any possible evolution of consciousness must be the product of a culture aimed at that evolution. This belief was partly an expression of Ouspensky's character. J. G. Bennett speaks of Ouspensky's "contempt for the illiterate masses,"[22] and we know Ouspensky rejected what he called *byt*—routine, everyday life. Ouspensky, however, was not alone in his recognition of two "types" of people, those who wish to evolve and those who do not, if we can simplify it in this way.

Ouspensky speaks of two cultures: civilization and barbarism. He sees history as the recurring rise and fall of these two opposites, with barbarism enjoying a slight but important edge. Originally, in the dim past, emissaries from the "Inner Circle," the esoteric directors of human evolution, set out to "civilize" early humans, but in the process allowed violence to enter and intermix with their aims. This muddying of the civilizing influence grew until the two cultures became ensnared in an ongoing battle. Civilization brings religion, science, philosophy, art, and a social order that allows individuals the freedom, security, and leisure to explore ideas and means of self-expression. Barbarism means violence, triviality, lies—all the base values that pervert and eventually destroy the work of civilization. But because civilization must incorporate certain elements of barbarism to maintain and defend itself—armies, police, the state—it is eventually overrun by these and finds itself more and more motivated by the values of barbarism, rather than its own values. Ouspensky believed that in his own day the spirit of true civilization was weak and fragile, "a pale, sickly growth."

Although the forces of barbarism may predominate among the masses (not necessarily in the form of violence, but in an acceptance of triviality and the glorification of ultimately unimportant values), they nevertheless form a strange symbiotic relationship with the individual, who for Ouspensky is the carrier of civilization. Ouspensky argues that by themselves, societies create nothing; only the individual can create. The tragedy of the individual, he says, is that he or she lives "within the dense mass" of society and almost all of his or her activity is harnessed to its aims. An individual's creative activity often runs "against the grain" of society. Anything new, different, exploratory is seen as a threat to the norm, and society resists it in various ways, trying to reduce the vision of the creative individual to something that fits the lowest common denominator. Higher values are unnecessary for the functioning of society, as we can see in the growing global success of our consumer culture.

Yet, as Ouspensky tells us, the individual man or woman is a "higher organism," capable of aims and motives that exceed society's needs. Although society attempts to absorb the whole of the individual's work, something nevertheless escapes. This small residue is what we call progress. Against its own wishes, society is "infected" with the values of the creative individual. Without this infection, a society would stagnate, come to a complete halt, and relatively quickly disintegrate. So in order to survive, the culture of barbarism must take on some element of the culture of civilization.

Fueled by his discovery of Theosophical literature, in 1908 Ouspensky embarked on his first journey in search of "esoteric schools." With his friend Sherbakov he set off on a voyage to the Orient, visiting Constantinople, Smyrna, Greece, and Egypt, writing about his travels for Moscow newspapers. In Constantinople he saw the Mevlevi dervishes. "Constantinople then was still alive," he would write. "Later it died. *They* were the soul of Constantinople."[23] In Egypt he felt fear and the terror of annihilation before the inscrutable visage of the Sphinx and made the curious remark that the Sphinx predated ancient Egypt. "This means that even for the most ancient of the ancient Egyptians . . . the Sphinx was the same riddle as it is for us today"—a comment in keeping with ideas popularized by contemporary writers like Graham Hancock.[24] Yet although he became convinced that the Sphinx was a "relic of another, a very ancient culture, which was possessed of knowledge far greater than ours," Ouspensky returned to Moscow without having found a school and, in essence, was no nearer to grasping the miraculous than before he left. Soon after his return, he moved from Moscow to St. Petersburg.

At this point Ouspensky reverted to an earlier obsession: the fourth dimension. Modern interest in the idea of a fourth dimension had begun with the philosopher Immanuel Kant. In his *Prolegomena to All Future Metaphysics*, Kant wondered if the odd difference between a hand and its mirror image wasn't the result of a limited perception of space. The two seem the same, yet clearly they're not, as they are reverse images of each other. In 1827 the German astronomer August Ferdinand Moebius—famous for the Moebius strip—suggested that an asymmetrical solid object, like a hand, could be reversed by rotating it through a "higher space." Scientists and mathematicians like Gauss, Lobatchevsky, Bolyai, Riemann, Mach, Minkovsky, and Einstein all devoted thought to this idea. In 1877, however, speculation about a fourth dimension took another turn when the physicist Johann Zollner argued that this possible "higher space" could account for the remarkable phenomena produced by the psychic Henry Slade. Zollner claimed that Slade achieved his results—like untying a knot in a sealed loop of rope, or writing on an sealed chalkboard—by summoning spirits who resided in the fourth dimension. When Slade was arrested on charges of fraud, many were surprised that a host of renowned scientists came to Slade's defense, including William Crookes, inventor of the cathode ray tube. Thanks to the sensational newspaper accounts of Slade's trial and the series of experiments, conducted by Zollner and the respected psychologist Gustave Fechner, designed to prove Slade's innocence, in the public mind the idea of a fourth dimension became firmly linked to the notion of a spirit world.

The name most associated with the fourth dimension in Ouspensky's time, however, was Charles H. Hinton, who popularized the idea in a series of books and magazine articles. Born in London in 1853, in the late 1870s Hinton had a kind of philosophical crisis; he felt a profound need—almost an obsession—to arrive at some form of absolute knowledge. He came upon a peculiar means of relieving his epistemological distress: he set out to memorize a cubic yard of one-inch cubes. He took a 36 x 36 x 36 block of cubes, gave each of the 46,656 units a two-word Latin name, and learned to visualize this structure as a kind of "solid paper." By adjusting its size so that it fit into this imaginary cubic yard, Hinton could visualize a solid structure by recognizing which of the named cubes it occupied. Hinton went on to memorize the positions of the cubes for each of the twenty-four possible orientations of the block as seen by an observer.

Hinton believed that through this exercise he had developed a means of seeing into higher space—the fourth dimension. He promulgated his ideas in a series of books; the first, *Scientific Romances* (1885), influenced probably the best-known fictional account of the fourth dimension, H. G. Wells's *The Time Machine* (1895). But perhaps most popular was the four-dimensional parlor game known as "Hinton cubes," a set of twelve cardboard cubes whose faces, edges, and corners sported different colors (eighty-one in all). Anyone interested in perceiving the fourth dimension was instructed to memorize the entire construction, as Hinton had, and then to move the little cubes about: this would demonstrate how rotation through the fourth dimension is the equivalent of a mirror image in our familiar three-dimensional world.

Hinton's cubes became a fad, turning up with astral vision and seeing auras in Theosophical circles in New York and London.[25] It's unclear exactly when Ouspensky discovered Hinton's work, but alongside his drawer of occult literature, Hinton's books became central items in his library of the miraculous. Later Ouspensky translated Hinton's work, along with that of another English metaphysical thinker, the mystical socialist Edward Carpenter, into Russian.

Like everything else he touched, Ouspensky brought his own insights to the idea of the fourth dimension. The purely mathematical approach, he thought, was a dead end; the spiritualist account was also limited. The fourth dimension, Ouspensky argued, was concerned with mysteries far greater than these: the mysteries of consciousness and of time.

In 1909 Ouspensky produced a book, *The Fourth Dimension,* later incorporated as one of the chapters in *A New Model of the Universe.* It was in many ways a dry run for his later, more influential work, but it immediately put him in the ranks of the important thinkers of his day. Ouspensky took from Hinton the idea that to perceive higher space, our consciousness itself must be altered. Hinton's cubes, though popular, were at best a starting point. They were supposed to help in what he called "casting out the self"—eliminating the subjective, relative perspective of the observer and allowing him or her to perceive the world "as it is." From Hinton, Ouspensky also borrowed an analogy to help us grasp imaginatively what perceiving the fourth dimension would be like. To a one-dimensional creature, a square of two dimensions would seem to exhibit properties that were "impossible." Likewise, to a square, a three-dimensional cube passing through it would flout all the known laws of its reality. So, the analogy suggests, for a three-dimensional creature like ourselves, manifestations of the fourth dimension would also appear impossible. Or, to use Ouspensky's favorite term, "miraculous."

Ouspensky concluded that the fourth dimension is not some mathematical hypothesis nor a dubious realm of spirits. It already exists, *in our own consciousness.* Yet trapped as we seem to be in a world of three-dimensions—the solid, predictable, and positively unmiraculous world of materialism, science, space, and time—we have no access to it. *Unless,* as Hinton suggested, we change our consciousness. Ouspensky, however, didn't have the patience to memorize Hinton's cubes. There were *other* means of changing consciousness, as his experiments with dreams had already shown. And in his little room in St. Petersburg he decided it was time to experiment again.

CHAPTER THREE

THINKING IN OTHER CATEGORIES

I N ST. PETERSBURG, Ouspensky lived at the corner of Nevsky
Prospect and Liteynaia Street, a fashionable neighbor-
hood in the heart of the city. His dwelling was small—a single
room with only a table, a chair, a bed, and a packing case over-
flowing with his library. Here were the French occultist and
freemason Papus; the decadent poet Stanislas de Guaita, who
wrote verse in the style of Baudelaire; and Eliphas Levi, "the
Professor of Transcendental Magic" responsible for the occult
revival of the nineteenth century. Here too were Hinton's
books as well as many others: *Cosmic Consciousness* by the
Canadian psychologist Richard M. Bucke, a volume of
Vivekananda, Edward Carpenter's *Toward Democracy,* the obligatory Nietzsche, some volumes of Dostoyevsky, and, of course,
Lermontoff.

One book Ouspensky found very useful was *The Varieties
of Religious Experience* by the philosopher and psychologist
William James. Published in 1902, this classic in the psychological study of religion was one of the few academic works to take
mystical experience seriously. James argues that the unusual
experiences given to mystics and saints throughout history are
a more fruitful foundation for understanding the nature of
religion than any dogma. James included accounts of well-
known saints and mystics from several religions, but he also
included accounts of mystical experiences of a different sort:
those produced by drugs.

In 1874 Benjamin Paul Blood, a New York farmer, body-builder, and calculating prodigy, privately published a highly eccentric account of his experiences under nitrous oxide, or laughing gas. In *The Anesthetic Revelation and the Gist of Philosophy*, Blood claimed that inhalation of laughing gas revealed to him "the Open Secret . . . the primordial, Adamic surprise of Life."

Blood sent copies of his pamphlet to as many influential people as he could, including members of the newly formed Society for Psychical Research in England. James, who was interested in psychic phenomena, came upon a version of Blood's account in *The Atlantic Monthly*. James was so impressed by Blood that he included an excerpt from *The Anesthetic Revelation* in his *Varieties of Religious Experience* (which, incidentally, also discusses the ideas in Bucke's *Cosmic Consciousness*).

James was not satisfied with a vicarious understanding of mystical consciousness. To fully grasp what the mystical experience was about, he'd have to have one himself. Sometime in 1900, he made arrangements to inhale the gas. Under its effects James experienced the reconciliation of opposites that Blood argued was the essence of the anesthetic revelation. "I have sheet after sheet of phrases dictated or written during the intoxication," James wrote, "which to the sober reader seem meaningless drivel, but which at the moment of transcribing were fused in the fire of infinite rationality. God and devil, good and evil, life and death, I and thou, sober and drunk . . . and fifty other contrasts figure in these pages in the same monotonous way." A sample of his notes gives an idea of what went racing through James's mind as the gas took effect:

What's a mistake but a kind of take?
What's nausea but a kind of—ausea?[1]

To the logical mind, such musings seem sheer nonsense. Yet James couldn't deny that his experiment was in some way important. "The keynote of the experience is the tremendously exciting sense of an intense metaphysical illumination. Truth lies open to the view in depth beneath depth of almost blinding evidence."[2] "Our normal waking consciousness, rational consciousness as we call it, is but one special type of consciousness, whilst all about it, parted from it by the flimsiest of screens, there lie potential forms of consciousness entirely different." "No account of the universe in its totality," he argues, "can be final which leaves these other forms of consciousness quite disregarded."[3]

Sitting in his little room on Liteynaia Street, a thirty-two-year-old Ouspensky agreed with James and firmly resolved that he would certainly not leave these other forms of consciousness disregarded.

Ouspensky tells us that the aim of his drug experiments was to answer some fundamental questions about the reality of magic. By 1911 he was familiar with the existing literature on Theosophy and occultism, and the scientist in him wanted to know what, if any of it, was real and what simply imaginary. By the time he set out on these investigations, Ouspensky had become a regular and much-respected figure in the Russian Theosophical community, contributing to its journals and lecturing to its followers on his travels. For the philosopher Nicolai Berdyaev, who was hostile to both Theosophy and Rudolf Steiner's Anthroposophy, Ouspensky was "the most independent and talented Theosophical writer we have." Yet Ouspensky was still grappling with the central questions of his life. He had experienced a taste of cosmic consciousness. In 1908, on board a steamship in the Sea of Marmora—an inland sea on the Asian side of Turkey—Ouspensky felt a fleeting instant in which his consciousness *blended* with the external world in a remarkable way. As he describes it:

[I] entered into the waves, and with them rushed with a howl at the ship. And in that instant I *became all.* The waves—they were myself: the far violet mountains, the wind, the clouds hurrying from the north, the great steamship, heeling and rushing irresistibly forward— all were myself . . . the unmerciful and unyielding propelling screw which pushed and pushed me forward . . . the rudder which determined all my motion—all this was myself: also two sailors and the black snake of smoke coming in clouds out of the funnel . . . all.

It was an instant of unusual freedom, joy and expansion. A second—and the spell of the charm disappeared.[4]

For a deeper understanding of cosmic consciousness, however, Ouspensky knew that more than brief moments were necessary. He was familiar with different methods of altering consciousness—yogic breathing, for example, or fasting and various physical exercises. But for a man eager to find the miraculous, these methods were too slow and time-consuming. Ouspensky was in a hurry; he was also a very modern mystic, willing to try new means of entering the unknown, like nitrous oxide and, if internal evidence can guide us, hashish as well. Armed with these two agents, over a period of at least a year, Ouspensky systematically attempted to induce higher states of consciousness.[5]

The change took place more quickly than he expected. Almost immediately he was faced with a problem: the unknown, he discovered, was truly *unknown.* "The new state of consciousness gave at once so much that was new and unexpected, and these new and unexpected experiences came upon me and flashed by so quickly, that I could not find words, could not find forms of speech, could not find concepts, which would enable me to remember what had occurred . . . still less to convey it to anyone else."[6]

Ouspensky's account has to be one of the most lucid reports about an absolutely "other" form of consciousness ever penned. One of the first signs of his approaching the "beyond" was a strange sensation of duality, as if his consciousness had split in two. He then found himself in a world that was entirely new. Nothing, he realized, could prepare one for this shift into *somewhere else*. He quickly saw that nothing he had read about the astral realm or the spirit world or the "higher spheres" was of any help in this totally different reality, the central characteristic of which was unity. In this new world nothing was separate. *Everything* was connected. To describe his first impression of any part of it, Ouspensky felt obliged to describe everything at once. During one drug experience, when he was accompanied by a friend, Ouspensky began to communicate something of his sensations. But the very act of speaking triggered so many associations and reflections that he found it impossible to continue. "Between the first and second words of my sentence, such an enormous number of ideas occurred to me and passed before me, that the two words were so widely separated as to make it impossible to find any connection between them."[7]

Ouspensky soon saw that the world he had entered was one of pure mathematical relations. In it, our usual distinctions between subjective and objective, inside and outside, were turned around. The external world of hard, material objects became unreal, while his inner world of thoughts, feelings, and sensations took on at times an overwhelming presence. Remaining to a certain extent "under the influence of Theosophical literature," Ouspensky realized that he had entered *Arupa*, the Sanskrit word for the formless, mental world. Here the invisible was present, while the visible world of everyday reality was nothing more than a symbol of the "higher" invisible world. The image of a gigantic lotus, its petals continuously unfolding, came to him, and he realized that this was a hieroglyph[8] of the world. Light, movement, color, music, emotion, knowledge, intelligence, and a sense of unceasing growth flowed from the center of this fantastic mandala, and a voice—as in his dream experiments—told him that this was an image of the Hindu god Brahma. But on the brink of entering the absolute, Ouspensky felt a sense of danger. Infinity stretched before him. It was frightening and fascinating. What if he entered it—and didn't come back? A "presence" warned him of the danger, and advised him to step back.

The danger of infinity could emanate from the most ordinary objects. And like James, Ouspensky tried to capture some sense of the strange reality he had entered. He tried to formulate the essence of it, to fix his insights in some verbal trigger. One day, sitting on a sofa and smoking a cigarette, Ouspensky chanced to look at his ashtray. "It was," he wrote, "an ordinary copper ash-tray." Yet as he gazed at it, it suddenly became unordinary. With a "certain wonder and almost with fear," he felt that he had never understood what an ashtray was before. A "whirlwind of thoughts and images" surrounded him. An infinity of facts and associations emerged from the ashtray, spreading out before him like a great web of relations. Everything to do with smoking and tobacco paraded before him. Then the ashtray itself: how it was made, where the copper came from, the history of metallurgy, how people had discovered it, through what processes it had to pass before it had arrived on his table. A flood of questions about his ashtray poured over Ouspensky, and, grabbing a pencil, he tried to capture some of what streamed through his mind. The next morning he read what he had written. The note said: "A man can go mad from one ash-tray."

On another occasion, when the gas had brought him to a peculiarly vivid state, he grabbed a pencil and sheet of paper.

The next morning he stared blankly at the single sentence he had scribbled down: "Think in other categories." As with so much of his experience, what exactly he had meant by those words had faded.

Ouspensky did, however, manage to retain something from the new insights. He generally made his experiments in his room, but on a few occasions he ventured out into the streets. As the effects of nitrous oxide pass in a few moments, it seems likely that on these occasions Ouspensky used hashish. Walking out his door, Ouspensky discovered that, like his ashtray, the ordinary world was not so ordinary. A strange emotional state came over him in which it was impossible to feel indifferent toward anything. Everything struck him with an unexpected force and significance. In this new world, where nothing was dead, nothing inanimate, he began to perceive things he had never perceived before. The houses he passed were living beings, and the people inside them were the thoughts, feelings, and moods of the houses. An ordinary cab horse on the Nevsky Prospect was not ordinary at all but was an "atom" of a great horse, just as a dog was an atom of a great dog and a man was an atom of a great man. But the most astonishing results came when Ouspensky thought about the dead.

It's not surprising that in his strange new state Ouspensky would try to gain some insight into the central mystery of life. Ouspensky speaks of the death of a certain person closely related to him and how, at the time, he tried to find some answer to the mystery of his passing.[9] Depressed over his loss, he found some comfort in a kind of dream fantasy. He "saw" two figures: one, that of the man as he knew him, and the other, the life of the man, which appeared to Ouspensky as a road passing over hills and through valleys into the distance. Now, during his experiments, Ouspensky thought of another loss, one that took place two years earlier.[10] He felt regret and remorse that he had not been near the person who had died "when he might have needed me." In the next vision he again "saw" the person, not as the individual he had known but as his entire life, his "Linga Sharira," the "long body of life." As in the case of the ashtray, everything about the person appeared to Ouspensky at once, and he realized that our lives are not merely a series of events, "one thing after another." From beginning to end they form a kind of living being that continues to exist after our physical, visible, sequential form passes. Our real selves are something much greater than the shadows we see before us. This insight, Ouspensky knew, meant something indeed. Time as we know it *does not exist.* What does exist is an "eternal now," which we do not see because our limited consciousness fragments it into the past, the present, and the future. Just as our consciousness normally limits the number of associations we can perceive in a given object, and in so doing enables us to function in the world, so too does it limit our perception of the true nature of time.

But after the rise comes the fall. Coming out of his transports, Ouspensky experienced something like a metaphysical hangover. "The strangest thing in all these experiences was the coming back, the return to the ordinary state." It was, he said, very similar to dying. These dark awakenings must have been very much like the unfruitful states of mind he entered when his attempts at inducing half-dreams resulted only in insomnia. Such states were "immersion in matter"—and it was precisely the thrall of Great Matter that he believed he had thrown off when he had plunged into the unknown. "Everything becomes flat, ordinary, prosaic; the voice of the mysterious and miraculous . . . falls silent and seems no more than a foolish invention. You notice only the discomforts—the ridiculous and unpleasant sides of everything and everybody. The mirror loses its luster and the world seems universally grey and flat."[11] In this "dead world" there was something extraordinarily oppressive, as if it was a vast wooden machine, with wooden wheels, wooden thoughts, wooden sensations, that moved and creaked and lumbered infinitely slowly. Years later, Gurdjieff would tell Ouspensky that the Earth was in a very bad place in the universe. On those mornings when he awoke from his mystical experiences, Ouspensky had already gleaned some hint of this discouraging insight.

Yet, perhaps even more than this sense of cosmic letdown, Ouspensky felt an immense frustration at his inability to hold onto anything of what he had seen. His experience ran through his fingers like sand. "So little remains," he laments. "I remember so vaguely what I have experienced." And what he could remember was almost impossible to communicate. What good were these sudden flares and illuminations if the world he glimpsed during them immediately became obscure? Between Ouspensky on his grim, wooden mornings and Ouspensky the *voyant* there seemed to stretch an impassable desert. He had seen *something*—of that he was sure. But exactly what? Having cut his moorings on the everyday, he found himself adrift in the infinite. His mind, finely honed and razor sharp, was a poor tool for grasping the import of the powerful emotions that rocked him. The rush of feeling proved too strong, too fast for words to grasp. What could he remember? Was it a dream?

Ouspensky concluded that for all their value as revelations of the possible, nitrous oxide and hashish were too elusive and uncontrollable to offer much more than a brief view from the mountaintop. In any case, if a man could go mad from one ashtray, a steady diet of the infinite would surely prove too much. Once again, the idea of schools came to him. If esoteric schools existed, then perhaps he might find one, and there find a teacher who would show him how to control these new, exciting states of consciousness. He would start on a long journey, he told himself.

But before he set out, Ouspensky gathered up what remained from his raids on the impossible and produced the work that would make his name. Its title was *Tertium Organum*.

TERTIUM ORGANUM

Ouspensky's *TERTIUM ORGANUM* was perhaps the single most effective counterblast to the reigning intellectual orthodoxy of the early twentieth century. A précis of the book is nearly impossible, as the ground covered includes Kantian epistemology, Hinton's cubes, animal perception, sex, Theosophy, cosmic consciousness, the superman, and Ouspensky's own experiences of mystical states. With its English translation as "The Third Organ of Thought"—set to supercede those of Aristotle and Francis Bacon—*Tertium Organum* argues for the need to move beyond logic and rationality in order to grasp the true nature of reality. Yet such a bare-bones summation of the book doesn't do justice to the wealth of detail, fine argument, striking analogies, and metaphors that illuminate Ouspensky's vigorous prose.

Perhaps a single quotation gives us the gist of Ouspensky's early work of genius as effectively as any lengthy exegesis:

> There is no side of life which does not reveal to us an infinity of the new and unexpected if we approach it with the *knowledge* that it is not exhausted by its visible side, that behind this visible side there lies a whole world of the "invisible," a whole world of new and incomprehensible forces and relations.[1]

We can see that Ouspensky's vision here shares the symbolism of his youth. That he had a sense of the "invisible" from an early age is clear from his love of Lermontoff's novel, *A Hero of Our Time*, with its magnificent mountain settings and vague hints of the numinous. Ivan Osokin tells Zinaida that he is fond of poems of one line, "for the more you leave to the imagination . . . the better."[2] Symbolism grew out of the work of the Scandinavian religious thinker Emanuel Swedenborg by way of the poet Baudelaire, who developed Swedenborg's notion of "correspondences" into a complete aesthetic philosophy.[3] Swedenborg himself carried on the tradition of the German mystic Jacob Boehme, who in a flash of heightened consciousness saw into what he called "the signature of things," the reality beneath the surface of the world. *Tertium Organum* brings a rigorous and convincing grounding in a systematic philosophy of consciousness to this fundamental insight.

Even when Ouspensky is least convincing—in his arguments on animal perception, for example—it's clear that what interests him about the fourth dimension is not, as with Hinton, the possibility of perceiving objects "aperspectivally," as the cultural philosopher Jean Gebser would phrase it.[4] Ouspensky believes that perceiving things in higher space will lead us to thinking about them in a different way, to "thinking in other categories"—to new concepts and new analogies and a new *language* with which to speak about reality. As he knew from his experiments with half-dream states and with drugs, this is what is most essential.

Subtitled "A Key to the Enigmas of the World," *Tertium Organum* is rightly seen as a classic of higher space and higher mathematics. Yet its sometimes forbidding passages on different dimensions and on the "consciousness" of a line, a square, and a cube are a kind of red herring. Ouspensky's starting point is his intuition that positivism, the intellectual orthodoxy of his day, was woefully inadequate to account for the most important aspects of human existence. That orthodoxy has changed names many times, but to this day it remains the official explanation of things. It states that what is real can be measured, through our own sensory organs or through the many extensions of these developed by science. Only that which is visible is real.[5] At one time positivism was a radical development, a fresh break with the past, an agent of progress. But positivism, like Theosophy and occultism, had hardened into a "Chinese wall" of dogma, restricting the growth of new knowledge and new perceptions. *Tertium Organum* smashed through that wall and opened a path for the "new"—for Ouspensky, another name for the invisible.

Tertium Organum did more than develop Hinton's and others' ideas about a fourth dimension. Ouspensky's aim is to convince us that there is good evidence for the existence of the "invisibles" science regards as nonexistent. In fact, he tells us that they are even *more* real than the material reality that science tells us explains them away. Since the time of William Blake, who cleansed the doors of perception and saw a world in a grain of sand, poets have made this same point in different ways—the Romantics, as well as the Symbolists of Ouspensky's generation. What Ouspensky did was to make the argument philosophically strong.

In doing this, Ouspensky secured a place for himself in the annals of higher mathematics and subsequent discussions of hyperspace. In fact, aside from books about Gurdjieff and the Fourth Way, the other area where Ouspensky's name turns up is in popular science books on other dimensions—sometimes with humorous results. For instance, in *Hyperspace* the physicist Michio Kaku remarks on Ouspensky's profound interest in multidimensional space and the influence his ideas had on writers like Fyodor Dostoyevsky.[6] Given that Dostoyevsky died in 1881, when Ouspensky was three years old, his influence must have been great indeed, making itself felt well before any of his books had been written.

Yet even without mistakes like these, confining Ouspensky to the niche of hyperspace philosopher ignores a good half—maybe more—of his argument. What draws Ouspensky on in *Tertium Organum* is the notion of the miraculous, the sense that an entire *other* world exists that we participate in yet are unaware of. Geometric analogies are useful to Ouspensky because they help us arrive through reason at an insight that *transcends* reason, or at least transcends the artificial limits set by positivism. Once we transcend those limits, the invisible, the fourth dimension, is suddenly found everywhere.

In nature, for example: "In the changing of season; in the yellow leaves of the autumn with their smell and the memories they bring; in the first snow dusting the fields and adding a peculiar freshness and sharpness to the air; in the waters of spring, in the warming sun and the awakening but still bare branches through which gleams the deep blue sky; in the white nights of the north and in the dark, humid, and warm tropical nights spangled with stars"—in these Ouspensky perceived the thoughts, feelings, and moods of a "mysterious being."[7]

In sex, too: "The voice of sex also contains a great deal of this mystical sensation of nature. The feeling of sex places man in the most personal relationship with nature. The feeling of woman by man or *vice versa* is often compared with the feeling of nature. And indeed it is *the same feeling* which is produced by the forest, the steppe, the sea, mountains, only in this case it is more vivid; it awakens more inner voices, touches more inner strings."[8]

Love, too, inhabits the invisible world. It is "a cosmic phenomenon, in which people, mankind, are merely accidental."[9] Love is a creative force that opens in men and women parts of themselves they are unaware of. People who "run away from love, run away in order to keep their masks." The most important part of love is "*that which is not,* which is completely non-existent from an ordinary everyday materialistic point of view."[10]

Everyday things, the "ordinary," are really portals opening onto the fourth dimension, the invisible world of meaning:

> The mast of a ship, a gallows, a cross at the cross-roads
> . . . may be made of the same kind of wood, but in real-
> ity they are *different* objects made of different material
> . . . They are nothing but the *shadows* of real things . . .
> The shadows of a sailor, a hangman and a saint may be
> completely identical . . . Nevertheless they are different
> men and different objects . . . A poet understands . . .
> the difference between a stone from a wall of a church
> and a stone from the wall of a prison . . . He hears the
> voice of the silence, understands the psychological dif-
> ference of silence, realizes that *silence may be different.*[11]

This poetical understanding of things needs to be developed, Ouspensky tells us, because only through it do we come in contact with the real world. Art is a means of doing this, because all art is concerned with representing the "differences" that positivist thought, in its focus on the purely measurable, denies. "At our present stage of development we possess no other means for the perception of the world of causes, which is as powerful as the one contained in art."[12] Echoing the poet Arthur Rimbaud, Ouspensky tells us that the artist must become "clairvoyant, he must see that which others do not see."[13] He must also be a magician and make others see what they would otherwise ignore.

The artist helps us see the differences between things that elude the measuring devices of science. He reminds us that we have our own innate means of "measuring" the meaning of things, our emotions. Emotions, Ouspensky tells us, are "the stained-glass windows of the soul." And our strongest emotion is the yearning for the unknown. In a certain sense, all of Ouspensky's subsequent work on increasing consciousness can be seen as an attempt to refine and harness the energy of emotions. Certain kinds of knowledge, he would later argue, cannot be had without achieving a certain emotional state.

One means of harnessing the power of emotions is morality, which is really a form of aesthetics. Through morality we organize our emotions and see their true relation to our life; we cultivate impersonal, unbiased emotions, which can increase our knowledge of the reality of things, and we inhibit the growth of purely personal, biased emotions that show us only a distorted view of the world. Morality can also aid in linking our thoughts to our deeds, our actions to our words. Through a morality fed by our awareness of the invisible world we can unify our life, and no longer think one thing but do another, no longer call a society or nation "civilized" that gives lip service to love, peace, and tolerance yet devotes its energies and investments to war.

I highlight these aspects of *Tertium Organum* because it is too easy to forget that even with his excursions into higher mathematics Ouspensky was still a poet and romantic. His remarks about nature, sex, and love could easily have been made by Ivan Osokin, as could his comments on the function of art and poetry. And although Ouspensky believed he had gained few definite results from his nitrous oxide experiments, his glimpses of higher consciousness and his brief forays into the unknown had clearly provided him with an inner compass and a powerful sense of direction. Higher consciousness, the fourth dimension, the unknown were aspects of reality available to a new type of person that Ouspensky, in keeping with the terminology of his time, thought of as the superman. It was towards the superman that he was slowly moving.

He was not the only one. In addition to William James, Charles H. Hinton, and a variety of Theosophical authors such as Madame Blavatsky, Annie Besant, C. W. Leadbeater, G. R. S. Mead, and Johan van Manen (as well as lesser-known Russian thinkers like M. V. Lodizhensky and Ouspensky's friend, A. L. Volinsky), Ouspensky also drew heavily on two English-speaking authors who also explored the possibility of an evolution in human consciousness. Edward Carpenter's *From Adam's Peak to Elephanta* describes his experiences of "consciousness without thought" during his travels in India and Ceylon. Carpenter believed that this new form of consciousness would slowly spread throughout the planet. In his massive *Cosmic Conscious-ness* R. M. Bucke, a disciple of Carpenter and a follower of the poet Walt Whitman, developed Carpenter's idea and charted the growth of cosmic consciousness from the first groping sensations of primitive life forms to the mystical ecstasies of the saints.

Yet Ouspensky gave the notion of cosmic consciousness a peculiar twist. With Carpenter and Bucke, he agrees that history shows evidence of a form of consciousness beyond the rational and logical mind. But its appearance in the future, he argues, is *not* inevitable. On the contrary, cosmic or higher consciousness can only be the result of discipline and effort. It is a product of culture and the possession of the few—not of the entire race. Ouspensky's view is decidedly not democratic. For him, the kind of consciousness he experienced during his experiments, or for that brief moment on the Sea of Marmora, had to be earned.

THE STRAY DOG

B ECAUSE OF HIS fluency in English—at least with the written word—for Russian readers Ouspensky became the main source of information about occult and Theosophical developments in England and America. Along with translating Hinton and Carpenter, he wrote introductions for their books, and through *Tertium Organum* itself many Russians became familiar with works otherwise inaccessible to them. The book made Ouspensky's reputation, and from 1911, when it was published, until 1917, when the revolution clamped down on mystical literature and societies, Ouspensky was one of the most widely read popularizers of occult and esoteric thought, a self-image very different from the one he would present years later to his students in London. After *Tertium Organum,* he published several short books on a wide range of occult or mystical topics—yoga, the Tarot, the superman, the Inner Circle (esotericism)—most of which found their way years later into *A New Model of the Universe.* His articles appeared in several Theosophical journals and magazines, his lectures attracted hundreds, sometimes thousands, of people, and his opinion on a variety of mystical matters was widely sought.

One group powerfully influenced by *Tertium Organum* were the artists of the Russian avant-garde. Interest in mystical and occult ideas among artists and poets had been widespread since the Symbolists. But whereas the earlier generation was satisfied with vague hints and allusions to the unknown,

Ouspensky's contemporaries wanted a more direct approach. His first book on the fourth dimension, *The Fourth Dimension* (1909), subtitled "An Experiment in the Examination of the Realm of the Immeasurable," was in keeping with the sensibility of the new generation. Where the Symbolists rejected science outright, the Cubo-Futurists (an ungainly amalgam of French Cubism and Italian Futurism) believed its insights could be combined with those of art and mysticism. Science, they agreed, was incomplete, but this was no reason to ignore it. Ouspensky's mathematical approach to the beyond was appealing to a generation discovering the liberating powers of abstract art. His declarations that "Art is a powerful instrument for the knowledge of the noumenal world,"[1] and that "Art in its highest manifestations is a path to cosmic consciousness,"[2] appealed to a generation of artists eager for direct contact with Reality.

At least two artists quoted Ouspensky directly in manifestos on their work. In "New Ways of the Word," the poet Aleksie Kruchenykh referred to Ouspensky's ideas about the inadequacy of ordinary language and the need for a new "language of the future." Like the Dadaists in Zurich, the poets of the Russian avant-garde experimented with language, attempting to break free of logic and rationality in order to reach a kind of "pure" speech of experience, a vocabulary of "nonsense" that would bypass meaning and grasp reality directly, a notion very similar to Zen.[3] One poet particularly associated with *zaum*, the name given to this new language, was Velimir Khlebnikov. Like Ouspensky, Khlebnikov was obsessed with the mystery of time and wrote several theoretical works dealing with the cyclical nature of history. Mikhail Matiushin, a St. Petersburg musician, composer, and painter, wrote an article for the arts journal *Union of Youth*, praising Ouspensky's work. Matiushin speaks of the "regal moment of the passage of our consciousness into a new phase of dimension" and, echoing

Ouspensky, announces that "artists have always been knights, poets and prophets of space in all eras."

Matiushin was the first to link Ouspensky's ideas on the fourth dimension to similar notions being put on canvas by the Cubist school in France; he includes extracts from *Tertium Organum* in his translation of a central Cubist text *Du Cubisme* by Gleizes and Metzinger. But perhaps the most famous painter influenced by Ouspensky's work was Kasimir Malevich.[4] Like Ouspensky, Malevich was eager to storm the gates of the unknown, and his Suprematist canvases, depicting weird nonrepresentational figures, are like higher-dimensional landscapes glimpsed through cracks in our three-dimensional world. There's good reason to suspect that Malevich as well as other artists attended the several lectures Ouspensky gave in St. Petersburg and Moscow between 1912 and 1915. If nothing else, Ouspensky was very popular, and the themes of his lectures were in keeping with the fashion of the time. In February and March of 1915, after his trip to India— about which we will hear more shortly—Ouspensky gave a series of lectures in St. Petersburg (then renamed Petrograd). At the same time, an influential Russian Futurist exhibition, *Tramway V,* featuring works by Malevich and the Constructivist Tatlin, was also held. By the end of the year, Malevich held his *0.10 Last Futurist Exhibit,* and of the thirty-nine paintings included, five dealt with the fourth dimension.

But the avant-garde and Ouspensky didn't necessarily see eye to eye. Malevich, a supporter of the revolution, was critical of Ouspensky's relations with the Theosophical Society, which was seen as a reactionary group linked to high society. Ouspensky, of course, had no interest in radical politics. And for all his belief in the ability of art to convey the invisible, in the second edition of *The Fourth Dimension* Ouspensky grumbled about "futurist artists" who were trying to paint the fourth dimension, which to him was like "trying to make a sculpture of a sunset." He also linked them with the various "occultists" and "spiritualists" who sought physical manifestations of the astral plane and so on as proof of their beliefs.[5]

After his meeting with the literary critic A. L. Volinsky, Ouspensky became a regular among the artistic *demimonde* making up St. Petersburg's bohemian crowd. Volinsky's writings introduced aspects of the new art and literature to a wide reading public, and through him Ouspensky was introduced to a world of poets, artists, musicians, and *poseurs*. Unlike other fast sets, their late-night carousing was accented by a passionate quest for the Absolute. This was the milieu of Berdyaev's God-Seekers, who wouldn't leave a café because they hadn't yet decided whether God existed. One central watering hole for these metaphysical all-nighters was a grimy, foul-smelling, and ill-lit establishment called The Stray Dog.

Opened in 1912, The Stray Dog was a place where, in Ouspensky's words, "one could do no wrong." It was, in effect, his real academy. It's more than likely that in this seedy bar, housed in the cellar of a house on Italyanskaya Street and Mikhailovskaya Square, not far from the Nevsky Prospect and Ouspensky's own room, the ideas of *Tertium Organum* were discussed by more inspired would-be mystics than had actually read it. Here, surrounded by an assortment of eccentric characters, Ouspensky held forth on the superman, cosmic consciousness, time, and, of course, the fourth dimension. Ouspensky became so associated with this possible other realm that he was known to the Stray Dog crowd as "Ouspensky Fourth Dimension"—an apt nickname and one that suggests a warm familiarity: Ouspensky's years at The Stray Dog were more than likely the most cherished of his life.

Ouspensky's reputation as an authority on the fourth dimension commanded considerable respect. On one occasion, a figure no less that Leo Tolstoy listened patiently while, over lunch, Ouspensky drew a series of multidimensional diagrams on the tablecloth. Tolstoy countered with some remarks about his experiences with Freemasonry and how they featured in his novels. But the artistic circles that moved within The Stray Dog were much more radical. Here was a kind of private club for the "artists of the future." Guests signed a book bound in pigskin. As in many fashionable haunts, there was an "in crowd" who didn't have to pay for admission, while the rest doled out to be where the action was. Some name characters frequented this dark underground. The ballerina Tamara Karasavina, for example, danced on a giant mirror. Banging on an immense drum and dressed as a gladiator, the poet Vladimir Mayakovsky announced the arrival of his friends. Another poet, Vasilik Gnedov, recited verse by making circular movements with his arms. The stale air, smelling of cheap tobacco, was filled with *zaum,* the non-sense language, accompanying the strains of works by the composers Ilya Sats and Arthur Lourie. "We began to imagine that the whole world was in fact concentrated at The Stray Dog," said the poet Anna Akhmatova. "Dead people performed there," replied still another poet, Alexander Blok. Andrei Bely, Valery Briussov— at the time, anyone who was anyone must have passed through its portals and entered its depths.

One seeker after the miraculous who braved the descent was a young classical pianist named Anna Butkovsky (later Hewitt). Like many of the stray dogs, she was interested in Theosophy; more importantly, she had actually read *Tertium Organum.* Nursing a mystical hunger since the age of nine, Anna had come across Ouspensky's book in a library. Here was someone who shared her passion and had actually made some headway into the beyond. Her next encounter with Ouspensky was less vicarious. At a meeting of the Theosophical Society, the twenty-something Anna was startled when she heard Madame Kamensky, an important member, ask Mr. Ouspensky for his opinion on some mystical matter. She saw a square-built, impressive frame of medium height stand up. His close-cropped white hair and near-albino coloring were accented by a pince-nez, which later became a symbol of imperturbable scrutiny. All heads turned toward the distinguished writer and journalist. Ouspensky, however, declined to comment, on the grounds that he was in the process of arriving at his own views on the matter; to speak now would be premature. Anna knew an opportunity when she saw one and approached Ouspensky after the meeting. She started up a conversation that lasted for the next four years.[6]

Ouspensky was always susceptible to attractive, intelligent women, and when Anna asked him, he admitted that his real reason for not answering Madame Kamensky was that he was planning on leaving the society. He even confided that he had been asked to join their "inner circle" but had declined.

"The ordinary members are 'sheep,'" he explained. "But there are probably even bigger sheep in the 'inner circle.'"

"You sound as though you are sorry there are no wolves," she replied.

"Exactly! At least wolves display strength. Sheep are simply sheep, and it is hopeless for them to pretend to aspire to be the image of God, and to develop the hidden, higher faculties."[7]

When Anna asked if he was planning any other books, Ouspensky smiled and replied that to answer her question properly would require some time. Would she like to meet him for coffee tomorrow morning? Did she know Phillipoff's Café?

Situated on the corner of Trotsky Street and Nevsky Prospect, not far from Ouspensky's flat, Phillipoff's Café was another central meeting place for St. Petersburg's intelligentsia. When Anna arrived the next morning, Ouspensky was already there, contemplating the empty coffee cups sitting before him. A well-known regular, Ouspensky had devised an ingenious method of ordering his drinks: the waiter was instructed to bring another whenever Ouspensky's cup was empty, and a certain gesture of the hand signaled that he had had his fill. "Better to decline once than to order several times" was the eminently logical reasoning. By the time Anna sat down, the waiter had placed a glass of strong coffee "a la Varsovienne" before her. When she had finished that, he brought another.

Anna asked again if Ouspensky was planning on another book, and he explained that before writing *Tertium Organum* he had started an earlier book but soon felt it would take at least twenty years to complete. Its working title, *The Wisdom of the Gods* (later *A New Model of the Universe*), suggests that, however dissatisfied Ouspensky had become with the Theosophical Society, theosophy itself—"god-wisdom"—was still very much on his mind.

Understandably, Anna found his estimate of twenty years a bit exaggerated. And even if it took that long, she asked, wasn't it still worth writing?

"What I wanted to say in that book," Ouspensky explained, "was so difficult and elusive that I did not feel equal to it." "I *must* always feel equal to anything I tackle." He admitted that the realization of his inadequacy hurt his pride, and he confessed that he "knew [he] lacked something necessary to do it."[8] Nevertheless, some of the ideas found a home in other works, which he was then preparing for publication.

After that morning, the two met at Phillipoff's every day at noon, and talk always centered around the same subject: how they could find a teacher who could lead them to the "Miracle." The Miracle was superconsciousness—*sverkhsoznanie*, a term popularized by the writer M. V. Lodizhensky. Everything they spoke of—the fourth dimension, Wagner, the Holy Grail, Vivekananda, alchemy, yoga, Nietzsche, magic, samadhi, and the rest—led back to the necessity of transforming consciousness. And for Ouspensky this meant finding someone who knew how to do this.

Through Anna's account it is clear that she and Ouspensky became lovers. In her, she tells us, Ouspensky had found a fellow seeker. He recognized in her a "driving force" that he too possessed, and the discovery made him feel "eighteen," although he was in his mid-thirties. This "boyish" quality came through in other ways, most endearingly in his enthusiasm for the unknown. "Sometimes one can put one's foot forward over the edge of a precipice, and propel oneself across to the other side without falling," he told her. She agreed. "We shall find the Miracle, I know it," he told her. Then he smiled and added: "I never feel, I *know*."

Ouspensky asked her to play the piano for him. He found her performance moving, full of a creative force that affected him. He likened music to a kind of language, like the "signs in heaven." There were, he told her, "signs everywhere, but we cannot read them." Given that Ouspensky admitted on a few occasions to a lack of musical appreciation, he may have been indulging in some metaphysical sweet talk; either that, or Anna is embellishing her account. Ouspensky linked their hunger for the Miracle to the Russian fairy tale of the Firebird, which the avant-garde composer Igor Stravinsky had recently used as a basis for a ballet score. Ever elusive, the magical Firebird drops a feather from its glowing tail and burns the hand of its pursuer: although it cannot be caught, it nevertheless leaves proof of its existence. Those who follow the Firebird, Ouspensky told her, may be frustrated in their hopes, but the pursuit itself brings joy and peace and the courage to continue the quest.

Anna saw in Ouspensky's face a "radiant countenance filled with a youthful happiness." No one else, she remarks, ever witnessed this. In this happy mood, his inspiration and vision were at their strongest, and in later years, when they met in Berlin, London, or Paris, she saw that this youthful innocence had hardened into an impenetrable outer shell. Why, she asks, had Ouspensky crushed the "gentle, poetic radiance of his St. Petersburg days?" Could it be that he saw this side of himself as a weakness?

For the meantime, however, it was Peter and not Demian who was most present during their affair—a supremely self-confident and perhaps slightly arrogant Peter. "I don't think that among your friends you have anyone as *interesting* as I am," he announced. And Anna had to agree, although she had already seen a great deal of life, having been married and gone through a few affairs. Ouspensky feigned shock at these revelations, but they didn't prevent the two of them from walking the streets until dawn and then, perhaps alone or perhaps with Volinsky and other stragglers from The Stray Dog, settling down at the Nikolaevski Station for one last coffee or a final glass of tea.

Ouspensky was usually the last to head home, after walking Anna to her door on Nikolaevski Street. Then, after a few hours sleep, the routine would start again. On one occasion, Ouspensky invited Anna to his room. As she had invited him to hear her play, he explained that he would like to return the gesture and show her his books. Aware that more than a love of deep reading was involved, Anna nevertheless agreed. She glanced through the titles and selected three to take home: Bucke's *Cosmic Consciousness,* Hinton's *The Fourth Dimension,* and a volume on yoga by Vivekananda. Ouspensky told her that if Vivekananda's books were translated into Russian, they would certainly sell. Anna took his remark to heart and got in touch with a friend, Nina Souvorina, niece of the publisher Alexei Souvorin, who had published Ouspensky's book on the Tarot *(The Symbolism of the Tarot: Philosophy of Occultism in Pictures and Numbers)* and his short work on yoga *(The Search for a New Life: What is Yoga?),* both of which were later included in *A New Model of the Universe.* Souvorin combined a sharp editorial brilliance with an unbalanced personality. He did have a good sense of what would sell, though, and his editions of Vivekananda's works, with their bright purple covers and yellow lettering, became very popular.

According to Anna, Ouspensky himself was working on two books: his novel, then called *Cinemadrama Not for the Cinematographer,* and his collection of novellas, *Conversations with the Devil: Occult Stories.* The original title for *Ivan Osokin* shows us a side of Ouspensky little known to his later readers: his humor. This is even more evident in his occult stories, one of which, "The Inventor," includes a hilarious tongue-in-cheek account of a Black Mass in *fin-de-siècle* Paris, a milieu Ouspensky knew well. This, too, is a side of Ouspensky we rarely encounter.

By this time Ouspensky's determination to find a teacher had reached a crisis point. A friend who had emigrated to Australia suggested he join him, but Ouspensky knew he wouldn't find what he was looking for there. With the yogis in India he could possibly find a way, and no doubt his conversations with Anna revolved around this obsession. Finally, she suggested he do what he had already decided upon.

Ouspensky obtained a commission from three Russian newspapers to travel to India and write about his journey. He was convinced that much of value still remained in the East; certainly there was more there than could be found in Europe. He admitted that an element of romance influenced this view; in his thoughts India and the Miracle seemed to coalesce.[9] He didn't doubt that schools existed, but in what form or shape he was unsure. He sometimes thought he could make contact with schools on a *different plane,* through somehow altering his consciousness. But if this was the case, then he needn't journey anywhere. At other times he believed the reports of various yogi schools he had heard, suggesting that remnants of an ancient tradition were still preserved: it was possible to encounter an unbroken esoteric line, one that reached back to the builders of Notre Dame, the pyramids, the Sphinx. Space and time would vanish upon contact with the source of wisdom. The miraculous would be open to him.

In the event, Ouspensky was disabused of these romantic notions. The journey, however, was not totally without profit. For one thing, at every port he came to, Ouspensky encountered a strange phenomenon. At each step of his journey—in London, Paris, Genoa, Cairo, Colombo, Galle, Madras, Benares, and Calcutta—he met people who shared an interest in the ideas that drove him on. They seemed to speak the same language, and between himself and these new acquaintances Ouspensky felt an immediate rapport and understanding. In *Tertium Organum* he had written of a "new race," those for whom cosmic consciousness was a distinct possibility. Now, thousands of miles from home, he found himself meeting individuals who made up if not a race, then certainly an uncommon community, a new category of person, motivated by values vastly different from the ordinary materialistic aims and purposes. He thought of himself as a kind of connecting link, tying together these disparate souls into an informal unity. Some of these contacts, like those with A. R. Orage and G. R. S. Mead, would prove invaluable in later years.

There were many moving experiences along the way. Standing before the cathedral of Notre Dame in Paris, Ouspensky was convinced that parallel to the known history of humanity, what he called "the history of crime," there was another history, written by the esoteric masters who had designed the cathedral. In doing so they had conquered time, transmitting in the structure's massive stone the hidden knowledge of the ages. In Ceylon, standing before a statue known as "the Buddha with the Sapphire Eyes," Ouspensky realized that he was in the presence of a miracle. The face of the Buddha was alive, and its eyes *saw him*—saw, that is, all that was hidden in the depths of his soul. Under the Buddha's gaze, all that was small, anxious, and unnecessary in him rose to the surface. It *understood* him in a way that no human countenance could, and the effect was to dispel the gloom that lay like silt in the bottom of his soul. Ouspensky, too aware of the "wooden world," too prone to passivity and lassitude,[10] now found himself filled with a mysterious, "miraculous" calm. And sitting before the Taj Mahal one moonlit night, he felt that the everyday reality in which we live had somehow dissolved and in its place was another reality, one that we rarely see but which is nevertheless more real and more true than the world we take for granted.

Ouspensky had many impressions of "the miraculous," but these were not what he had gone in search of. Schools, a teacher, a definite way to superconsciousness—these had eluded him. He met interesting people, like Sri Aurobindo, who was then establishing himself in Pondicherry. There were disciples of Ramakrishna, nice people who he liked but whose way of devotion and slightly sentimental morality could offer him nothing. There were yogis who knew how to create in themselves unusual states of consciousness but seemed unable to pass their knowledge on to others. There were also many "miracles" of a frankly dubious nature—fakirs who could lie untroubled on a bed of nails, holy men who saw visions, and charlatans of every stamp who preyed on the gullibility of European travelers filled with tales of the magical East. Of all that he experienced, only the reports of a certain type of school, which he had failed to make contact with, suggested anything like the possibility of achieving his goal. But even these schools had drawbacks. To enter them, one had to give up *everything, at once,* which meant that Ouspensky would have to forget his past, his work, his life, and remain in India for an unknown length of time. This he couldn't do. What he heard about these schools impressed him, but in the end he felt that "a man had the right, up to a certain point, to know where he was going," a sentiment that would surface again and cause him no little disturbance.

"Are there ever any real results achieved by Yoga?" Leslie White, the protagonist in "The Benevolent Devil," one of Ouspensky's "occult stories," asks an Indian holy man. "Or does it all come down to travelers' tales of India?"

I want to know whether all these miraculous happenings I have read about in books on Yoga ever really took place—clairvoyance, second sight, mind-reading, thought-transference, knowledge of the future, and the like. I often wake up at night and think, can it really be true that somewhere there are people who have achieved something miraculous? I know I would drop everything to follow such a person. But I must be sure he has succeeded. You must understand me. I cannot believe in words any longer. Too often have we been deceived by words, and I cannot deceive myself any more, nor do I want to. Tell me then, are there people who have attained something and what is it they have attained, and could I attain the same and how?[11]

Ouspensky did not find what he was looking for. Leaving India, on his third visit to Colombo, he wondered what the next phase of his search would be. Would he meet again the man who had offered to introduce him to certain yogis? Would he return to Russia? Or would he venture even further, to Burma, Siam, Japan, and perhaps America? But when his ship touched dock, all these thoughts were forgotten. The world of obvious absurdities and the history of crime had decided to interfere with his plans. It was August 1914, and the world, Ouspensky found, was at war.

CHAPTER SIX

THE INCOMPARABLE MR. G.

O USPENSKY RETURNED to Russia in November 1914, disappointed by his fruitless search for schools. An international journalist, he must have known that war was on its way. Yet like so many others, he had tried to avoid facing its reality. Now that was impossible. "All the mud was rising from the bottom of life,"[1] he said, as the serenity he had found in the sapphire gaze of the Buddha was replaced by the wild rhetoric of war. The culture of barbarism was triumphant, and the fragile threads he had drawn across the globe, linking himself and the bearers of the new consciousness, were severed. All bets were off and everything was thrown into disorder.

"Why on earth did I ever go to India?" he asked Anna when, once again, they began daily appointments at Phillipoff's Café. "I found nothing there that I have not read before in books, or heard rumored in some way . . . nothing new, *nothing*."[2] His personal disappointment must have been great, and amidst the confusion and madness of war it must have seemed doubly painful. Here were the anti-values of barbarism, championed by newspapers and politicians, fueling the base passions of hatred, nationalism, and violence. And the one way out of the history of crime, the one escape route from the insanity, seemed closed to him. Did it ever exist? he must have asked himself. Wasn't it, like so much else he encountered on his journey, an illusion? Wasn't he simply believing in lies, like the rest? Different lies, certainly, but stories, myths, fantasies all the same?

It would have been easy to drift into cynicism. But Ouspensky's conviction that the only way out of "the labyrinth of contradictions in which we live" was via some "entirely new road, unlike anything hitherto known or used by us," was too great. "Beyond the thin film of false reality" there was "another reality"—there was, as he and Anna had told each other time and time again, the miraculous.[3] If nothing else, the failure to find what he was looking for in India allowed him to finely tune his requirements. All that was "fantastic" in his thoughts about schools had now evaporated. Ideas about "nonphysical contact"—the possibility of communicating with schools in the ancient past or on some other plane—dissolved. He discarded all such dreams and fantasies as signs of weakness, and recognized them as "one of the principal obstacles on our possible way to the miraculous."[4] If he was going to find a school, it was going to be real, solid, concrete, and its teachers, however knowledgeable, would be flesh and blood, just as the teachers of any ordinary school would be.

In the event, the ordinariness of the surroundings in which Ouspensky eventually did find his "school" would prove one of the strangest and most unusual things about it.

He was not, however, entirely free from the normal human reaction to bruised dreams. In the late winter of 1915, during the "generally catastrophic conditions of life in the midst of which we have to live and work,"[5] Ouspensky gave public lectures on his travels at the Alexandrovsky Hall of the Petersburg Town Duma. These were well attended; more than a thousand people came to each lecture, among them, as we've seen, members of the Russian avant-garde. The talks seemed to serve two purposes: to distance Ouspensky from the still-prevalent notions that the key to solving the spiritual dilemma of the West could be found by foraging in the East, and to sever his ties with the Theosophical Society. By all reports, he was successful. In its review of Ouspensky's lectures, the leading Russian Theosophical journal reported:

> P. D. Ouspensky's three lectures attracted a huge audi-
> ence, but they evoked perplexity. The lecturer
> promised to talk about India. In fact he talked only
> about his disillusionment in seeking the miraculous
> and about his understanding of occultism at variance
> with its understanding by Theosophy and the
> Theosophical Society. With indignation he said that
> the Theosophists selected ethics and philosophy, not
> occultism, as their field of effort, and that ethics and
> philosophy are unnecessary to the Society and unrelat-
> ed to occultism . . . He also accused the Theosophical
> Society of arrogance and sectarianism.[6]

It wasn't only in his search for schools that Ouspensky found India wanting. Hunting for material to fill his newspaper column, he tried to track down evidence of some of the well-known, though less edifying, "miracles" that the mystic East was famous for. But here too he drew a blank. Of the legendary rope trick, for example, in which a fakir throws a rope into the air upon which a young boy climbs, he could find no trace at all. Not only did he find it impossible to locate a fakir capable of such a feat, Ouspensky was unable to find a single traveler who had seen it in person: everyone he questioned knew of it only by hearsay. Even reports from the educated Hindus whom he spoke with about it were not to be believed, not because they wanted to deceive, but because they were reluctant to disappoint yet another European in search of Indian magic. That a phenomenon with *no basis in fact* should command belief by numbers of otherwise intelligent people suggested to Ouspensky that human beings have a propensity to accept a lie because doing so is easier than seeking out the truth. Ouspensky, however, constantly submitted himself to the acid bath of experiment and observation. His decision to search for a teacher who could lead him to the miraculous was motivated, he admitted, by a desire to avoid what he considered "amateurish attempts at 'work on oneself.'"[7] As Leslie White announced, "I cannot deceive myself anymore, nor do I want to." Although he believed in the miraculous, Ouspensky wanted facts.

It isn't surprising, then, that while in Moscow in December and January of 1914–15 Ouspensky cast a bemused eye at a curious advertisement he had found in a newspaper. Doing editorial work for a journal he had written for while in India, Ouspensky spied a notice for a ballet entitled "The Struggle of the Magicians." The title itself would have caught his attention. Even more intriguing, its author was a "certain 'Hindu,'" and the performance promised to present a complete picture of all that Ouspensky had just failed to find on his journey. Set against the backdrop of India, the ballet would include fakir miracles, sacred dances, and much more. Having just discovered the "truth" about India, Ouspensky was critical of the advertisement's claims. But the irony of the coincidence must have amused him. Acknowledging that Hindu ballets were something of a rarity in Moscow, he decided to include the notice in the next issue of his paper, adding to it the caveat that the ballet would provide all that is unavailable in India, but which travelers journey there to see.

Ouspensky's St. Petersburg lectures had been successful enough that he was able to repeat his performance in Moscow. In India, he told his audience, the miraculous was not sought where it should be sought. The known ways were useless. The miraculous passed us by and we did not notice it. The miraculous, when it appears among ordinary humanity, always wears a mask, and only the very few succeed in penetrating it.

One wonders if Ouspensky was speaking to himself. For as fate would have it, he was about to have an opportunity to put his theory into practice.

During his Moscow lectures Ouspensky was approached by two men, Vladimir Pohl, a musician, and Sergei Dmitrievich Mercourov, a sculptor. They told him of an occult group to which they belonged, and which, oddly enough, was led by the "certain Hindu"—actually a Caucasian Greek—responsible for the ballet scenario "The Struggle of the Magicians," the notice for which Ouspensky had come across a few months earlier. They spoke of the work the group was engaged in, and of "G's"—the Greek's—aims. To Ouspensky it seemed heady, confused, and extremely doubtful material. As a noted journalist, highly successful lecturer, and author of a popular and influential book—which was about to go into a second edition—Ouspensky had heard it all before. Tactfully he listened, but no doubt looked for a polite way to escape. By now Ouspensky had had enough of the kind of self-hypnosis associated with all such occult groups. People, he ruefully reflected, "invent miracles for themselves and invent exactly what is expected of them."[8] It was all a brew of "superstition, self-suggestion and defective thinking," and Ouspensky, having just returned from a long, profitless journey, wanted no part of it.

Mercourov, however, was persistent, and it was more than likely out of the desire to quiet his entreaties than out of any real interest that Ouspensky finally broke down and agreed to meet the mysterious Mr. G.

It was, without doubt, the most fateful decision of his life.

"Georgei Ivanovitch Gurdjieff was born . . . and here all pretensions to accuracy stop."[9] So begins James Webb's exhaustive biography of the man Ouspensky was about to meet. What proves a nightmare for a biographer is a godsend for someone set on presenting himself as an enigma. As with many gurus, mystic teachers, and occult masters, Gurdjieff's past is, as the cliché goes, shrouded in mystery. Up until 1912 or 1913, all that we know of him comes from his own hand, and even the most devoted follower must admit that what Gurdjieff tells us about himself is at the very least open to multiple interpretations. Our sources for material on Gurdjieff's early years are his autobiographical account, *Meetings with Remarkable Men;* the unfinished *Life Is Real Only Then, When I Am;* and an earlier effort that, if nothing else, must go down as one of the strangest publications ever to see the light of print, *Herald of Coming Good.*

Ouspensky's early years are difficult to piece together, but the difficulty arises out of the normal ravages of time and the dispersal of material: a diligent researcher, armed with patience and a command of Russian, could burrow through the Moscow and St. Petersburg periodical archives and more than likely uncover a great deal of interesting material about Ouspensky's days as a journalist. The same cannot be said of Gurdjieff. He invented and reinvented himself so many times, left so many false trails, and encouraged so many myths and mistakes about exactly who he was that uncovering the truth about his past would take a lifetime. And very likely the whole dizzying business would leave even the most tenacious researcher wondering if it was not in some way planned. Gurdjieff is a man with no loose ends. There is, it seems, no way *into* him as there is into Ouspensky or other mystic figures of the Golden Age of Western Occultism, like Madame Blavatsky and Aleister Crowley. Both Crowley and Blavatsky were fond of creating myths about themselves, but these amounted to tall tales and improbable claims, often made with tongue in cheek. Gurdjieff had his share of these, but something more was added: a sense that he wanted, and exerted, an absolute control over his identity. As he once told an impressionable student, C. S. Nott, "the sign of a perfected man . . . must be that in regard to everything happening outside him, he is able to . . . perform to perfection externally the part corresponding to the given situation; but at the same time never blend or agree with it." Gurdjieff had worked hard and long at so "perfecting" himself, and we are left to wonder exactly when the separation between his inner and outer worlds that he deemed so important began. And unless, like William Patrick Patterson, we accept every word of Gurdjieff's as holy writ and see him as a "Messenger from Above," with all the religious overtones such a belief implies, we are also left asking why. Why did Gurdjieff cover his tracks so efficiently? Why was it so important to reach a state where nothing from "outside" could touch him internally? And what does this tell us about him?

The Gurdjieff story, however, is this:

We have, to date, three candidates for the year of Gurdjieff's birth: 1866, 1872, and 1877; this would make him either twelve, four, or only one year older than Ouspensky. As Gurdjieff himself destroyed all his private papers and documents, including birth certificates and passports, on the eve of a trip to America in 1930, there is no concrete evidence for any one year being accurate. The year 1877 has acquired a certain preference, since it is the date on Gurdjieff's passport. All the evidence, however, suggests that Gurdjieff could fake a date on a passport, so while official recognition of 1877 gives it some weight, there's still no guarantee that it's accurate. The day of his birth accepted by his biographers is December 28, although followers of the Fourth Way celebrate his birthday on January 13, making allowances for the Old Russian calendar.

The ambiguity over the year of Gurdjieff's birth makes his nationality equally ambiguous. Depending on which year we accept, Gurdjieff was either Turkish or Russian, as the place of his birth in the Caucasus was either called Gumru, and was under Turkish rule *before* 1877, or Alexandropol, and was under Russian rule *after* that year. His parents' nationality is clearer: his father was Greek, his mother Armenian. In 1878, a year (or more) after his birth, his family moved to Kars, a near-by town. Captured by the Russians in 1877, most of its Turkish population had been slaughtered. When it became Russian, a large flood of Russians arrived, while the remaining Turks left. Colin Wilson makes the point that Gurdjieff grew up in an ethnic melting pot, in a society that was by necessity multi-cultural. While the young Ouspensky suffered personal loss but lived in an ethnically and culturally, if not politically, sta-ble world, Gurdjieff grew up in a world with few or no boundaries and nothing like a Western sense of order. The unpredictability of his surroundings taught him to think on his feet—a lesson that, years later, he would try to pass on to his students.

Gurdjieff's father was a carpenter whose real love was poetry and storytelling, and Gurdjieff would listen while his father recited from memory one of the epics of the past. He was a bard, and Gurdjieff was impressed when he read in a magazine that archaeologists had recently discovered ancient tablets containing fragments of the epic *Gilgamesh;* this was one of the traditional tales that Gurdjieff's father had memo-rized and often recited. Gurdjieff's father had been taught *Gilgamesh* by another bard, who had learned it from one before him, and so on, going back countless generations. This notion of the reality of an ancient oral tradition kept alive for cen-turies would later play a major part in Gurdjieff's own teaching.

At an early age Gurdjieff showed a fascination for the occult. Early on, he witnessed a variety of strange phenomena: table-rapping, fortune-telling, faith healing, even vampirism. The death of his sister raised questions about life beyond the grave. When he was around eleven years old (accepting 1877 as the year of his birth), he witnessed a remarkable sight. The sound of screaming brought him to a group of children. There he saw a young Yezidi boy standing within a circle that had

been drawn on the ground. The Yezidis are a religious sect—
erroneously considered devil worshippers—and are prone to
an inexplicable phenomenon: if placed within a circle they are
unable to leave it. The young boy was screaming, trapped within the ring the children had drawn around him. When
Gurdjieff rubbed out part of the circle, the boy fled.
Inquisitive, Gurdjieff asked everyone he knew about the experience, but no one could explain it. Years later he
experimented himself, drawing a circle around a Yezidi
woman. She too was unable to leave it, and when Gurdjieff and
another man finally pulled her from it, she collapsed into a
state of catalepsy.

Meetings with Remarkable Men is filled with other, equally
unusual experiences. The young Gurdjieff investigated each
one, trying to find an answer to its mystery. He read all he
could get his hands on and questioned everyone. Finally, he
concluded that although human beings seem to understand
themselves and the world, they are almost totally lacking in
knowledge of either. Just as Ouspensky would conclude years
later, Gurdjieff realized that laziness and lack of curiosity
allowed people to accept whatever story seemed simplest and
freed them from seeking the truth.

Gurdjieff studied for the priesthood, and as the head of
his school insisted that all students have medical training, he
also studied medicine. Gurdjieff soon manifested a remarkable
talent for mechanical work; he was a natural "Mr. Fix It." He
spent a great deal of his adolescence taking things apart and
putting them back together. Often times he would see how
some machine or tool could be improved and would make the
necessary adjustments. As we will see, his later life centered
around fixing "machines" as well. As his family was poor, for a
time he earned money as a traveling repairman.

Religious questions, the paranormal, and mechanical
skills informed Gurdjieff's early years. To these were added an

enviable knack for making money and a cheerful disregard for the legalities involved. As a teenager he worked for a railway company, surveying a proposed route between Tiflis and Kars. He knew in advance which towns were slated for a station, and would approach the town elders suggesting that, for a price, he could arrange for the train to stop there. Naturally the city fathers were pleased, and Gurdjieff's pockets were filled. On another occasion, Gurdjieff caught sparrows, dyed them different colors, and sold them to gullible customers as a rare breed of "American canary"—making his escape quickly, before a sudden shower washed the dye off. In later years this talent for making money was applied to diverse activities, from selling carpets and curing drug addicts to running cinemas and restaurants.

With a friend, Sarkis Pogossian, Gurdjieff spent long evenings discussing the central questions of human existence. They visited "sacred sites" and through their reading became convinced a "hidden knowledge" existed. They also believed that traces of this lost wisdom could be discerned in the relics of the past—a belief, we know, that Ouspensky had absorbed from Theosophy. After they made enough money to give up their jobs—Pogossian, too, worked for the railway—the two purchased a library of ancient Armenian texts, then moved to the ancient city of Ani. Here they built a hut and plunged into their studies and explorations of the ancient Armenian capital.

They discovered a monk's cell in an underground passage. Within it were old parchments inscribed in ancient Armenian. They brought these to Alexandropol, hoping to decipher them. It turned out that the parchments spoke of an ancient secret society, the Sarmoung Brotherhood, and they recalled the name from one of the texts in their library. This brotherhood, it seemed, flourished in about 2500 BC; the parchments dated to around 600 AD. Gurdjieff and Pogossian concluded that remains of the Sarmoung Brotherhood might still be found in an area about three hundred miles south of present day Mosul (Iraq). Convincing a society of Armenian patriots to finance their expedition, they embarked on their own quest for the miraculous.

They seemed to be in luck. An Armenian priest who housed them mentioned a map he had in his possession. A Russian prince, he said, had wanted to purchase it, but the priest wouldn't sell it and only allowed the prince to make a copy. He showed Gurdjieff the map; it turned out to be of "pre-sand Egypt." Understandably, Gurdjieff was excited by the discovery and, when the priest was out, made a copy of the map. The Russian prince had paid for this privilege, but as Gurdjieff would later tell Ouspensky, it is sometimes necessary for a seeker to "steal" knowledge.

A series of events brought Gurdjieff to Alexandria (Pogossian abandoned the quest along the way). From Egypt he went to Jerusalem, where he worked as a tourist guide. Gurdjieff fails to tell us whether he had discovered any evidence of the Sarmoung Brotherhood or what he made of the map of pre-sand Egypt. But back in Egypt, Gurdjieff sat by one of the pyramids studying the map. A man approached and, peering down at him, with great emotion asked how he had come across it. This, it turned out, was the same prince who had tried to buy the map from the priest.

At this point Gurdjieff became involved with a group of questers, the Seekers of Truth, whose leader was the Russian prince. Their adventures took them to several sites in Asia, some inaccessible to Europeans, where they discovered the "hidden knowledge" the existence of which Gurdjieff had suspected years before. Gurdjieff tells us that he did eventually make contact with the present-day Sarmoung Brotherhood, spending time at their monasteries in the Himalayas and Turkistan. It was there that he learned the ancient secrets of human existence and the methods of achieving a higher state of consciousness.

All of which makes for a wonderful story, the reliability of which is difficult to corroborate.

Gurdjieff's account of his formative years can be read on a variety of levels: metaphor, allegory, pure tall tale, metaphysical fiction, autobiography, or simply invention. Given the milieu in which he surfaced in Moscow, it's understandable that he would want to present himself as a mysterious figure with a series of mystical adventures under his belt. He had other accomplishments as well: during this period he may have spent some time as a secret agent working for the Russian government during their political chess match with the British known as the Great Game.[10] He also worked for a period as a professional hypnotist and wonder-worker—a kind of traveling magician, the equivalent today of a television psychic. But the Gurdjieff who targeted Ouspensky and sent his students to draw him in was determined to present himself as one thing and one thing only: a man who *knows*.

It seems likely that in St. Petersburg in 1913 he presented himself as a certain "Prince Ozay" and made the acquaintance of the Englishman Paul Dukes, a twenty-four-year-old traveler and musician. The friend of Lev Lvovitch—significantly, a professional healer and hypnotist—Dukes, who later knew Ouspensky, was informed that Lvovitch had met the Prince while on military service in Central Asia. The Prince, Lvovitch told Dukes, was a man like no other. Upon meeting him, Dukes had to agree. At a house not far from Nikolaevski Station—a short walk, we know, from Ouspensky's own apartment—Dukes was led to a large and sumptuously appointed room. Oriental carpets adorned the walls, the windows were covered in rich curtains, and wrought-iron lamps fitted with colored glass hung from the ceiling. The atmosphere was appropriately exotic and oddly reminiscent of the magician's room in Ouspensky's novel. A hole in Dukes's sock prompted the Prince to remark on the virtues of ventilation: "Good thing—nothing like fresh air." It's the kind of thing Gurdjieff would say. But more commanding evidence are the occult lessons that Dukes received from the Prince. Most seem to have concerned diet, breathing, sex, and other standard fare in mystical disciplines. The Prince told Dukes the musician that he was a musical instrument and spoke of the importance of being "in tune." This suggests both Gurdjieff's later use of musical terms like "octave" and his tendency to approach each student through a subject familiar to them.[11]

But before appearing as Prince Ozay—if indeed he and Gurdjieff were one—Gurdjieff had already made forays into the occult milieu of *fin de siècle* Russia. Writers on Gurdjieff's life suggest that by 1909 or 1910 he was ready to make his mark on the world; the only question seemed to be where. From Central Asia he could have gone to Constantinople, where he knew people, knew the language and where—as Ouspensky had found on his first journey to the East—a living spiritual tradition still existed. Instead he chose Russia. Some commentators argue that this is because going to Russia was the greater challenge. Perhaps. But Moscow and St. Petersburg were the most European of Russian cities, and Gurdjieff more than likely aimed at eventually bringing his work to Europe. It's also true that, as we've seen, Russia at that time had a thriving occult market, and devotees of a variety of teachings filled the major cities. Gurdjieff had already tested himself in the spiritualist and Theosophical circles of cities like Tashkent. Like Ouspensky, Gurdjieff had little good to say about his mystical competition, though it's clear he borrowed liberally from their work. The knowledge that Gurdjieff would present to Ouspensky was without doubt impressive and, in the form Gurdjieff gave it, unique. But it was not absolutely original.

In Tashkent, Gurdjieff's success as an occult master was considerable. He tells us that within six months he "succeeded not only in coming into contact with a great number of these people ('occultists'), but even in being accepted as a well-known 'expert' and guide in evoking so-called 'phenomena of the beyond' in a very large circle."

No doubt Gurdjieff, with his deep desire to get to the bottom of life, found that many in these circles were simply sensation seekers and bored dilettantes, eager for some distraction. He spoke of the occult hysteria of the time as a psychosis, simply another manifestation of the laziness common to human beings. He also confirmed this in practice; part of his success, he tells us, involved his "skill in producing tricks," which suggests that he wasn't above sleight-of-hand when necessary. His aim in infiltrating these circles was to acquire a group of serious students upon whom he could test the knowledge he had acquired during his search. As he himself admitted, he needed guinea pigs.

In Tashkent the types available weren't sufficient, and his experiments demanded work with a much wider variety. So he moved to Russia after closing down his groups as well as the considerable business ventures he was involved in at the time, the liquidation of which netted him a million rubles. He first went to St. Petersburg where, decked out in the appropriate Oriental garb, he met the world, perhaps as Prince Ozay. Then, for reasons best known to himself, he went to Moscow. Here, too, Gurdjieff looked for types—new guinea pigs—but also for something else. Unlike Madame Blavatsky, or the highly successful Rudolf Steiner, Gurdjieff was apparently uncomfortable presenting himself to the world at large: his predilection for disguise suggests this.[12] But for a man eager to make his mark on the world—and this certainly was Gurdjieff's intention—a good presentation is a necessity.

What better candidate for the position of Gurdjieff's public relations man than a well-known, highly respected, supremely talented writer, journalist, and lecturer?

When Ouspensky agreed to the meeting, he had no idea who "G" was. The same was not true of Gurdjieff. He knew precisely who Ouspensky was, and it's likely he placed the notice for his "Hindu ballet" in the hopes that it would attract Ouspensky's attention. Certainly he sent Pohl and Mercourov to Ouspensky's lectures with the express purpose of enticing him to a meeting. Gurdjieff had paid particular attention to Ouspensky's writings, reading his books and following his articles about his experiences in the mystic East. The papers had made much ado about Ouspensky's trip, and as he would soon tell Ouspensky, Gurdjieff had even given his pupils the task of reading Ouspensky's books to *determine who he was*. In this way, Gurdjieff said, they would know in advance exactly what Ouspensky would find when he got to India. Ouspensky doesn't tell us what Gurdjieff's pupils had to say on this matter; as he himself believed he had found nothing, he may not have raised the question. Of the journey to the East itself Gurdjieff had little to say. "It is good to go for a rest, for a holiday," he told Ouspensky. "But it is not worth going there for what you want. All that can be found here."[13]

"Here" meaning Russia and Gurdjieff himself.

"This is not an exotic city," Ouspensky had told Anna. "But there must be *someone* here of the kind that I am seeking."[14] Writing sixty years after the fact, it's understandable that Anna might arrange the pieces of the puzzle so that they fit together more neatly than they may have at the time. But apocryphal or not, Ouspensky's remark was soon proved true.

CHAPTER SEVEN

MEETING A REMARKABLE MAN

T HE MIRACULOUS, OUSPENSKY believed, could be found in the most ordinary things. Even, it seems, in a small Moscow back-street café.

> We arrived at a small café in a noisy though not central street. I saw a man of an oriental type, no longer young, with a black mustache and piercing eyes, who astonished me first of all because he seemed to be disguised and completely out of keeping with the place and its atmosphere. I was still full of impressions of the East. And this man with the face of an Indian raja or an Arab sheik whom I at once seemed to see in a white burnoose or a gilded turban, seated here in this little café, where small dealers and commission agents met together, in a black overcoat with a velvet collar and a black bowler hat, produced the strange, unexpected, and almost alarming impression of a man poorly disguised, the sight of whom embarrasses you because you see he is not what he pretends to be and yet you have to speak and behave as if you did not see it.[1]

By this time, Gurdjieff had abandoned the exotic role of Prince Ozay for the dreary appearance of a small businessman. Yet beneath the bowler hat something of the prince still remained. The drab but not quite effective covering may have made the suggestion of hidden romance and adventure even stronger than any obvious display. Gurdjieff *knew* Ouspensky, knew he had "journeyed to the East" and that he had been disappointed. More than likely he also knew that if he presented himself as Prince Ozay, or some variation thereof, he would scare Ouspensky off. Yet he also knew that Ouspensky was still looking, and that a slight hint of the miraculous would be more effective than any of the standard props and accoutrements.

Ouspensky says Gurdjieff spoke Russian incorrectly. Anna Butkovsky-Hewitt says he spoke it fluently. In any case, Gurdjieff's strong Caucasian accent seemed totally inappropriate for the kind of conversation they had. And what did they speak of? India, esotericism, schools. Gurdjieff spoke of his travels, mentioning places that Ouspensky had wished to visit but was unable to; later when Ouspensky pressed him for more details about his journeys, Gurdjieff demurred. Ouspensky next asked Gurdjieff what he knew about drugs, "narcotics." Clearly his own experiments were still on his mind, and perhaps a feeling of guilt remained because of them. Drugs could be good for self-study, Gurdjieff said, to have a "look ahead," to know possibilities beforehand. But that was all. He told Ouspensky that when a man is convinced that what he knows theoretically *really exists,* he can work consciously to attain it. Ouspensky was no doubt heartened by this thought, as this was exactly what he wanted to do.

Gurdjieff then invited Ouspensky to meet his pupils.

On the way, Gurdjieff talked about the great losses he had incurred because of the war, of students, equipment, and money. He mentioned the expensive nature of his work and the sumptuous apartments he had taken in order to conduct his classes. His work, he said, had interested several well-known people in Moscow: writers, artists, professors. Yet when Ouspensky—who "knew everyone"—asked for names, Gurdjieff fell silent.

Ouspensky was surprised to find that Gurdjieff's "expensive" apartment was really some cheap, unfurnished rooms given to municipal schoolmistresses. Several of Gurdjieff's students were present, and that two of the women were indeed schoolmistresses confirmed Ouspensky's suspicion. Why, he wondered, had Gurdjieff so obviously lied to him about the apartment? It wasn't his, and such places were either rent-free or cost practically nothing. What was the point of the clumsy story? At that point, he tells us, he found it difficult to look at Gurdjieff.

When Ouspensky asked Gurdjieff's students about their work, they replied in a strange, unintelligible terminology, and he could get little out of them. Perhaps, one suggested, it would help if they read a story that one of Gurdjieff's students, not present at the moment, had written?

Ouspensky agreed, and one of them began to read aloud from a document known as "Glimpses of Truth."

Ouspensky's sense of déjà vu must have been piqued, for very soon into the tale, the same notice for the Hindu ballet "The Struggle of the Magicians" that Ouspensky had come across was mentioned. It even appeared in the same newspaper Ouspensky had seen it in, *The Voice of Moscow*. Other aspects of the tale suggest that, like the ballet advertisement, the story may have been written precisely for him to hear. "Strange events, incomprehensible from the ordinary point of view, have guided my life," its narrator declares. In every "exterior result" only the "hidden cause" interests him—a remark straight out of *Tertium Organum*. The narrator studies occultism, as Ouspensky did, and in it he sometimes sees a "harmonious philosophical system," as did Ouspensky. And like Ouspensky, the narrator has glimpses of vast horizons which inevitably fade from view. He has searched for truth, but his efforts proved useless. His grasp of the philosophy of occultism is complete, yet he sees only the outline of a "majestic structure." Books, he knows, will never bring him to the reality he seeks.[2]

The narrator searches for others who may "know," yet he is disappointed. In his quest for truth he visits India, Egypt, and other lands. Then, through a friend, he hears about the mysterious ballet "The Struggle of the Magicians" and of its equally mysterious author, G. I. Gurdjieff, an orientalist well-known in Moscow. (Until that evening, of course, Ouspensky had never heard of him.) He resolves to meet Gurdjieff and mentions this to another friend, who is somewhat cool about the idea. Eventually this friend admits that he knows Gurdjieff and may be able to arrange a meeting, although this would be difficult. He mentions Gurdjieff's expensive country home, a retreat that no one but he, and now the narrator, knows about, hinting at secrets and initiations.

When the narrator finally meets Gurdjieff, it seems he is still in his Prince Ozay phase. He finds a man of oriental complexion whose eyes particularly attract his attention "not so much in themselves as by the way he looked at me, not as if he saw me for the first time, but as though he had known me long and well."[3] Gurdjieff is sitting on a low ottoman against a wall, his feet crossed in Eastern fashion, smoking a water pipe. The atmosphere of the room is "unusual to a European." Every inch is covered with carpets and rugs, even the walls. Brilliantly colored ancient silk shawls cover the ceiling, in the middle of which hangs a light covered by a glass shade in the form of an immense lotus flower. Musical instruments, carved pipes, and a collection of antique weapons, daggers, and yataghans decorate the walls. Huge cushions litter the floor. An icon of St. George the Victor, set with precious stones, stands in one corner, and near it a cabinet containing ivory figures of Christ, Buddha, Moses, and Mohammed. A coffee pot and heating lamp sit on a small ebony table, and the air is filled with a "delicate scent" that combines pleasantly with the smell of tobacco.

The narrator remarks that after taking in the room he looks at Gurdjieff, who seems to size him up in an instant, taking him in the palm of his hand and weighing him—a suggestion, perhaps, that the same feeling should come to Ouspensky.

After some small talk, Gurdjieff suggests that they not waste time and asks the narrator what he really wants. The narrator, too, notices that Gurdjieff speaks Russian badly. Yet as the conversation goes on this ineptitude vanishes, and by the end of their meeting, during most of which the narrator's friend acts as an interpreter, Gurdjieff's vocabulary and command has improved remarkably. Gurdjieff then explicates some aspects of his teaching. Taking the hermetic dictum "as above so below" as a starting point, Gurdjieff remarks that he has begun this way because he knows the narrator is a student of the occult. As in the case of Paul Dukes, Gurdjieff is gearing his pitch to his audience.

The rest of the story is too long to go into. Gurdjieff expounds on early formulations of several aspects of his teaching that Ouspensky himself would later develop into a clear, lucid system, the "law of three," the "law of seven," and the idea that everything in the universe is material, including ideas. He speaks of the different kinds of food necessary for man, the need for a new language and a new understanding, and the notion of an objective art, one that avoids the subjectivity of the art of Gurdjieff's time. On this last note, Gurdjieff mentions a sculptor, a companion of his early childhood, who is now a famous artist in Moscow—the very Mercourov he had sent to entice Ouspensky. He also remarks that Mercourov became involved in his activities after Gurdjieff asked a certain "P"—Vladimir Pohl—to "interest" him.[4]

As "Glimpses of Truth" is some thirty pages long, Ouspensky showed considerable patience in sitting through it. As he remarked, it possessed no particular literary value. The writing was clumsy and at times confused. It did, however, make an impression on him. He also discovered that it wasn't written by one of Gurdjieff's pupils who was then absent, as he was told, but by two students present in the room. If this was not confusing enough, he was eventually told that the idea for the story came from Gurdjieff. It's possible that Gurdjieff himself wrote it, but the style, though awkward, is different from that of his books.

During the reading Gurdjieff sat on a sofa "Eastern fashion," smoking and drinking coffee. Again Ouspensky saw him in the light of his "search": he would have preferred to meet him not in this dreary room but in Cairo, Ceylon, or India. He was impressed by his feline grace, which set him apart from the others. Gurdjieff, it seems, had made an impression.

When Gurdjieff asked him what he thought of the story, Ouspensky replied tactfully. He said it was interesting but he pointed out that its point was not particularly clear. Gurdjieff's students took argument with this, and when Ouspensky asked for more details about their "system," they replied hesitantly about "work on oneself." Ouspensky may have smiled; it was precisely amateurish attempts at work on oneself that he wanted to avoid. He found Gurdjieff's students artificial, as if they were playing roles. He also remarked to himself that they didn't compare with their teacher. They were nice, decent people, but they were not the type of person he believed he would meet on his way to the miraculous.

Gurdjieff asked if Ouspensky thought "Glimpses of Truth" could be published in a newspaper. It might be a good way to acquaint the public with his ideas. Ouspensky said no, as it stood, no paper would touch it.

Gurdjieff may have been disappointed at this news. He was interested in publicizing himself, and he must have seen Ouspensky as an opportunity to do this. Then again, he may not have been disappointed at all, and the story's flaws may have been merely a means of suggesting to Ouspensky that he could write one much better. In any case, the real aim of the reading had been achieved. As the meeting ended and Ouspensky was about to go, the thought that he *must at once* ask to meet with Gurdjieff again suddenly flashed through his mind. In the light of later events the question of exactly *whose* thought this was comes to mind. In any event, Ouspensky did ask, and Gurdjieff replied that he would be at the same café tomorrow at the same time.

On leaving Gurdjieff with one of the students, Ouspensky's first reaction was to make some remark about Gurdjieff's odd behavior and the long, boring reading. But something stopped him. A strange giddiness came over him, and he felt an urge to laugh or sing. It was, he remarked, a feeling as if he been released from detention. He had felt something similar before, when his discovery of occult literature made him feel like a condemned man who suddenly sees a chance of escape. For the rest of his stay in Moscow, Ouspensky met Gurdjieff every day at the same time at the same noisy café. He tried to get Gurdjieff to tell him more about his travels, but Gurdjieff was not forthcoming. Though disappointing, this reticence was negligible compared with what Gurdjieff did talk about. Gurdjieff seemed to know a lot about everything, and his answers to Ouspensky's questions suggested that they stemmed from a *system* of some kind, a coherent, organized body of knowledge that Gurdjieff kept in the background, but nevertheless informed each of his increasingly fascinating remarks. Gurdjieff also spoke of certain practical aspects of his work. His students, for example, were required to pay a thousand rubles a year—a considerable sum. When Ouspensky remarked that such an amount might be too dear for many people, Gurdjieff replied that those who found it difficult to pay such a sum would also find it difficult to pursue his work, and that people do not value something they do not pay for. His own time was too valuable to waste on people for whom it would do no good. Ouspensky accepted this, but Gurdjieff pressed the point, and Ouspensky found it odd that Gurdjieff seemed intent on convincing him of something about which he needed no convincing. Ouspensky knew that the kind of research he had engaged in required money, and already the thought came to him that if he became more involved in Gurdjieff's activities, he could more than likely help obtain the necessary funds. Even more important, he could bring to Gurdjieff a better type of student.

Without a word from Gurdjieff, Ouspensky was already writing himself into the story. Gurdjieff, he felt, had already accepted him as one of his students—he had not said so in so many words of course, but his intention was plain. Ouspensky was clearly pleased; but there was one problem: he had to return to St. Petersburg to prepare several books for publication. Gurdjieff replied that he often came to St. Petersburg and would let Ouspensky know the next time he planned to visit.

There was, however, one other consideration. Before everything else, Ouspensky was a writer, and he had to retain absolute freedom to choose what he would write about. On two other occasions he had had opportunities to join similar groups but had declined; if he joined them, he would have had to keep secret everything he learned. Ouspensky knew that, sooner or later, his discussions with Gurdjieff would touch on matters that he himself had thought about and worked on independently—ideas of time, higher space, and other dimensions. He was sure that notions of this sort must play a part in Gurdjieff's work.

To all this Gurdjieff simply nodded.

"Well," Ouspensky continued, "if we were now to talk under a pledge of secrecy, I should not know what I could write and what I could not write."

Gurdjieff agreed to this, but added that too much talk was

undesirable. Some things, he said, were only for disciples. He conceded, however, to the condition that Ouspensky could write about that which he understood fully.

Ouspensky asked if there were any other conditions.

Gurdjieff replied that there weren't and added that in fact there could be no conditions at all, as the starting point of his work was that "man *is not.*" Man as he is, Gurdjieff told an increasingly astonished Ouspensky, is incapable of making agreements, of deciding anything for the future, of keeping promises and obligations. "Today he is one person and tomorrow another."[5] To keep promises and fulfill obligations, a man must first know himself, and he must *be.* "And a man such as all men are is very far from this,"[6] Gurdjieff remarked. The reason for this, Gurdjieff told Ouspensky, is that all men are *machines.*

"Have you ever thought about the fact that all peoples *themselves* are machines?"[7] he asked.

Familiar with the current trends in psychological thought, Ouspensky replied that yes, from the scientific point of view people are simply machines. But as he himself had argued in his writings, such a view leaves out the most important aspects of human existence—art, poetry, thought, all the phenomena of the fourth dimension. These, he replied, cannot be adequately explained by a strictly mechanical view of human beings.

Gurdjieff disagreed. "These activities," he told a shocked Ouspensky, "are just as mechanical as everything else. Men are machines and nothing but mechanical actions can be expected of machines."[8]

Ouspensky was not entirely convinced. His whole drift had been toward discovering some means of resisting what he saw as the increasing mechanization of human life. *Tertium Organum,* the summation of his thought, argued in a variety of ways that love, art, poetry, ideas—all the things this mysterious Mr. Gurdjieff has just shrugged off—were powerful weapons in his philosophical arsenal. Now he was being told that they were just as mechanical as a pocket watch.

Conceding the point for the moment, Ouspensky asked if there were no people who were *not* machines.

"It may be that there are," Gurdjieff replied. "You do not know them. That is what I want you to understand."

"All the people you see, all the people you know, all the people *you may get to know,* are machines, actual machines working solely under the power of external influences."[9]

It was a powerful thought. Yet Ouspensky still wasn't convinced, and he found it strange that Gurdjieff was so insistent on this point. What he said was, in one sense, obvious; one had only to spend time in a large modern city like London, as Ouspensky had on his way back from the East, to see that life in such places was becoming more and more mechanical. It was clear that this was the "way of the future." At the same time, Ouspensky had always been suspicious of such all-embracing metaphors; they left out the *differences* which he knew were the most important things in life. It was precisely because the scientific view wiped out these differences that he fought against it. Why did Gurdjieff insist on an idea that was fruitful as long as it was not made too absolute?

Not everything Ouspensky heard from Gurdjieff in those first meetings was satisfying. Gurdjieff's refusal to discuss his travels was annoying, especially for someone who had journeyed much himself. About "The Struggle of the Magicians," Gurdjieff mentioned that as several "sacred dances" were involved the performers would have an opportunity to "study themselves." It seemed an interesting idea; but Ouspensky remarked that Gurdjieff's notice for the performance said certain "well-known" ballet dancers would take part. Surely they would not dance in order to "study themselves?" The matter, Gurdjieff explained, was not yet decided, and the person responsible for the advertisement had not been completely informed. Everything might be quite different—all of which seems a hurried attempt to avoid the inconsistencies Ouspensky had noticed. In any event, "The Struggle of the Magicians" was soon set aside and wouldn't surface again for another five years.

Even more disturbing were Gurdjieff's remarks about his companions during his years of travel in the East, his fellow Seekers of Truth. Gurdjieff explained that each school has a specialty which its students must study: art, music, dancing, astronomy. There are no "general schools," and in order to study everything it would take several lifetimes.

How then had Gurdjieff studied?

"I was not alone," he said. Each one in his group was a specialist, and each studied his own discipline. Later, they pooled their knowledge and put together what they had found.

And his companions, Ouspensky asked, what became of them?

"Some have died, some are working, some have gone into seclusion."

"Seclusion"—this word from monastic language made Ouspensky feel uncomfortable. He also felt Gurdjieff was again "acting," deliberately saying things to shock him. This "acting" would eventually lead to many difficulties between them. Gurdjieff shocked Ouspensky in other ways. He told him that the war, which was on everyone's mind, was not the result of economic or political causes but of certain cosmic conditions. Planetary influences were causing several million machines to slaughter each other. The planets were living beings, and when they passed too close to each other, certain tensions in the cosmic order were created; on Earth, this resulted in wars, massacres, bloodshed. When Ouspensky asked if nothing could be done about this, Gurdjieff answered no. Man the *machine* could do nothing. Man as he is *does nothing*. He cannot *do.* Everything is done to him. For man as he is, *everything happens.* He does not think, he does not feel, he does not will. Rather, for him, *it thinks, it feels, it wills.*

It was beginning to sound like a refrain. No matter what road Ouspensky started on, all conversations led to the same place: human beings, as they are, are nothing but machines. Whether it was art, psychology, or man's ability to act, the punch line to every discussion was identical. Ouspensky doesn't say it, but clearly the thought must have been on his mind: And what about myself? Am I nothing but a machine too?

For once, Gurdjieff didn't speak bluntly. But his remarks were straight to the point.

"Take yourself for instance: you might already know a great deal if you *knew how to read.* If you *understood* everything you have read in your life, you would already know what you are looking for now. If you understood everything you have written in your book, I should come and bow down to you and beg you to teach me. But *you do not understand* either what you read or what you write."[10]

What the respected author, journalist, lecturer, and translator thought of this is unknown. That language was an inadequate tool for grasping the reality of things he knew from experience, so perhaps Gurdjieff's outrageous remarks did not strike him as too extreme. But it's difficult to think that Ouspensky didn't take this, and many of Gurdjieff's more radical comments, with a very large grain of salt. Ouspensky's remarks during their last meeting before he returned to St. Petersburg suggest as much. Although much of what Gurdjieff said introduced new and stimulating ideas, the essential thing, Ouspensky knew, was "facts." Only if he saw real and genuine facts would he believe he was traveling on the right path. And by "facts" he meant, of course, the miraculous.

Gurdjieff, I imagine, smiled. *There will be facts,* he assured him. But there would be much else too.

CHAPTER EIGHT

FINDING THE MIRACULOUS

O USPENSKY RETURNED to St. Petersburg excited by his talks with Gurdjieff. It seemed that the "new or forgotten road" that would lead out of the false world of contradictions lay before him. The way to the miraculous seemed clear and he had perhaps already taken a few steps on it. If so, the timing was right. St. Petersburg that summer was a strange city, its atmosphere tense with the expectation of catastrophe. The war had reached Russian soil, and the suicidal tendencies latent in the Russian soul were surfacing. Everyone knew that something was on its way, and Ouspensky feared that the storm would hit before he could get his work finished. When the anxiety grew oppressive his thoughts turned to Moscow, and the idea that he could throw it all overboard and return to Gurdjieff calmed him. More than likely it was an idea that came to him frequently, as he found his work delayed by printers' strikes and other disruptions to the normal flow of everyday life.

It wasn't until the autumn that he heard from Gurdjieff again. Gurdjieff had come to St. Petersburg and telephoned Ouspensky. They met briefly and talked, and before he left for Moscow, Gurdjieff told Ouspensky he would be back soon. Not long after, he returned, and again they met and spoke. Ouspensky mentioned that he knew other people who would surely be interested in Gurdjieff's ideas, and Gurdjieff remarked that this would be good, as he was planning on starting a group in St. Petersburg similar to those he had in Moscow.

One of the first people Ouspensky spoke to about Gurdjieff was Anna.

One morning, waiting at Phillipoff's Café, Anna was surprised that the usually punctual Ouspensky was late. When he finally arrived, she found him in an unusual emotional state. Without even saying "Good morning" or bothering to sit down, he breathlessly explained why he was not on time.

"I think this time we've really found what we need! I must tell you all about it. I have found the Miracle!"[1]

Ouspensky mentioned his meeting with Mercourov and Pohl and, reminding her of the strange man he had met through them, he explained to the mystified Anna that this man was here, in St. Petersburg, waiting for them at another branch of Phillipoff's across the road. His knowledge, Ouspensky explained, went far beyond mere theory. He was a real teacher, and already Ouspensky had learned a great deal from him. For example, he had already understood his central idea that man cannot *do* because in a sense he doesn't really *exist.*

"What I am trying to say," an excited Ouspensky related, "is, there is not one 'I' but many . . . A man might have twenty-two 'I's' . . . He is passive, does not *do* things personally, but . . . everything in him is *done,* mechanically . . . But I mustn't try to tell you it all here . . . He's across the road, waiting for us now!"[2]

Eager to meet the Miracle, Anna agreed. When they reached the other Phillipoff's, she saw the man who had turned the usually reserved and self-assured Ouspensky into a tongue-tied schoolboy.

She could tell he was of Greek ancestry; his fine, virile features told her that. His oval head was surmounted by a high astrakhan cap, his skin was of an olive complexion, and he had a black moustache. But it was his eyes that struck her most forcefully. As she peered at the Miracle across the room, they seemed to hold her. And as she walked toward the table in the far corner, where he sat alone, she knew Peter Demianovich was right. Like so many others who met Gurdjieff, she felt that his eyes, black as his moustache, "looked right through her."[3] Calm, relaxed, speaking quietly with few movements, he seemed to emanate a sense of agreeableness, and after a few moments, she found it pleasant merely to be sitting with him. She could tell Russian was not his first language, but he spoke it with an odd fluency, and his phrasing was careful and picturesque. It seemed to her that he put his sentences together slowly, as if they were specially made for this meeting alone. Sitting there, listening to Gurdjieff speak in his "lazy voice," it was not long before Anna, like Ouspensky, felt she "was at last in the presence of a Guru."[4]

She told Gurdjieff that she had been looking forward to meeting him with much joy.

"But you do not know me," Gurdjieff replied. "Perhaps I shall bring some evil on you. What you are saying is mere empty courtesy."[5]

Ouspensky quickly came to Anna's defense. No, he explained. Anna was young, surely, but like himself, she was a serious seeker.

"To live the way I am living now," she told the Guru, "seems to me very shallow, and I am not satisfied."

Gurdjieff looked at her. With a note of benevolence he asked: "Is it so unbearable?"

"Yes!" Anna replied, repeating the word. "*Unbearable!*"

Then, Gurdjieff told her, "It is better than I thought."[6]

For the rest of Gurdjieff's stay in St. Petersburg, Anna and Ouspensky met him at Phillipoff's every day. Soon to their ranks were added other seekers of the miraculous. As Gurdjieff began to make the long journey from Moscow regularly, more and more people would attend his talks. Ouspensky organized groups and arranged for Gurdjieff to speak at the homes of various acquaintances. At times up to forty people came to sit at Gurdjieff's feet. Gurdjieff's methods of dealing with these groups were unusual, and the orderly and organized Ouspensky often found himself at his wit's end trying to pull people together at the last minute. For example, Gurdjieff would say he was leaving for Moscow the next morning, but the next day he would announce that he would stay until the evening. The day would be spent talking in cafés. Then, just before his train, Gurdjieff would decide to stay on longer and suggest to Ouspensky that they have a meeting. Ouspensky would then hurriedly telephone everyone, but by that time most had made plans, and if they wanted to hear Gurdjieff, they would have to cancel their arrangements and rush to wherever Gurdjieff would be. Like his use of noisy cafés, and the fee of a thousand rubles, it was another example of his creating difficulties so that people would value what he was giving them.

Out of the many who came to meetings or listened to Gurdjieff at Phillipoff's, a small group was formed, a nucleus of serious seekers. These Anna dubbed the Six. They never missed an opportunity to talk with the Miracle, and when he was absent, they met together to discuss his ideas. As we might expect, they were an unusual group. Charkovsky, an engineer in his early fifties, had a knowledge of occult and mystical literature that rivaled Ouspensky's. Between the two, esoteric sparks would fly as they tried to outdo each other in arcane sparring matches, arguing about the Tarot, Theosophy, and other mystical philosophies. Dr. Stoerneval, also in his fifties, was a successful, stout physician with an interest in hypnotism; his wife, much younger than himself, didn't share his interest in Gurdjieff. He enjoyed the good life, but his manner was businesslike, unemotional, and levelheaded. The railway engineer Zakharov was a younger member of the group. Like Ouspensky, he was adept at mathematics, but Zakharov had no talent for expressing himself in words, and his inner world remained a mystery to them. Nicholas R., a patient of Dr. Stoerneval, was a man in his late sixties. Highly emotional, with white hair and a long patriarchal beard, he was of a nervous disposition, and his hands constantly fidgeted. It was only in the presence of Gurdjieff that he approached anything like calm.

As with his groups in Tashkent, Moscow, and St. Petersburg, Gurdjieff brought together a variety of types, a select group of "guinea pigs" ready for experimentation. His effect on each was different. For Anna, Gurdjieff was a powerful masculine figure, a kind of spiritual father who offered her a chance at the Miracle. For Ouspensky, he was the man who *knows*. On the phlegmatic Dr. Stoerneval Gurdjieff produced the most pronounced effect. Once, during a group meeting in Finland at the country home of one of the doctor's wealthy patients, Stoerneval announced to the astonished Six that for him "Georgei Ivanovitch is not less than Christ himself!" Gurdjieff was quick to cut the doctor off, but on other occasions he was less reluctant to take on the mantle of a religious figure.[7] Such outbursts, however, would be embarrassing for a man intent on winning over the fastidious Ouspensky to his cause.

What Ouspensky himself thought of the Six is unclear. It seemed to him that at the meetings many people heard something entirely different than what Gurdjieff said. Some paid attention to the inessentials, and for the most part what was really important escaped them. Of the group, only Anna and Ouspensky have left records, and for all its value as a document of the time, Anna's account doesn't exhibit a particular intellectual rigor. (That she wrote it at the age of ninety must of course be taken into account.) Yet it would be unusual for a man of Ouspensky's abilities not to feel he was somewhat "different" than the others. And it was precisely this difference that he sought to convey to Gurdjieff. When Ouspensky agreed to organize the St. Petersburg groups, there were two conditions: Ouspensky would decide who would be a good candidate to join, and he himself would stand apart from the group. He had always remained independent of groups, whether spiritual or literary; his decision to leave the Theosophical Society, even when offered a high rank, suggests as much. Gurdjieff dismissed all this with a sneer. For him, all of Ouspensky's accomplishments meant little, except insofar as he could use them for his own purposes. By now Ouspensky must have had some inkling of this. But the promise of "facts," combined with Gurdjieff's charisma and the ideas he had already received, proved too strong an attraction. That the "man's man" Gurdjieff must have appeared as some sort of father figure to the romantic intellectual Ouspensky also cannot be ruled out.

And how was Ouspensky seen by the Six? We have only Anna's word on this, and at some point during this time their affair came to an end. Why it did, and how Ouspensky met and formed a union with the more formidable Sophie Grigorievna, is unclear. But it's difficult not to suspect that in Anna's description of Ouspensky there isn't a slight bit of malice. On all accounts he comes across as a wordy, abstract know-it-all, whom Gurdjieff nicknames "Wraps Up the Thought," because of his obsessive need to tie all the loose ends of a discussion together. Like some of Anna's other pronouncements, we need to take this with a grain of salt. But it's clear that if Ouspensky prided himself on his intellect and independence, then Gurdjieff, intent on showing Ouspensky that he was, *like everyone else,* a machine, would hammer away at these relentlessly. Which is exactly what he did.

For Anna, Ouspensky was all "outward manifestation." "Behind his quasi-scientific phrases there was no real significance or deep meaning." He made a show of all the knowledge he had so industriously acquired. "Names of leaders, countries, philosophers, heroes, mystic books, all poured forth in non-stop speech in a characteristic avalanche." Anna remarks that after Ouspensky had been speaking for a while, Gurdjieff would look at him and smile. "Wraps Up the Thought could certainly go on," we can imagine him saying. Yet something in Anna's account suggests that more than a desire for accuracy is at work. "I, too, had a very good memory and could rehearse all the names of these books that Ouspensky loved to discuss," she assures us. But "in spite of all his erudition . . . Ouspensky, any more than the rest of us, still did not possess the key" to the "human machine," as Gurdjieff did. Yet obviously without Ouspensky she would never had found that key. Why should she want us to know that he was no better than she, unless perhaps she had suspicions that he was?

Yet for all his showy erudition, Wraps Up the Thought was the driving force behind the St. Petersburg group. He asked the most questions, kept the conversation going, and most likely talked more than anyone else because he had more to say. He organized lectures and meetings, introduced new and "better prepared" people to the ideas, and acted as a highly efficient and powerfully motivated public relations man. He even went out of his way to mollify a disgusted Gurdjieff when the teacher stormed out of a meeting, fed up with the dim-wittedness of his pupils. According to Anna, Ouspensky chased Gurdjieff down the street and begged him not to give up on his flock. Playing hard to get seemed to work, and the next day at Phillipoff's a chastened Anna and Ouspensky awaited their master, hoping he had forgiven them.

From Anna's account, Gurdjieff could be bullying, exasperating, and dictatorial as well as fatherly, mysterious, and provoking. Yet as Boris Mouravieff would remark, "One can say, without exaggeration, that without Ouspensky, Gurdjieff's career in the West would probably not have gone beyond the stage of endless conversations in cafes."⁸

As it was, Gurdjieff's talks introduced Ouspensky and the others to a new and very different way of looking at themselves and the world. Discussions would begin with a standard occult or mystical topic—the astral body, immortality, reincarnation. Well versed in these ideas, Gurdjieff gave them a characteristic twist that turned them in the direction of his work. Whereas occult thinkers like Rudolf Steiner taught that all people possessed an astral body, Gurdjieff argued that we must acquire one through effort. Immortality? But of whom do we speak? The man-machine who can do nothing? How can he hope to be immortal? Reincarnation? But what is there to reincarnate? Can a machine have a soul? If you desire these things, you must work for them, you must understand your machine and struggle against it. Man has possibilities beyond anything he could imagine, but to actualize them requires an immense amount of work, pain, and suffering. "There stand behind you many years of a wrong and stupid life, of indulgence in every kind of weakness, of shutting your eyes to your own errors, of striving to avoid all unpleasant truths, of constant lying to yourselves, of self-justification, of blaming others, and so on and so on."⁹

It was not a cheery doctrine, yet somehow Gurdjieff got it across. Taken out of context, it sounds like a helping of old-fashioned fire and brimstone. In context, it meant something more. The world Gurdjieff gradually revealed to Ouspensky and the others was a weird science-fiction universe of living planets and strange complex laws. The Law of Seven, for instance, was responsible for the discontinuity in the world, why a process that starts in one direction can find itself going in a totally opposite direction, pursuing totally different goals, and yet still believe it's following its original aim. The Law of Three stated that all phenomena require the presence of three forces, not two, as was recognized by orthodox science. Both laws were related to the vast cosmic scheme Gurdjieff called the Ray of Creation, a kind of "ladder of being" reaching from an unthinkable Absolute down to its lowest level, situated in the moon. In the diagram Ouspensky would later use to illustrate the idea, the Ray of Creation resembles earlier cosmological schemes reflecting what is called an "emanationist" view of the universe—one in which various worlds or levels of existence emanate from a central, nonmanifest source. Such ideas can be found in Gnostic, hermetic, and kabbalistic cosmologies, all of which were known to both Gurdjieff and Ouspensky. Each level on this vast "octave" was constrained by a number of laws, the necessary and irrevocable conditions of its being. Placed here on earth, man was limited by forty-eight laws, merely one level higher than the lowest and most limited, the moon, which was subject to ninety-six. The aim of the work was to free man from the constraints of one set of laws and so place him under the conditions of a higher, less restricted level. No one can be "free" in an absolute sense, Gurdjieff told his astonished students, but we can choose which set of laws we wish to obey.

But to do this wasn't easy. Man's position was perilous. The Earth is in a very bad place in the universe. Man is a machine. He is in prison. He cannot do. He is trapped in the illusion that he possesses the very things he must struggle and sweat to acquire: free will, knowledge, and consciousness. Most of all, consciousness. Man is not conscious. He is not awake. He is, in truth, asleep.

This situation, Gurdjieff told his pupils, was created by nature itself. Ouspensky had already reflected on the prevalence of the "culture of barbarism" in the modern world, and until he met Gurdjieff, he believed that against barbarism values of a higher sort could stand. Gurdjieff disabused him of this error: all that Ouspensky believed was "higher" is merely a more complex form of mechanicalness. All human activity is controlled by the necessities of the cosmic order. Human beings, and indeed all organic life, are really nothing more than a kind of thin film coating the earth, a necessary insulation for the transmission of certain cosmic energies, a requirement of the inescapable Ray of Creation. The illusions under which human beings live, their ideas of "evolution," "progress," and "civilization," are a kind of dream, a hypnotic spell maintained by the cosmic order so that these energies could be processed most efficiently. Human beings are really "food for the moon," a kind of cosmic fertilizer whose only purpose is to give up their vital forces to enable the Ray of Creation to continue growing. Their lives, desires, hopes, dreams, and ideals in themselves mean absolutely nothing.

For a man who believed that life was a trap, this was stiff confirmation. Ouspensky had of course already given up on the usual ideas of evolution, progress, and civilization, but Gurdjieff's rejection of these was even more absolute. Unequivocally, there was no evolution, no progress, no civilization, not even of the rare, elite kind that Ouspensky had placed his hopes on. "*There is no progress whatever,*" Gurdjieff told him. "Everything is just the same as it was thousands of years ago." Man is exactly the same as nature made him from the start. Civilization and culture count for nothing. Violence, slavery, and fine words were the reality of human life. Ouspensky felt much the same, but Gurdjieff pressed the point with a peculiar insistence. His words must have affected Ouspensky deeply. One day, he saw two huge trucks carrying an ominous cargo: immense piles of new wooden crutches— preparations for *limbs not yet blown off,* the result of the "progress" of the "civilized" nations then locked into an absurd but deadly war. More than any of Gurdjieff's words, this sight, yet another "obvious absurdity," must have driven home the earnestness of the situation.

CHAPTER NINE

YOU DO NOT REMEMBER YOURSELF

I F GURDJIEFF'S COSMOLOGY was new and startling, his psychological ideas were even more so. It was difficult, at least at
first, to observe and test notions like the Law of Seven or the
Ray of Creation. But what Gurdjieff told his students about
their own minds, their identities, their selves was something
they could experience firsthand. His fundamental theme was
the notion that human beings are made up of two parts, what
Gurdjieff called "personality" and "essence."[1] Essence was
what was *one's own*, the core of one's self, given at birth—one's
natural tastes, likes, dislikes, joys, and fears. Around this grew
a kind of accretion: personality, which was everything one
acquired from others through education, imitation, emula-
tion, or simply habit. For the most part, personality was made
up of lies, fantasies, and bad habits, and Gurdjieff's aim was to
cut through these layers to reach the essence below. Doing this
was hard and entailed considerable suffering. What Gurdjieff
had in mind can be seen in an exercise he put to the Six: they
were asked to relate the worst thing they had ever done. Anna
recounts how difficult this was for Dr. Stoerneval. Always correct, reserved, and, in his position as a doctor, someone of
authority and control, Stoerneval was now compelled to show
himself in a humiliating light. Almost at once Anna and the
others were convinced that no matter what the doctor might
tell them, it wasn't the truth. He spoke abstractly and imper-
sonally and related the event at such a distance that it was

clear he was holding something back. Stoerneval squirmed for a time and then, receiving a "piercing" look from Gurdjieff, stopped. Twisting the knife, as it were, Gurdjieff remarked, "Another time, doctor, you will be sincere, and recall these matters accurately."[2]

Ouspensky doesn't tell us how he fared at this test, although he does relate that when given the challenge to tell the story of their lives, each of the Six failed miserably. Such "encounter group" tactics seem familiar today, in an era of tell-it-all talk shows and "humiliation TV," yet to the reserved and aristocratic Ouspensky it must have been an unpalatable experience.

Ouspensky nevertheless had a clear experience of his essence when, after repeated attempts, Gurdjieff failed to force him to overcome his dislike of milk.[3] Another requirement of the work may have proved difficult for Ouspensky as well. Gurdjieff impressed on them all the necessity of not expressing negative emotions, which is not the same as not having them. For a man aware of the drawbacks of a "wooden world," a "history of crime," and a "culture of barbarism," not speaking of these or of the dozens of minor irritants that plague ordinary life must have been a strenuous undertaking. Talk, Gurdjieff emphasized, was one of our most mechanical actions, and, given Anna's account, he may have directed his comments more than once in the direction of Wraps Up the Thought.

Gurdjieff was persuasive, and when he asked them to observe themselves, to see their mechanicalness, to convince themselves that they were asleep, they had to admit he was right. But how to escape from the prison? How to wake up? Was it possible not to be a machine?

There were three traditional ways to reach true consciousness, Gurdjieff told them. There was the fakir: through physical torture he compels his body to obey his will. There was the monk: through religious devotion he compels his feelings to follow his faith. And there was the yogi: through rigorous study he compels his mind to increase his understanding. Yet however effective, these paths are incomplete. For the fakir's mind and feelings are undeveloped, the monk's body and mind are undeveloped, and the yogi's feelings and body are undeveloped. All three also suffer from the drawback that Ouspensky encountered on his travels: the need to sacrifice one's current life and devote oneself exclusively to the way. Only a few could do this, or even wanted to.

Our position would be desperate indeed, Gurdjieff assured them, if not for an additional way, one not known to many people and rarely recognized. It was the Fourth Way, also sometimes known as "the way of the sly man."

The sly man, Gurdjieff said, knows a secret the fakir, the monk, and the yogi do not know. How he learned this secret is unknown. He may have found it in some old books. Someone may have given it to him. He may have bought it. He may even have stolen it. No matter. The sly man has *knowledge,* and with it he can achieve all that the fakir, monk, and yogi achieve with less pain and much more quickly, perhaps as simply as taking a pill.

The Fourth Way differed in other aspects as well. For one thing, it was the only way that allowed one to remain in the world, in one's everyday life. There was no need to throw everything aside and enter a monastery or retire to a cave in Tibet. One's immediate conditions of life provided the best environment to follow the Fourth Way. In this sense, it was the most "convenient" way of all.

There was, however, a catch.

To follow the Fourth Way, one must find a group. Nothing, Gurdjieff impressed on them, can be accomplished alone. Working alone, however intelligent, motivated, and knowledgeable, one was still a victim of lies and illusions. Working alone, one could never escape from mechanicalness, from the grip of what Gurdjieff called his "false personality." Working alone was in fact merely another form of sleep.

For the fiercely independent Ouspensky this idea must have been difficult to swallow. Yet he had already come to the conclusion that on his own he was getting nowhere: this was why he had embarked on his search for schools in the first place. Now that he had found the possibility of one, he knew he had to submit to its conditions. For all his dislike of groups, there seemed no avoiding being part of one.

There was more. In order for the group to be effective, it must have a teacher. Unlike the students, the teacher is a man who has *woken up*. He has escaped from prison, has overcome his mechanicalness, and can lead others out of the trap. But in order to be freed, the pupils must relinquish their will, which in any case is illusory, and submit wholly to the will of the teacher. The first step was to recognize unequivocally their absolute nothingness; until they do they will still feel that they have a right to their own ideas, their own judgments, their own views on how work on themselves should go, in which case nothing can be done for them. "When he begins work on himself," Gurdjieff told them, "a man must give up his own decisions." He must no longer think for himself. This will be difficult for a man who has not realized that in submitting to another he loses nothing because in reality he has nothing to lose. He must first realize that, as he is, *he does not exist* and, as such, should have no fear regarding submitting himself to the will of another. The consciousness of one's nothingness, Gurdjieff impressed on them, is the first step on the Fourth Way.

Acknowledging one's nothingness may have seemed a difficult requirement. Ouspensky, who even before Gurdjieff was an astringent critic of his own shortcomings, more than likely swallowed it with several grains of salt. And yet hadn't the pupils already had a sense of it? Hadn't Anna told Gurdjieff that her life was unbearable? It was this feeling of disappointment that Gurdjieff looked for in potential initiates. When the composer Thomas de Hartmann, another seeker, was brought to Gurdjieff by Zakharov, Gurdjieff asked why he had requested a meeting. Was he perhaps unhappy in his life? This general rule applied to everyone who came to the Fourth Way: something somehow must not be "right," something must be *missing*, without which life became, as it had for Anna, unbearable.

This was reflected in one's aim, in the reason why one came to the Fourth Way, the goal toward which all one's efforts would be directed. Characteristically, Ouspensky told Gurdjieff that his aim was to know the future. A man, he said, ought to know how much time is left to him. It was humiliating not to know this. What good was it to begin work if one had no idea whether it would be finished or not?

Gurdjieff's answer was equally characteristic: The future is easy to know. It will be exactly like the past, unless one works on oneself today.

Perhaps to counterbalance the insistence on their nothingness, Gurdjieff showed Ouspensky how a conscious man could act. His performance must have been impressive. Gurdjieff was a man who knew everything and could do everything. He told Ouspensky of his life, relating the story of the Seekers of Truth and of his travels. Gurdjieff was again vague and evasive about exactly which monasteries and inner sanctums he had visited, and Ouspensky soon saw that much in Gurdjieff's account was contradictory and hardly credible. He would later tell his own students that he had asked about the sources of the teaching ten times a day and each time Gurdjieff gave him a different answer. Ouspensky accepted that, at least for the moment, no ordinary standards of truth could apply to Gurdjieff. One could take nothing for granted with him, be sure of nothing. What was affirmed one day was denied the next. Yet he was an inordinately capable man, able to play a remarkable number of roles. For example, there was Gurdjieff the carpet dealer. Seeing that the demand for exotic carpets was higher in St. Petersburg than in Moscow, Gurdjieff always traveled with a bale of carpets that, depending on which story, he either came upon during his travels or simply bought in Moscow. In either case, he was adept at getting the best price for them, and Ouspensky saw that Gurdjieff was not averse to using his knowledge of human psychology to his advantage. There was Gurdjieff the *gourmand* and *bon vivant.* Gurdjieff often gathered his St. Petersburg pupils and treated them to a lavish feast, buying large quantities of food and wine, of which, Ouspensky tells us, Gurdjieff had very little. In later years, having lunch or dinner with Gurdjieff would become the stuff of legend, the key ingredient of which was the liberal "toast to the idiots" made with a potent vodka. Ouspensky recognized that during these feasts Gurdjieff had an opportunity to observe his students in a different setting, and getting someone tipsy is of course an age-old method of uncovering their "real self."

Gurdjieff also had a curious ability to create unusual psychological effects, a result in part of his "acting." Ouspensky had observed Gurdjieff's acting at their first meeting. It was a trait that practically everyone who came into contact with him noticed. When Thomas de Hartmann was finally granted his audience with Gurdjieff, it was, as in Ouspensky's case, in another seedy café, perhaps even seedier than the one Ouspensky had to frequent. At least from Gurdjieff's reckoning it was one that usually had "more whores."[4] De Hartmann also remarks that on one occasion Gurdjieff told Ouspensky to arrange for a talk at a "fashionable lady's drawing room," only for Ouspensky to discover that it was really held at a public school.[5] These and other exasperating antics make up the repertoire of the "crazy guru." Like the Zen monk's whack on the head in answer to a "deep" question, Gurdjieff's tactics were aimed at shocking his students into a new level of awareness. They often worked, but perhaps just as often they didn't.

At least for Ouspensky, who as a known writer and journalist was putting his reputation on the line acting as Gurdjieff's lieutenant, Gurdjieff sometimes acted too much.

Yet he couldn't deny Gurdjieff's knowledge. And very soon Ouspensky found that Gurdjieff had introduced him to an "*entirely new problem which science and philosophy had not, so far, come across.*"[6] "Not one of you has noticed," Gurdjieff remarked, "that *you do not remember yourselves.*"[7] None of them, he said, felt "I" in anything they did. They did not feel themselves, they were unconscious of themselves—a variation of the fact that they did not exist. Self-remembering was the only means of overcoming this absence. Only through self-remembering would they gradually develop a sense of presence, of "being there" at all times. And Gurdjieff urged them all to make attempts at remembering themselves.

Ouspensky worked at it. And he soon discovered that although self-remembering was a strange, new idea, the sensations that his attempts at remembering himself produced were oddly familiar. He discovered that attempts at remembering himself—at having the clear feeling that *he* was walking, *he* was doing—stopped his thoughts. When concentrating on the sensation of "I," he found he could do little else. He was familiar with this sensation from earlier attempts at certain yogic practices described by Edward Carpenter in *From Adam's Peak to Elephanta*. The one difference was that in self-remembering, consciousness was divided; attention was split between the effort to stop thoughts and the awareness that you are doing this. Such "duo-consciousness" must have been familiar to Ouspensky from his experiments with half-dream states.

His attempts at self-remembering produced in Ouspensky "a very interesting state with a strangely familiar flavour."[8] He realized that such states do occur fairly often but we do not understand them. They occur, for instance, in moments of crisis when one has to keep one's head; one seems to see and hear oneself objectively, from "outside." They also occur when traveling, when one finds oneself in new or unexpected surroundings and the feeling suddenly comes: "What? *Me, here?*" It was also clear to Ouspensky that his early vivid memories were in fact memories of self-remembering. Our ordinary memories are of abstract facts: I was here, I did this, and so on. The vivid memories that self-remembering brings are not abstract at all, but are full of detail and "life"—the kind of memories that Ouspensky's contemporary Proust used as the basis for his gigantic novel. As the "chief absurdity of life" for Ouspensky was the fact that we forget so much, for him, self-remembering was a major discovery.

During his attempts at remembering himself, Ouspensky had experiences very similar to those from his drug experiments. Wandering through the streets of St. Petersburg, he would "sense" the houses and find that they were "quite alive." He also found himself in some comical situations. Ouspensky discovered that on fairly quiet streets his attempts were usually successful. Deciding to test himself, he turned toward busier roads and after a while began to feel "the strange emotional state of inner peace and confidence which comes after great efforts of this kind."[9] He remembered that his tobacconist was nearby, and still remembering himself, he decided to get some cigarettes.

Two hours later he *woke up* in another part of town. He was in an *izvostchik* (a kind of carriage) heading to his printer. The feeling that he had just woken up was quite strong. In between buying his cigarettes and "coming to," he had performed a variety of tasks: he had gone back to his apartment, spoken to his printer, written letters, decided against visiting another place, and flagged down his carriage, all in a state of "sleep." It was while driving in the carriage that a strange disquiet came over him. Then he suddenly remembered that he had forgotten to remember himself.

Here, Ouspensky knew, was one of the facts that Gurdjieff had promised. Gurdjieff had told him that the central fact of man's being was sleep, and until now this had been little more than a striking metaphor. But now he had seen it for himself. Gurdjieff would later elaborate on this idea, telling Ouspensky and the others that in man there existed four possible states of consciousness, contrary to the two recognized by orthodox science. There was sleep in its ordinary sense, the state Ouspensky had explored during his experiments with half-dreams. There was what was called the waking state, which Gurdjieff had shown them was really another form of sleep. There was this strange new state of self-remembering, brief moments of which Ouspensky and the others were beginning to experience. And there was what Gurdjieff called "objective consciousness," a variation on the cosmic consciousness that Ouspensky had already experienced during his nitrous oxide experiments. Mystics had passed down various accounts of this rare state, but of the third state, self-remembering, there was little information. Yet this state was the key to all else. Without it, man could achieve nothing and would spend his life in dreams and illusions. For years Ouspensky was searching for a method, a discipline that would help him and others toward becoming superman. It seemed that now he had found what he was looking for.

CHAPTER TEN

"I" AND OUSPENSKY

ALTHOUGH HE WAS already convinced that Gurdjieff had in some way got hold of a secret knowledge, Ouspensky's work on self-remembering was the first concrete evidence that Gurdjieff could make good his assurance that he would get "facts." He should have been happy. But this evidence only helped increase the pessimism that had accompanied his entry into this strange new world. If, as his attempts seemed to make clear, he didn't remember himself, then the rest of Gurdjieff's teaching became even more persuasive. The cosmological lectures continued, and Ouspensky was particularly fascinated by a strange system of inner chemistry, a kind of contemporary alchemy, that involved substances Gurdjieff called "hydrogen," "carbon," "nitrogen," and "oxygen" but seemed to have no relation to the ordinary chemicals these names usually refer to. Gurdjieff spoke of "impressions" as a form of nutrition, along with food and air. He explained how making efforts at becoming conscious *changes* our impressions, and how this change creates a shock that enables us to transform coarse substances into finer materials. Eventually, after much work, these finer materials accumulate, and with them we can attract even finer substances from which we obtain the energy to transform ourselves.

To Ouspensky, it made sense. He had already experienced a change in his impressions when, trying to remember himself, he walked St. Petersburg's streets and felt that the houses were alive. Certainly his vivid childhood memories were of moments in which his impressions were particularly strong. The "table of hydrogens" Gurdjieff presented reminded him of the experiences he had had under nitrous oxide. Then he had seen that the universe is fundamentally an expression of underlying mathematical laws. Gurdjieff's hydrogens, his Ray of Creation, the Law of Octaves, and much else seemed to corroborate this. Wherever it came from, Gurdjieff's system had a rigor and internal logic that continually impressed Ouspensky.

Yet as they went on, the Six and the others who came to Ouspensky's apartment—where many of Gurdjieff's talks were held—were increasingly aware of the great obstacles they faced. The goal they had set themselves seemed to recede further and further away. The rewards of waking up were many, yet the very first step toward consciousness required a sacrifice of terrific proportions. They had, in effect, to sacrifice their selves, to give up the idea that they possessed any ability to think, choose, act, will, or decide for themselves. "To awaken," Gurdjieff told them, "means to realize one's nothingness, that is, to realize one's complete and absolute mechanicalness and one's complete and absolute helplessness."[1] Years later in Paris, Gurdjieff impressed on his students that they were *merde de la merde,* shit of shit. In St. Petersburg his language was less rough but the intent was the same. Gurdjieff hammered this point with an almost ferocious insistence. It was necessary to be convinced of one's absolute nothingness, he told them, because only through this could one conquer the fear of giving oneself over completely to another's will. It is necessary to give one's will over to another because, while destroying all the illusions, lies, and falsifications that he has hitherto lived under—what Gurdjieff called "buffers"—a man is left absolutely helpless, adrift. It's a state of complete disorientation, and the worst thing possible is for a man to believe in his own power to act, think, or decide. He must free himself of these illusions. He must, in effect, turn himself into two people, achieve a kind of willed schizophrenia in which he is "I," his real self, and *another*, who is not really himself but an automaton fashioned from all his mechanical habits and behaviors. He must become, in Ouspensky's case, "I" and "Ouspensky."

In this case, the "I" was weak, feeble, passive, and wholly in the grip of the mechanical, sleeping, forgetful Ouspensky. He must free himself of "Ouspensky," but as he is weak and feeble, he cannot—unless another man helps him. This other man, the teacher, is awake and can tell when Ouspensky is "Ouspensky" and when he is his real self. Ouspensky himself can never know this, at least not until he has thoroughly rid himself of his false personality and his illusions about will and all the other fantastic powers he believed he possessed. "This is a very serious moment in the work," Gurdjieff impressed on them. "A man who loses direction at this moment will never find it again afterwards."[2]

If Ouspensky felt that in all this there was a hidden agenda aimed particularly at him, he would not have been mistaken. Although of the Six he remained the most adept, it's also true that he was the most resistant. Anna, with her sense that life was unbearable, more than likely welcomed the opportunity to throw off the burden of being responsible for herself. Dr. Stoerneval, for whom Gurdjieff was tantamount to Christ, probably felt much the same. Many people who seek a teacher do so for precisely this reason. But not Ouspensky. What he wanted from a teacher was knowledge, not freedom from himself. He had already experienced a sense of such freedom in his love of knowledge and the search for it. It was this in Ouspensky that Gurdjieff failed to see. And even if he did, it probably wouldn't have made much difference. Gurdjieff seemed unable to have a relationship with anyone unless he already in some way dominated them. He may have believed that this domination was for their own good. But it prevented him from accepting that anyone could have any real sense of their own value and worth. That would have meant they were not as mechanical as he believed. In any case, Gurdjieff seemed to have a need to stimulate in others a feeling of their worthlessness. "So long as a man is not horrified at himself he knows nothing about himself."[3] Gurdjieff did everything he could to horrify Ouspensky.

For one thing, he made a point of impressing on Ouspensky that his high regard for himself as a writer was worthless. "It is possible to think for a thousand years," he told him, "it is possible to write whole libraries of books, to create theories by the million, and all this in sleep, without any possibility of awakening."[4] In fact, all these books and theories only help to put other people to sleep. All such "knowledge" was worthless and had to be scrapped. To dot the i's and cross the t's, Gurdjieff gave a lecture on the different cosmoses that made up his universe. There were, he told the group, seven in all, ranging from the Protocosmos, the cosmos of the Absolute, to the Microcosmos, which was usually understood to be man but in Gurdjieff's system was the atom. Ouspensky knew practically every cosmological theory available at the time and was baffled by this odd change. He was struck by the fact that Gurdjieff's seven cosmoses were practically identical to a system he had developed himself, which he had discussed with Gurdjieff. It was not, he says "merely a coincidence of details" but "absolutely identical."[5] Ouspensky had never heard of seven cosmoses before, but his "period of dimensions" corresponded to it exactly.

When he mentioned this to Gurdjieff, the teacher merely shrugged. He then spoke more about the cosmoses, quoting long passages from Ouspensky's writing without acknowledging their source. Asked to speak on these matters from his perspective, Ouspensky delivered a flawless presentation of his theories on dimensions. As if to give his student a crumb,

Gurdjieff remarked that there was a great deal in what he had just said but it needed to be elaborated. Coming from someone who had just plagiarized him, this must have been difficult to absorb: if anyone had elaborated on these ideas, Ouspensky had. The experience affected him deeply. For one thing, he found it impossible to write.

Gurdjieff continued to impress on them all the difficulty of their position. In order to make it clear, he told them a parable, an Eastern tale about a magician and his sheep. The magician wanted to keep his sheep from running away, but he didn't want to spend any money doing so. The sheep knew the magician wanted their skin and flesh, and they took every opportunity to escape. The magician hit upon a brilliant idea: he hypnotized the sheep, told them he loved them and that they would come to no harm, and, to ensure that they wouldn't try to run away, convinced them that they really weren't sheep at all. They were, he told them, lions, eagles, men, even magicians. Thus they were happy and had no thought of escape. Meanwhile, whenever he needed to, the magician killed one and ate it.

This, Gurdjieff told his flock, was "a very good illustration of man's position," hypnotized by the forces around him.

Given his remarks about Theosophists, we can imagine what Ouspensky thought of this. One thing is odd: no one asked if Gurdjieff himself was not the magician of the story. He seemed to suggest as much. Speaking of the dangers of black magic, Gurdjieff said that a black magician was one who infatuated his pupils by playing on their weaknesses. The black magician uses people "for some, even the best of aims, *without their knowledge and understanding,* either by producing in them faith and infatuation or by acting on them through fear."[6] A black magician was one of the central characters in Gurdjieff's "ballet"—which to date had yet to be performed. And it's difficult not to see some element of infatuation in his pupils' responses to Gurdjieff's remarkable powers, his ability to *do*, his eyes that "looked right through you." It is also difficult not to see some element of fear at work in all that Gurdjieff told them about the dangers of sleep: he was, in his way, putting "the fear of the Lord" in them when he asserted that they had to be horrified before they could begin to work on themselves. Is it too much to suggest that Gurdjieff was warning them against himself? When discussing the relationship between the teacher and the pupil, Gurdjieff made clear that "a pupil can never see the level of the teacher."[7] And the teacher has an aim "which those who are beginning work . . . have no idea whatever and which cannot even be explained to them."[8]

Gurdjieff's aim was always a mystery. "I certainly have an aim of my own," he told Ouspensky. "But you must permit me to keep silent about it."[9] And yet, during a lecture on the Fourth Way, Gurdjieff remarked that "*no one can ascend onto a higher step until he places another man in his own place.*"[10] Was Ouspensky being primed for this position? If so, then in order to continue his own development, Gurdjieff needed Ouspensky to be in a condition that would serve his purposes. Speaking of the "three lines of work," Gurdjieff told the group that they could be useful to the work, and also useful to themselves, but they could also be useful *to him*. In what way useful? No doubt, Gurdjieff gained some greater control of his powers and a greater control of himself, as well as more insight into human psychology, through working with the group. Gurdjieff told them that while the teacher is indispensable to the pupil, the pupil is also indispensable to the teacher. Ouspensky himself later discovered that in teaching the system to others, he revealed to himself "new possibilities,"[11] new understanding and perceptions. But perhaps in Ouspensky's case "being useful" meant something more. Perhaps Ouspensky could be useful to Gurdjieff by taking his place.

And if Ouspensky decided not to? Gurdjieff's lectures at this time placed much emphasis on the fate of those who came to the work and then left it. The struggle against the "false I"—against, as it were, "Ouspensky"—was the most important part of the work. The teacher's role is to present certain barriers that the student has to surmount. At first they are small, but as he progresses more is required of him. Finally he gets to a point where he can no longer return to life, to sleep, and yet he is not yet awake. He is presented with a difficult barrier, and he cannot get over it. He may then "turn against the work, against the teacher, and against other members of the group."[12] He may repent and acknowledge the blame as his own, but then he changes his mind and again lashes out against the teacher. "Nothing," Gurdjieff told them "shows up a man better than his attitude towards the work and the teacher *after he has left it.*"[13] Sometimes he may be made to leave it intentionally; he may be put in such a position that he is *obliged* to leave, and for good reason. He is then watched to see how he will react. Generally, in such cases, the one who leaves turns against the work. When a student asked Gurdjieff what happens to such people, he replied, "Nothing." There is no need for anything to happen. They are their own punishment. As the fathers of the Inquisition said long ago, "There is no salvation outside the Church."

How much of this Ouspensky absorbed is unknown. He was, however, increasingly disappointed with his own progress. He had changed in some ways. When he thought back on his first meeting with Gurdjieff, he realized now how silly his questions were, how little understanding he had, or could have had, of all that was being revealed. When he met with Gurdjieff's Moscow group now, they no longer struck him as artificial or false. In fact, he looked forward to their visits and to exchanging ideas and insights with them. Oddly, it was he and the others who now seemed artificial and false to their friends. Gurdjieff had given them the task of talking with their friends about the work, and they were all surprised at the result: none of their friends could understand what they saw in it. Even Volinsky, who Ouspensky thought highly of, could find nothing important in self-remembering. Most of them found the ideas of the system repellent in some way. And they also found that their friends now in the work had *changed.* They had become less interesting, they lacked spontaneity, they no longer thought for themselves, they parroted everything they heard from Gurdjieff. They were becoming, in a word, *machines.* Ouspensky accepted this as a sign that he and the others had stopped "lying." He also felt a loosening of the self-confidence and assurance he had on his first meeting with Gurdjieff. To some extent this was compensated by a feeling of self-satisfaction that he shared with the Six when they attended meetings of new students. To hear the same naïve questions and see the same incomprehension suggested that they had at least moved on from there.

But Ouspensky wasn't satisfied. He wanted more "facts." In spite of all his efforts, he could not remember himself for more than a few minutes at a time. As in his nitrous oxide experiments, he felt he had reached something and then it vanished. He was left only with sleep. Efforts at other tasks were equally futile. He no longer understood what they were doing or what Gurdjieff wanted.

As usual, his disappointment emerged as irritation, and of course, Gurdjieff noticed this.

Later, when the two were sitting at a restaurant, Gurdjieff asked what was wrong. Almost petulantly, Ouspensky explained. He felt he was getting nowhere. He no longer understood where they were going, and Gurdjieff himself never answered questions.

Gurdjieff asked him to be patient, but Ouspensky only grumbled. Gurdjieff then offered to answer any question he would like to ask.

Ouspensky asked about eternal recurrence. Gurdjieff explained that, as in the case of his "period of dimensions," Ouspensky's ideas about recurrence, although close to the truth, were not *quite* the whole truth. He was near to it, though, and if he understood his—Gurdjieff's—reasons for not speaking more about it, he would be even nearer. But the point was, what good would it be to know whether recurrence was the truth or not if one did not change now, in this lifetime?

Ouspensky asked more, and Gurdjieff continued. He then reminded Ouspensky that "Possibilities *for everything* exist only for a definite time"—a message perhaps specifically meant for him.

Ouspensky was impressed by what Gurdjieff said, and imperceptibly his irritation faded. Much that Gurdjieff had just told him he had already guessed, and the fact that Gurdjieff had acknowledged his ideas was very encouraging. He began to see the outlines of a vast metaphysical system.

Then he looked at Gurdjieff. He was smiling.

"You see how easy it is to *turn* you," his teacher said. Perhaps, he continued, there is no recurrence? It was no fun to sit at lunch with a grumpy Ouspensky, so Gurdjieff had decided to cheer him up. Ouspensky wants answers? I will answer him. He will no doubt ask about recurrence: it is his hobby. Now Ouspensky has his answer, and he is cheered up.

Ouspensky didn't believe that Gurdjieff had simply made up what he had just told him. He was only acting again. Later Ouspensky felt he was right, as Gurdjieff introduced the notion of recurrence into his lectures. Yet even then he used recurrence to emphasize the lost possibilities of people who had come to the work—and then *left it.*

CHAPTER ELEVEN

THE MIRACLE

B Y AUGUST 1916, more than a year after meeting
Gurdjieff, Ouspensky was ready for more "facts." If he
hadn't yet embraced the idea of his own nothingness, he had
at least been brought fairly close to it. Eternal recurrence was
a hobby. His ideas about the fourth dimension were worthless.
He was asleep. His appreciation of the system was clear, yet in
himself there was still something that resisted giving up completely. Gurdjieff, it seems, was determined to break
Ouspensky, and it's probable that the remarkable experiences
he was about to undergo were designed to do just that.

Fired by a sense that time was running short, Ouspensky
added some exercises of his own to Gurdjieff's stiff regimen.
His own sense of failure, coupled with the growing gloom
about the war, propelled him into action. He began a series of
intensive fasts, the aim of which was to give a shock to his system. Along with these he practiced certain breathing
techniques he had already used with some success, as well as
meditation techniques to concentrate his attention. One of
these, the "prayer of the mind," a form of internal repetition,
he would in later years teach his students.

Along with Gurdjieff's talks and meetings, these practices
kept Ouspensky in a state of unusual tension, a prerequisite, it
seems, for the miraculous.

Once again the group met in Finland, at the home of
Madame Maximovitch, the very place where Dr. Stoerneval

had spoken of Gurdjieff as Christ. Ouspensky was in a rather nervous condition, light-headed and unsteady from his fasts and meditations. That evening Gurdjieff spoke about his pupils' inability to tell the story of their lives. He was, Ouspensky tells us, harsh and sarcastic, provoking them with taunts of weakness and cowardice. Then Gurdjieff announced to the group something that Ouspensky had told him in strict confidence about Dr. Stoerneval. It was a humiliating moment for Ouspensky; gossip was something he had always criticized in others. Yet it was a moment in which Gurdjieff truly overstepped his bounds and in which his lack of insight into Ouspensky is apparent. Ouspensky trusted Gurdjieff; tact and discretion were important values for him. His commitment to the work was undoubted. He didn't need to be tested, and in any case, Ouspensky already possessed a good amount of the inner freedom that the work aimed at achieving. Gurdjieff ignored all this. He was bringing Ouspensky to the brink, creating those conditions in which he would finally give way or be obliged to leave the work.

What Ouspensky felt at this moment is unclear; his remark that the experience was "unpleasant" is an understatement. Combined with his already highly unstable state, we can imagine he was in a very susceptible condition.

Later that evening, Gurdjieff called Ouspensky, Stoerneval, and Zakharov and sat with them in a separate room. He began to show them certain postures, positions, and gestures. They were nothing that a gymnast couldn't do; even Ouspensky, who had no pretensions to athleticism, could imitate them. Gurdjieff explained something about them and then moved on to the difficulty they had in telling the story of their lives.

It was then, as Ouspensky has told us, that "the miracle" happened.

Gurdjieff, he says, did not hypnotize him, nor did he

administer any drug—at least, he adds, not by any known method.

The miracle began by Ouspensky *hearing Gurdjieff's thoughts*. Sitting on the wooden floor, Gurdjieff began to speak of their "chief feature," the central characteristic of their personality, around which all of their lies and illusions revolved. It was impossible for them to tell the truth, he told them, and Ouspensky was disturbed by this. Then, among the words Gurdjieff was saying, Ouspensky heard *other* words, intended for him alone. These were not spoken: they were Gurdjieff's thoughts. Ouspensky "caught" one of these words and answered it, aloud. Gurdjieff nodded and paused. Then Ouspensky "heard" another thought. This time it was a question. Again he answered aloud.

Gurdjieff turned to the others and asked why Ouspensky had spoken.

More "questions" followed, difficult ones, and as Ouspensky answered them, Dr. Stoerneval and Zakharov were astonished at what they were witnessing. This went on for half an hour. Finally, Gurdjieff put to Ouspensky certain conditions which he had to meet or else leave the work.

Ouspensky answered that whatever Gurdjieff asked he would do. His commitment was complete.

Gurdjieff said something that affected Ouspensky strongly, and he went off into the forest, wholly in the grip of unusual thoughts and feelings. There he wandered for hours, wrestling with what Gurdjieff had said to him. He decided that Gurdjieff was right; what he thought was unshakeable in himself really did not exist. But there was something else, a new strength he had not known before. He knew Gurdjieff would only dismiss this as well, but for him it was indubitable. We can assume he did not mention this to Gurdjieff.

After a while he returned to the house and, thinking that the rest of the group had turned in, went to bed. Soon after, he began to feel a strange disquiet. His pulse raced, and he once again heard Gurdjieff's voice in his chest. This time he answered not aloud but mentally. Ouspensky tried to find some way to verify that what was happening was not a dream. After all, he had heard voices before, during his experiments with dreams and nitrous oxide. We have seen, in fact, that he was in some way prone to this phenomenon, and as he himself admits, at the time he was in a highly unstable state. The "impersonation" that he had found so remarkable in dreams could, he knew, "function in a waking state when a man is absorbed in himself or separates himself from the immediate influences of life."[1] Clearly his fasts and meditations, Gurdjieff's taunting, and their situation in a secluded country house met these conditions.

Ouspensky admits it could have been a waking-dream. He could find nothing that would prove that it was indeed Gurdjieff he was "speaking" with. But the feeling that it was a conversation was strong.

Then something Gurdjieff said frightened Ouspensky. He became paralyzed and began to shiver, and although he made terrific efforts, he couldn't reply.[2] He asked Gurdjieff to wait. But Gurdjieff saw that he was tired and told him to sleep.

The next morning the miracle continued. When Ouspensky saw Gurdjieff and some of the group, Gurdjieff asked one of them to ask him what happened last night. His off-hand manner bothered Ouspensky, and he walked off. Even the miracle, it seemed, was dismissed. But then he heard Gurdjieff's voice inside him once again, telling him to stop. Gurdjieff asked him to sit down. Ouspensky returned and sat, but he had no desire to talk. An extraordinary clarity of thought came to him, and he decided to concentrate on some difficult aspects of the system. He focused on a problem concerning the Ray of Creation. But then Gurdjieff turned to him and said out loud, "Leave it."

"That is a very long way away yet," he said, and advised Ouspensky to concentrate on his personal work.

Gurdjieff had apparently read his mind.

For the next three days Ouspensky found himself in an unusual state. Powerful emotions gripped him, and soon they became too much to bear.

He asked Gurdjieff how he could get rid of this burden, and Gurdjieff asked him if he wanted to "sleep." When Ouspensky said no, Gurdjieff told him that he was finally in the state that he had worked toward. He was, he said, "awake."

Ouspensky wasn't sure this was true. He realized that he must have seemed strange to the others. His words, he knew, often had no relation to reality, and later he found it difficult to remember much of what he said.

Gurdjieff went to Moscow, and, after seeing him off, Ouspensky took the train to St. Petersburg. During his trip, he "saw" Gurdjieff in his compartment and had another conversation. And on returning to St. Petersburg, for several weeks Ouspensky remained in a strange state, during which he saw "sleeping people." Walking along Troitsky Street, he saw a "sleeping" man coming towards him. Ouspensky said he could see his dreams move across his face like clouds. Ouspensky believed that if he could look at the man long enough he would probably even see what he was dreaming of. More sleeping people passed by, and Ouspensky realized that if he made an effort to remember himself, the sensations increased. And he discovered that when he ceased to see sleeping people it was because he had fallen asleep himself.

Ouspensky was unsure what exactly had happened during this time, but he was convinced that he had seen things that he had never seen before. He had, it seems, got his facts. He was also convinced that the type of experiences he had gone through, phenomena of a "higher order," as he called them, could be investigated and explored *only* while in the peculiar emotional state he had been subjected to. This is why all attempts to study the paranormal using ordinary scientific methods must ultimately fail, as such conditions exclude the very state necessary for the phenomena to appear.[3] Ouspensky also came away with certain insights into himself. After the miracle he felt a weakening of his fierce independence and individualism, and he began to feel a greater community with others—a result of the powerful emotions he had been subjected to. He also realized that there was an esoteric principle against the use of violence "to attain no matter what." Violent methods, even for the highest of aims, would, he saw, produce negative results.

With the world at war, such an insight was timely. Yet it could also have been a veiled criticism of his own teacher's methods.

One of the first things Gurdjieff talked about when he returned to St. Petersburg was his notion of "chief feature," or chief fault. In some people, he said, their chief feature was so entwined with everything else about them that they had to consider *themselves* as their chief feature. This was true in "Ouspensky's" case, which meant, effectively, that Ouspensky had to rid himself of "Ouspensky"—that is, commit a kind of suicide.[4] Gurdjieff had spoken of the need to "die" in order to be reborn: this was an outcome of the total recognition of one's nothingness. Gurdjieff also added that as there can be no mistake concerning one's chief feature, any disagreement about this merely showed that he was right—effectively putting the idea beyond criticism. One advantage to destroying one's chief feature, Gurdjieff said, is that one would then become capable of producing on people any impression one liked, a talent he clearly enjoyed himself.

Soon after this, Gurdjieff announced that it was time for people to decide what they wanted to do. The work had to change gears, and from then on he would demand absolute commitment. He was prepared to continue working only with those people who could help him to achieve his aim—which still no one knew—and this meant, of course, only with those people who had firmly decided to wake up. Out of the group, two people left. They, it seemed, had mysteriously changed their minds about everything. Specifically, they claimed that Gurdjieff himself had changed and that they could no longer trust him. Ouspensky was surprised at this attitude, but soon he would become more familiar with it.

Ouspensky went to visit Gurdjieff in Moscow. His small apartment on the Bolshaia Dmitrovka was covered in oriental carpets. It was a décor familiar to Prince Ozay, and within it Ouspensky recognized a peculiar atmosphere. In the silence that Gurdjieff and his students maintained, no one, he said, could tell *lies*. Any newcomer brought into this sanctum soon felt oppressed by the quiet and began to speak. And almost immediately it was clear that he was lying. Ouspensky even invited an old journalist friend to meet Gurdjieff, with, however, unexpected results. Gurdjieff laid out a wonderful buffet for his guest. Ouspensky's friend sat near the master and after enduring the silence for a few moments began to talk. He spoke nonstop for the entire lunch, without a word from anyone else. Then several hours later he thanked Gurdjieff for his marvelous "conversation" and left. Ouspensky felt bad for his friend. Gurdjieff had made a fool of him. But once again, it seemed that his belief in our mechanicalness was justified.

Ouspensky himself had an interesting conversation with Gurdjieff. Gurdjieff asked Ouspensky what he felt was the most important thing he had learned since starting work. Ouspensky replied that the miracle clearly was. If he was able to produce that state at will, everything else would follow. He knew, of course, that the miracle depended on the odd emotional state in which he had found himself. But he felt he was far from being able to achieve this, and he asked Gurdjieff how it could be done.

The state, Gurdjieff said, could come by itself, by accident. Or *he* could produce it for him. But if Ouspensky wanted to produce it himself, one thing was needed: sacrifice. And the most difficult thing to sacrifice, Gurdjieff told him, was one's suffering.

What Ouspensky thought of this is unknown.

CHAPTER TWELVE

NOAH'S ARK

GURDJIEFF RETURNED TO St. Petersburg, and the lectures continued. By this time Ouspensky had moved to a new apartment on Troitskaya Street, still near the Nevsky Prospect. Here new recruits were given the background on Gurdjieff's system. When Thomas de Hartmann arrived in late 1916, he found Ouspensky dressed in a soldier's uniform. Ouspensky had been drafted into the army as a Guard Sapper but had been demobilized because of his poor sight—the pince-nez attested to this. De Hartmann found Ouspensky "simple, courteous, approachable and intelligent."[1] Clearly, he made a strong impression. De Hartmann was even more impressed with the ease with which Ouspensky related Gurdjieff's complicated cosmology. Wraps Up the Thought had his virtues, it seems. Before he left, Ouspensky gave de Hartmann a copy of "Glimpses of Truth."

When de Hartmann returned home, he gave his wife the manuscript. Olga de Hartmann was stunned by what she read and expressed a strong wish to meet Gurdjieff.

In February 1917, that wish came true. On what was his last visit to St. Petersburg, Gurdjieff gave a talk at Ouspensky's apartment. At 8:30 in the evening on February 9, Olga and Thomas were among the group sitting before a sofa in Ouspensky's small living room. There were about fifteen people in all. Dr. Stoerneval asked for questions and reminded everyone of the last meeting's topic: what hindered self-development?

Suddenly a man of "oriental appearance" entered the room, "like a black panther."[2] He sat on the sofa with his legs crossed and asked what the group had been speaking about. When Stoerneval read the list of obstacles "on the path," Gurdjieff stopped him at "love." He then began an impromptu lecture on the different kinds of love, a theme that A. R. Orage would later develop into a celebrated essay. Olga had been worried that Thomas's determination to find a teacher would wrench them apart—he had already experimented with several—and she was relieved to hear Gurdjieff's words. As was often the case, she felt he spoke "just for her." Without looking at him, she knew his eyes were upon her. Later that evening, at a ballroom dance, the guests seemed like "puppets," and like Ouspensky, she felt that "something had hit [her] in the chest."[3] When she next met Gurdjieff, before she could say anything he asked her how she had felt when she went home that first evening. When she told him about the puppets, he was glad.

Soon after this, de Hartmann, who, like Ouspensky, had been mobilized, had to leave for the front. The days of the St. Petersburg group were drawing to a close. The next time the de Hartmanns saw Gurdjieff would be in Essentuki, several hundred miles away, in the Caucasus Mountains in Southern Russia.

St. Petersburg was then on the brink of collapse. Like everyone else, Gurdjieff must have felt this, and perhaps this is why he demanded of his pupils a deeper commitment. Time was running short. Possibilities for everything, including the work, were not infinite. Gurdjieff had told them that in times of great upheaval much knowledge is released into the world. Emissaries of the Inner Circle, the esoteric core of humanity, who Ouspensky believed directed the fate of civilization, allowed for this knowledge to reach some people. Then it was up to them. There were no guarantees, and the opportunity could disappear as quickly as it emerged. It was around this time that Ouspensky and the group began to speak of Noah's Ark, which for them was an allegory of esoteric knowledge. Ouspensky agreed, but thought it also had a more immediate application. The flood was on them, and it was called the Revolution.

Strikes had broken out. There were no trains, no newspapers, no electricity. The war had gone badly. Ill-equipped troops were slaughtered—a million of them—and the Tsar's strategy was to send out more. Many people believed that the Tsarina, who was of German birth, wished her homeland to win. At the close of 1916, Rasputin was assassinated by Prince Felix Yussupov. With an eerie clairvoyance Rasputin had predicted that if he was murdered by a member of the aristocracy, the monarchy would fall. This proved true. By March there was rioting in St. Petersburg, many troops had mutinied; indeed one group had threatened de Hartmann, who was an officer. Events, as Ouspensky remarked, were drawing nearer. Nothing, he thought, showed more clearly the truth of Gurdjieff's teaching than the extraordinary last days that were upon them. It was clear to him now that *everything* "happened," that *no one was in control.* At least not until the Tsar abdicated and Kerensky arrested the royal family and set up a provisional government. But this too was only temporary. In April, sent by Germany to topple Russia, Lenin arrived, and only a few months after that the Bolsheviks began their attempt to gain control.

Ouspensky knew the crash was approaching and that nothing could be done to stop it. He loved St. Petersburg perhaps now more than ever, in the last winter of its life. But the time of its possibilities, at least so far as the work was concerned, was ending.

At the end of Gurdjieff's last visit, Ouspensky and the others witnessed a remarkable sight. As they said farewell to the master at the Nikolaevski Station, he seemed like the Gurdjieff they had always known. But when the bell rang and he entered his carriage, the man they saw through the window had *changed*. He was not the same man who had just left them. Ouspensky saw a man of quite a different order; he could have been a prince or a prominent statesman. He seemed to emanate a strange new power, and as Ouspensky later found out, this was felt by Gurdjieff's companion in his compartment, who turned out to be a prominent journalist. In his column a few days later, he described sharing his journey with a strange Oriental who had struck him with his extraordinary calm and self-assurance. The Oriental ignored the crowds squeezing into the carriage, and the journalist was certain that at the least he had to be a millionaire. This was Gurdjieff's acting at its best.

After seeing him off, Ouspensky thought about his last two years with Gurdjieff. He had, he realized, failed to complete the plans he had made. None of his books were prepared, and he hadn't made the arrangements for foreign editions, although he was certain now more than ever that he would have to go abroad. In the past two years he had given all of his time to pursuing Gurdjieff's work and, he reflected, completely ignored his own affairs.

There was little he could do about that now. The situation grew gloomier by the day. Then it happened. "The great bloodless revolution" was upon them. Murders were taking place left and right but, a pessimistic Ouspensky observed, everyone still spoke of the glorious new world that was being born. More than likely, remembering his reflections on "Indian magic," Ouspensky saw that those around him who had put their hopes in revolution, like many of the Russian avant-garde, were incapable or unwilling to see what was actually taking place. This would have meant much effort and the loss of comforting illusions.[4] With his sister killed by the monarchy, Ouspensky had no love for the dynasty, although he did admit an odd admiration for Nicholas II; perhaps in him he recognized another gentle romantic. He refused to accept the lies that everyone else seemed to embrace. He knew that the liberation the newspapers spoke of was a "liberation from the possibility of eating, drinking, working, walking, using tramways, reading books, buying newspapers."[5] What it really meant, Ouspensky believed, was the end of Russian history, and that realization affected him deeply. He would never recover from its loss. With the Tsar gone, everything, the whole bureaucratic machine, would topple, as if Nicholas II had been a kind of buffer holding all the contradictions at bay.

Ouspensky gathered the group together and put the facts before them. They had to go abroad. To stay in Russia was pointless. Not everyone agreed. What caused the most hesitation was that they had yet to hear from Gurdjieff. Only one letter had reached them from Moscow, and it was obvious that he had gone somewhere, but no one knew where. So they waited.

Finally, a postcard arrived. It was a month late, having been lost in the mass confusion. Gurdjieff was going to Alexandropol, and he advised Ouspensky to continue the groups until he returned at Easter.

It was evident to Ouspensky that Gurdjieff had written the card before the revolution and that his plan to come at Easter could not be relied on. There was nothing he could do but wait, aware that each day possibilities diminished. Easter passed without Gurdjieff's arrival. Then a telegram from Gurdjieff announced he would return in May. Ouspensky took advantage of the time to think more deeply about the cosmoses.

In June another telegram came. Gurdjieff was in Alexandropol, and he told them to come.

Two days later Ouspensky left St. Petersburg.

Ouspensky's train arrived at Tiflis five days later; the usual three-day journey was extended because of the confusion. He arrived at night, and as there was a curfew, he was obliged to stay at the station. There he witnessed further evidence of madness. Soldiers filled the station, many of them drunk, and throughout the night they held "meetings." These turned out to be kangaroo courts, during which three men were shot—one for theft (three rubles), another for being mistaken for the first, and a third for being mistaken for the second. Looking at the bloodstained bodies lying on the platform, Ouspensky mused that this was only the beginning. After another day he caught the train to Alexandropol. When he arrived the next morning, he found Gurdjieff setting up a generator for his brother.

Ouspensky met Gurdjieff's family; for a man who had lost his own, it was more than likely a moving experience. Ouspensky was particularly impressed by Gurdjieff's relationship with his father. Past eighty, the old man was still alert, and Gurdjieff spent hours with him, listening to him. In later years, filial piety became for Gurdjieff an essential on the path to awakening.

Ouspensky discovered something else: a photograph of Gurdjieff that made his former profession unambiguous. It showed a curly-haired Gurdjieff (he was then almost bald) dressed in a black frock coat, his remarkable eyes staring straight into the camera. It was a photograph of Gurdjieff during his years as a hypnotist. For some reason, Ouspensky remained reticent about his discovery and kept it to himself.

Gurdjieff didn't agree with Ouspensky about the state of affairs in Russia. He thought things would quiet down and that they would soon be able to work in Russia again. This was either a dig at Ouspensky's worries or evidence of Gurdjieff's lack of political insight—something that a later student,

J. G. Bennett, would remark on. Ouspensky was keen to persuade Gurdjieff to go abroad. He would, he tells us, have already done so himself, but he didn't want to leave Gurdjieff. But Gurdjieff was waiting; more than likely he didn't know what to do himself. Ouspensky cooled his impatience by admiring the scenery; he was particularly impressed by a view of Mount Ararat, where the original Noah's Ark struck land. The travel writer in him was piqued, and he took in Alexandropol's different quarters. Finally, after two weeks, Gurdjieff announced that they were going back to St. Petersburg. But while in Tiflis, a conversation with a general who had come to the St. Petersburg group changed Gurdjieff's mind. At another station, Ouspensky pressed Gurdjieff about his plans. What did he intend to do? "A man," he knew, "had the right to know where he was going." In any case, it was clear they could do nothing in this madness.

Again Gurdjieff disagreed. It was only now, he replied, that they could do something. In five years, he told Ouspensky, this would be clear to him. Ouspensky later writes that even after *fifteen* years, what Gurdjieff had spoken about had become no clearer.

At another station Ouspensky asked Gurdjieff how he could strengthen the feeling of "I." Gurdjieff replied that the sense of "I" should be the result of all his efforts, and he suggested that even then, Ouspensky should be feeling his "I" differently.

Ouspensky had to admit that he didn't. This was a discovery that would come later. Three days out of Tiflis, Gurdjieff directed Ouspensky to return to St. Petersburg alone while he would carry on to Kislovodsk. Ouspensky was to stop at Moscow first, and in both cities he was to tell the groups that Gurdjieff was beginning new work. Those who wished to should come.

On the way to Moscow, Ouspensky acknowledged that his plans for going abroad were finished. And when he arrived, the newspapers were full of reports of shooting. This time it was the Bolsheviks. Their time had come. Promising to stop the war, they gained the support of the people, although Ouspensky knew that they would say or do anything to win power. The culture of barbarism was on the rise.

In Moscow and St. Petersburg he delivered Gurdjieff's message. Less than two weeks later he was back in the Caucasus. Others followed, the de Hartmanns among them, and by August 1917 a dozen apostles had gathered in Essentuki.

CHAPTER THIRTEEN

SUPER EFFORTS

L OCATED IN THE valley of the Podkumok River some thirteen hundred miles south of St. Petersburg, until 1917 Essentuki was not even a city. Founded in 1798, it became a fortress in 1830, and what there was of it when Gurdjieff's students arrived had been built up out of an old Cossack village. Its mineral springs and rejuvenating air gave it a reputation as a health spa, but Gurdjieff's band wasn't there for a rest cure. They had come to work.

Besides Ouspensky, others who made the trip included his wife, Sophie Grigorievna, and her daughter from a previous marriage; Gurdjieff's "wife," Julia Ostrovsky;[1] Anna Butkovsky; Zakharov; Dr. Stoerneval and his wife (under duress, one suspects); Charkovsky; Stoerneval's patient Nicholas; and the de Hartmanns. Anna had by this time met her future husband, whom she would marry at the end of the year. She would soon return to St. Petersburg, but would again work with Gurdjieff in France. (Oddly, during their first day in Essentuki, the group ran into the theatrical producer Evreinoff, with whom Anna had the affair that shocked Ouspensky. For a brief time, Evreinoff, too, became part of Gurdjieff's entourage.)

Thomas and Olga de Hartmann were an important catch for Gurdjieff. Both were members of the Russian artistic aristocracy. Olga was a celebrated opera singer, and Thomas's ballet, *The Pink Flower*, had been produced by Diaghilev, with

Nijinsky and Karasavina in the cast. That Gurdjieff went out of his way to dispel Olga's fears about losing Thomas to the work suggests that, as in the case of Ouspensky, he was keen on bringing them into the fold. The best way for him and his ideas to become well-known was to attract people who already were. Gurdjieff was always on the lookout for intelligent, articulate followers to act as his spokespersons. Although Ouspensky had agreed to the conditions Gurdjieff had telepathically communicated to him, the master more than likely was covering his bets. He may have seen de Hartmann as a backup lieutenant in the event Ouspensky defected.

Over the next six weeks, Gurdjieff introduced a new, intensive regimen, setting the pace for the atmosphere he would create a few years later in France. Ouspensky and half of the group lived with Gurdjieff in a small house on the outskirts of the village. They did all the housework themselves—no mean feat for middle-class intelligentsia who had probably never lifted a broom before.[2] Gurdjieff allowed them little sleep—in the ordinary sense—and he often presided over the cooking, showing yet another of his remarkable abilities. The meals, Ouspensky says, were wonderful, and each day they dined in the style of some foreign land, Gurdjieff being a deft hand at Tibetan, Persian, and other cuisines. Other times they ate little, which may not have been too difficult for Ouspensky, accustomed as he was to fasts. In fact throughout his life, although he clearly enjoyed food, Ouspensky was not a large eater. He once told Maurice Nicoll that one meal a day was sufficient, and that he had lived on appetizers his entire life.

Gurdjieff moved quickly, and as he unfolded the whole of the work to them, he introduced a variety of physical exercises. These included breathing techniques, periods of silence, and a method of relaxation that interested Ouspensky. It began with relaxing the muscles of the face and included "feeling" different parts of the body, what Gurdjieff called "circular sensation."[3] Much of this Ouspensky had already discovered himself, through his own work with breathing techniques. During his nitrous oxide experiments he had felt his pulse simultaneously throughout his whole body. This, he knew, was the sign that he was about to enter the "other" state of consciousness. On some the relaxation exercises had a healing effect; one was cured of a neuralgic complaint, and practically everyone felt that they slept better—a welcome discovery, no doubt, given the little rest the master allowed them.

Another new idea was the "Stop" exercise, which Gurdjieff would use to great effect in the future as the finale to public performances of his "movements," which were also introduced at this time. (On their first day at Essentuki, after tea, the de Hartmanns were surprised when Gurdjieff shouted "March!" and the group immediately began to run around the room; later they witnessed Mr. and Madame Ouspensky struggling through a series of military turns.) In this exercise, the teacher would shout "Stop" at some arbitrary moment, and everyone was required to freeze in the exact position they were in. Although dangerous—Gurdjieff told a tale about one of the Seekers of Truth almost drowning because of it—it was essential for study of one's "moving center," that part of the "machine" in charge of one's learned movements. One had a limited repertoire of positions and postures, and the "Stop" was intended to catch a student in between these. The uncomfortable state allowed one to see oneself more clearly. In a way, it was a variation of Gurdjieff's early remarks about roles, and how when we are put in an unfamiliar situation and are unable to find our "place"—one of the many personas we adopt to deal with the world—we can see who we really are. Gurdjieff created as many unfamiliar situations as possible, and his students were rarely comfortable.

The accelerated pace was linked to another exercise: "super efforts." Gurdjieff had earlier told them about "accumulators," a kind of energy reserve that we rarely use but in special circumstances can be tapped. Accumulators contain an enormous amount of energy, and when in touch with them a man can perform miracles. Reaching them requires immense effort; one has to exhaust one's usual energy supply first. Yet when one student wondered if making such efforts was dangerous, Gurdjieff shrugged off the thought. It was more dangerous not to make them, he said. It was much easier to die from laziness.

Essentuki then became a place for super efforts. These could take different forms, like carrying out a task in half the usual time. The idea was to do *more* than necessary to perform some job, like washing the dishes. A more austere variation would be to walk an extra two miles after already hiking for twenty-five. And as in all things, the student could not rely on his own judgment, since, being lazy, he would invariably go easy on himself. It was the teacher who decided when to make a super effort. He would show the pupil no pity. Gurdjieff found many opportunities to do this.

For one thing, in addition to the rounds of housework, he gave them complicated physical exercises to perform. Sitting on the ground with knees bent and his palms together between his legs, Ouspensky had to lift one leg and count to ten by saying "Om." Then he would count to nine, then to eight, and so on, all the time "sensing" his eye, ear, thumb, or some other part of his body. Not only the physical effort was demanding; Ouspensky had to remember the sequence of movements, of "Om's," of the parts of his body he sensed, and so on. When this was mastered, breathing exercises were added. While Ouspensky struggled, Gurdjieff casually remarked that on his travels he had known people who worked at these contortions for *days*.

Gurdjieff kept them busy, forcing them to work double time while fasting. It was a mistake, he said, to conserve energy

while fasting; on the contrary, one had to work even harder.
Gurdjieff put his theory into practice, never leaving them at
peace, forcing them to march in place, stand with extended
arms (a punishment for tardiness at lectures), or run in the terrific heat. They had very little chance of dying from laziness.
There were other exercises as well. When the de Hartmanns
arrived they witnessed an unusual sight: after tea, Gurdjieff
ordered Zakharov "to his place." This turned out to be a corner of the room. There he knelt, and when Olga, unable to
restrain her curiosity, asked what he was doing there, he
barked angrily, "What bloody business is it of yours!"[4]
Zakharov was too gentle and considerate, Gurdjieff said, and
needed to learn to be rough. When Gurdjieff noticed that
Thomas took sugar with his tea, he made him stop. It was probably at this time that he tried to get Ouspensky to drink milk.

On another occasion he put up a notice requiring everyone to give up their possessions. Then he devised a series of
movements for the arms and legs. These formed the letters of
the alphabet and Gurdjieff ordered that all communication
had to be done using these movements, even in private. The
de Hartmanns found themselves unable to speak normally,
even in whispers, in their room; they would, they thought, have
been failing the teacher. Each day Gurdjieff posted new
requirements and orders; then he sat and watched the reac-
tions of the group. Sometimes he appeared the loving, tender
father, "the dearest man in the world."[5] Other times he was the
fierce taskmaster. Olga reports how "proud" she and the others felt when, to one of Gurdjieff's impromptu questions,
they could provide the correct answer. An incorrect one
evoked his displeasure. Yet even here his response was unpredictable. When one student was clearly distraught over
failing to give a correct answer, Gurdjieff softened the blow by
taking him to a café in the evening. He used the stick and the
carrot well, and it's no wonder that in later years Ouspensky

had a "strange feeling" whenever he thought of this period.

Ouspensky took part in all of the activities, but he also had his own plans. While the de Hartmanns and the others clearly regarded Gurdjieff as a father figure whose approval they desired, he kept his original aim in view: how to achieve that "other" state he had entered under nitrous oxide. With this in mind he set himself to make his own super efforts. Alone in his room, he began to run in place, simultaneously practicing a breathing technique. He continued for a time but soon recognized that he would have to give up and begin breathing normally. Pouring with sweat, his head spinning, he felt he would collapse, but he carried on. He was about to stop when he felt something "crack" inside him. Suddenly his breath flowed evenly, without effort and he felt an extraordinary pleasant sensation. He shut his eyes and the feeling of strength and renewed energy grew. Waves of "joyful trembling" passed over him; this, he knew, was the precursor to the "opening of the inner consciousness."

Unfortunately, at that moment someone entered the room, and he stopped. Yet clearly Ouspensky was capable of super efforts on his own. But when he spoke of his experience to Gurdjieff, the master predictably dismissed it as mere chance. An Ouspensky who was able to tap his accumulators himself wouldn't need someone to do it for him.

Then, just as everything seemed to be moving toward some climax, Gurdjieff pulled the rug out from everyone by suddenly announcing that all work would stop and the group would disband. The others could do what they liked, but he was heading to the Black Sea coast with Zakharov. Gurdjieff gave no reason for his decision, aside from some internal disturbance within the group. Given the close quarters and unusual circumstances, some friction was inevitable; and in any case, Gurdjieff thrived on it. So maybe his announcement was another shock. Or maybe he had run out of ideas—it's difficult not to suspect that much of what Gurdjieff had put his group through for the past six weeks was made up on the spot: he was "experimenting" with his guinea pigs again. Gurdjieff claimed he had learned the movements and the Stop exercise during his tenure in the Sarmoung monastery; but then, one wonders, why he didn't include them in the work much earlier?

The absurdity of stopping work just as it was reaching new levels certainly shocked Ouspensky. Most of the group didn't think Gurdjieff was serious. It was yet another case of acting. But by now Ouspensky had had enough. What was the point? Was there one? If not, there was no reason to stay with Gurdjieff. Try as he might to avoid it, Ouspensky had to admit that his confidence in Gurdjieff was fading. All along he had put his doubts to one side, but this was too much. He came to a conclusion: there was Gurdjieff, and there was the work. He no longer felt sure about Gurdjieff—or, more accurately, the reservations he had put aside could no longer be ignored. But he had no reservations about the work. So he separated the two. It was a rift that would last the rest of his life.

Ouspensky followed Gurdjieff to Tuapse, then headed to St. Petersburg, where he thought to collect some of his belongings, mostly his library. It was, of course, gone; whether confiscated or looted is unknown. In a city facing famine and total breakdown, Ouspensky could escape with only a few essentials. He remained in St. Petersburg longer than he expected and left on October 15, just a week before the Bolshevik Revolution. It was, he said, impossible to stay there. Something "disgusting and clammy was drawing near."[6] "A sickly tension" was felt in everything; rumors spread each day, each one more absurd than the last. "The dictatorship of the criminal element"[7] was at hand, and Ouspensky would hate it for the rest of his life.

In Tuapse there was still relative calm, and Ouspensky found that Gurdjieff had moved to the coast and rented a house about fifteen miles from Sochi, overlooking the sea. The place was surrounded by roses and had a view of snow-capped mountains in the distance. It was idyllic, but Ouspensky found the atmosphere of the group tense; it was not at all like Essentuki. An absurd quarrel had broken out between Gurdjieff and some neighbors, and this had affected Zakharov. When Ouspensky had left, Zakharov was full of enthusiasm (his assertiveness training had apparently helped) and he had urged Ouspensky to return swiftly. Now Ouspensky discovered that Zakharov was intending to go to St. Petersburg. This seemed madness. When Ouspensky asked Stoerneval what had happened, the doctor replied that Gurdjieff was displeased with Zakharov and told him he had better go.

Ouspensky eventually discovered that during the quarrel with the neighbors, Zakharov had said something that displeased Gurdjieff, and from then on Gurdjieff had made it clear that Zakharov had to leave.

Ouspensky considered it the height of idiocy to send anyone to St. Petersburg. There Zakharov would find famine, riots, looting, and worse. Ouspensky would not have let a dog go there, he said. But here was Gurdjieff sending one of his most loyal students into the abyss. When Ouspensky persuaded Zakharov to try to reconcile with Gurdjieff, Zakharov relented. But Gurdjieff only replied that since Zakharov had decided to go, he had better do so.

There had been other developments as well. For one thing, the civil war had broken out throughout the country; for another, the de Hartmanns and Zakharov had learned very precisely what Gurdjieff meant by super efforts. He had invited them to accompany him on an "expedition to Persia." This meant a long and arduous trek across war zones and mountains. The group walked inland for days, Olga de Hartmann wearing high heels. Gurdjieff kept them at a brisk pace. When, after hours of strenuous hiking, they finally arrived at an inn, instead of letting them rest, he decided that the night was too fine to waste on sleep so they should continue. Eventually, after days of rugged and ill-equipped walking, with little rest and less food, they found themselves at a village not far from Tuapse, having traveled practically in a circle. One outcome was that Thomas came down with typhoid. Another may have been that Zakharov had had enough of Gurdjieff.[8]

After Ouspensky joined them, Gurdjieff moved the group around for months, trying to avoid being trapped by the opposing Red and White Armies. Finally, they ended up back in Essentuki. Here, in February 1918, Gurdjieff sent out a circular letter, over Ouspensky's signature, inviting the rest of the Moscow and St. Petersburg groups to join them. Forty people showed up, including Zakharov.

Gurdjieff found a house, and another stiff regimen was set in place. No one was allowed to leave the grounds, and orderlies were established. Work of the "most varied kind" was begun.

Gurdjieff introduced music, dervish dances, and breathing techniques as before, as well as a series of exercises in "psychic phenomena." Basically, this meant learning how to fake paranormal abilities like thought-reading, clairvoyance, and mediumship. Gurdjieff explained that the study of "tricks" was part of the training at a school. But then Gurdjieff had already had a career as a traveling magician, and he may have learned his routines from another source. Money at this time was scarce—the Bolsheviks had confiscated everything—and Gurdjieff made a virtue of necessity by sending de Hartmann and the others out to neighboring towns to sell silk, which he had presciently saved for just such an occasion. When Gurdjieff told de Hartmann to head to a particular town, he balked, explaining that he had many friends there; he would obviously be embarrassed if he was seen selling silk. Gurdjieff disagreed. All the better: you can sell it to your friends, and in the meantime learn not to "identify." Silk was a rarity then, and de Hartmann proved a successful salesman.

Gurdjieff decided that the "colony," as Ouspensky called it, had to have a name. Ouspensky offered "The Society for the Struggle against Sleep." Gurdjieff thought this too obvious, but I suspect Ouspensky's tongue was in his cheek. Finally they decided on "International Fellowship for Realization through Work," giving a nod to the proletarian fashion of the times. More strict requirements were set. All members had to break all ties with each other. Each hour of the day was given over to a particular exercise. Ouspensky, the doctor, and a student named Petrov were named full members of the fellowship; de Hartmann soon made the grade as well. Public lectures were begun. Ouspensky gave the first one and then lectured a few more times on Sundays. But just as the fellowship was beginning to establish a respectable reputation, Gurdjieff began once again to "act," this time posting notices announcing that "Dr. Black," a fictional mountebank depicted in the satirical papers, would be lecturing as well. Ouspensky doesn't mention this in his account of this time; by then he had no doubt already seen too much of it. Ouspensky, in fact, was beginning to feel that Gurdjieff's acting was out of control, that it had become automatic—another word for mechanical.

Gurdjieff decided it was time for another expedition, and he showed considerable panache in getting both the permission and all the equipment for it from the new Soviet powers. The real idea was to escape from Essentuki; Gurdjieff had finally realized that if the work was to continue, they had to leave Russia. But Gurdjieff convinced the Bolsheviks that he was setting out on a scientific expedition to seek out archaeological sites and, perhaps more fetching, gold. Ouspensky advised that they would need alcohol in order to wash the gold, and this, though scarce, was supplied as well. They had everything for the journey, and Gurdjieff set out to cross the dangerous and bandit-ridden Caucasus with fourteen of the faithful. But not Ouspensky. Madame Ouspensky's daughter was expecting a child, and Ouspensky had more immediate responsibilities to attend to.

In any case, by this time Ouspensky's "personal position"[9] in the work had changed. For the last year the feeling had been building, and now he knew he *had to go*. He had no doubts about the ideas; of their value and significance he was convinced. But he felt strongly that for him, and for many of the group, it was no longer possible to work with Gurdjieff. He does not say exactly why this was so. In his account of his decision to leave he does say, however, that he had ascribed many things to Gurdjieff incorrectly, and that if he remained with him now, he would no longer be going in his original direction, which led him to Gurdjieff in the first place. His octave,[10] following the Law of Seven, would be deflected, turned off course. He was not the only one who felt this way; the rest of the small group had reservations too.

The simple fact is that Gurdjieff's methods did not suit him; Ouspensky had had enough of "acting" and, given his own experience of super efforts and accumulators, more than likely felt he was not as helpless as he had originally thought. In any case, after much soul-searching and meditation, Ouspensky came to the conclusion that Gurdjieff's way, the way of the sly man, was not *his* way after all.

He moved into a separate house and did what he hadn't done for two years: he wrote. Among the few possessions he managed to salvage from the "flood" was the manuscript of *The Wisdom of the Gods*.

THE BREAK

OUSPENSKY KNEW HE had to go abroad, but he didn't want to leave before Gurdjieff. That would be like abandoning ship. He wanted to make sure he had done everything he could to help Gurdjieff before he took care of his own affairs. His solicitousness cost him dearly. When Gurdjieff and his troupe headed for the mountains, Ouspensky stayed behind; by then it was too late. The history of crime was upon him. He was trapped. Cossacks had attacked the railway line, and the Bolsheviks had begun their "requisitions"—basically, looting. Ouspensky was forced to remain in Essentuki for another year. He felt foolish: he had had the chance to get away and missed it, something the sly man would never have done. It was a difficult time, but Ouspensky was philosophical: only two in his family contracted typhoid; miraculously, no one died. They weren't robbed. Although it was a time of famine and want, Ouspensky was able to find work, first as a porter, then a schoolteacher. At one point he convinced the local Soviet to let him set up the Essentuki Soviet Public Library with books that had been "requisitioned" from their owners, no doubt remembering the loss of his own collection. Ouspensky showed his own brand of panache and resourcefulness when the White Army "liberated" Essentuki and he hastily tore down the word "Soviet" from the library's sign.

What he heard of Gurdjieff was minimal and intermittent. Gurdjieff had, it seemed, made his way by rail to Maikop, then reached Sochi by foot, subjecting his group to another series of super efforts. Ouspensky may have felt some satisfaction when he discovered that in Sochi practically all of the Essentuki group decided they had had enough. Only four remained with Gurdjieff and his wife: the Stoernevals and the de Hartmanns. Zakharov, Petrov, and the rest had jumped ship, just as Ouspensky had foreseen. Gurdjieff and his reduced band had made their way to Tiflis. Here, through the de Hartmanns, he would meet the artist Alexandre de Salzmann (like de Hartmann, a friend of the Theosophist Wassily Kandinsky), and the work would take on another character. In Tiflis, Gurdjieff would make his first attempt to establish the entity with which he would finally make a name for himself: The Institute for the Harmonious Development of Man.

Ouspensky, meanwhile, passed from the frying pan into the fire. It wasn't until June 1919 that he managed to escape from Essentuki. Still trying to get abroad, like Gurdjieff, he found himself moving from place to place—Rostov, Ekaterinodar, Novorossiysk. At Rostov he was delighted to discover his old journalist friend Bechhofer-Roberts, with whom, we know, he had once shared some homemade vodka. Roberts found Ouspensky living in miserable conditions, in a drafty, ice-cold apartment with no coal and little food, body and soul kept together by his minimal belongings: a worn overcoat, a few shirts, a pair of boots, some socks, a blanket, a towel, a razor, a file, and a whetstone. Given the situation, Ouspensky thought he was extraordinarily lucky to have even these. Back in Ekaterinodar, Ouspensky finally stopped moving, but his landing place taxed his reservoir of optimism. Everything about the revolution filled Ouspensky with a deep physical disgust, and in Ekaterinodar that inner nausea found its outer correlate. Then considered the "capital of Russia," for Ouspensky Ekaterinodar was "the most God-forsaken place one could imagine." Built in the Age of Reason according to

Enlightenment ideals, its streets, all running at right angles, were now filled with the rotting carcasses of animals, the foul smell of which filled the air.

Through some miracle Ouspensky was able to get a series of letters describing the revolution through to A. R. Orage, the charismatic editor of *The New Age* whom he had met in London on his return from the East. Ouspensky's training as a journalist served him well, and his *Letters from Russia 1919* is a sobering read for anyone sympathetic to the Soviet experiment. Ouspensky tells the *New Age* readers that "During this period we have lived through so many marvels that I honestly pity everybody who has not been here, everybody who is living in the old way, everybody who is ignorant of what we know."[1] What he and others knew was the true meaning of words like "revolution" and "Socialist state": they meant thuggery, murder, political bullying, "the dictatorship of the criminal element." Here, in this filthy, soulless place, Ouspensky had an ideal opportunity to observe the clash between culture and barbarism and to witness the struggle between individuals and the "big two-dimensional creature" determined to absorb them: the state. He knew that "the whole life of individual men and women is a struggle against these big creatures . . . A Nation is a creature standing on a far lower stage of development than individual men and women."[2] Ouspensky placed states at the level of zoophytes—mindless, amorphous masses whose only aim was to eat each other. Here, too, Ouspensky had a chance to see the Law of Seven (see chapter 8) at work. Speaking of the Law of Opposite Aims and Results, he makes clear how the ideals of brotherhood and freedom that fueled the revolution became justifications for murder and tyranny. According to this law, "Everything leads to results that are contrary to what people intend to bring about and towards which they strive."[3] One can't help wondering if Ouspensky ever thought of his relationship with Gurdjieff in this light.

When Orage recognized Ouspensky's plight ("I personally am still alive only because my boots and trousers and other articles of clothing . . . are still holding together")[4] he got in touch with his friend Major Frank Pinder, who was on the staff of General Denikin, leader of the White Army. Pinder hired Ouspensky as a bulletin writer and generously paid him wages out of his own pocket.

When not typing out field reports, Ouspensky started doing what would occupy him for the rest of his life: lecturing on the work. He gathered a handful of people and began to give talks, linking Gurdjieff's ideas to philosophy and psychology. Gurdjieff himself had written him, inviting him to come to Tiflis and take part in Gurdjieff's institute. Enclosed was its prospectus. In high-blown, inflated language—what would become Gurdjieff's unmistakable style—Ouspensky's still-not-quite-ex-teacher announced that "the Institute for the Harmonious Development of Man based on G. I. G.'s system . . . accepts children and adults of both sexes . . . The subjects of study are: gymnastics of all kinds . . . exercises for the development of will, memory, attention, hearing . . . and so on." Furthermore, the announcement continued, this celebrated system was already in operation in Bombay, Alexandria, Cabul, New York, Chicago, Christiania, Stockholm, Moscow, Essentuki, and a host of other places.

Predictably, Ouspensky was not amused by Gurdjieff's acting, if only in print. He was also not pleased to find his name listed along with other specialist teachers. Among these was another ex-member of the group then residing in Novorossiysk who Ouspensky knew had no intention of heading to Tiflis.

Ouspensky had little enthusiasm for the institute, perhaps recalling Dr. Black and other inharmonious episodes. Gurdjieff's invitation to come and work, regardless of "past difficulties," was typical, but Ouspensky held fast. Leaving his teacher had cost him dearly and he was not about to abandon his decision lightly. And in any case, as the prospectus showed, the sly man was up to his old tricks.

Ouspensky himself had found a new seriousness. Running into an old St. Petersburg friend, Ouspensky talked about his experience with Gurdjieff, and the friend asked the obvious question. Were there any practical results of his work with Gurdjieff? Ouspensky thought about it and answered yes, there were, and chief among these was a new sense of confidence. Two years before, Gurdjieff had asked if he had yet begun to feel his "I" differently, and Ouspensky had had to answer no. That had changed. The self-confidence he had acquired was not the ordinary kind; it was rather a recognition of the unimportance of the ordinary little self, that knot of wants and complaints, which, he hastened to add, was still present and would no doubt remain so. This new self-confidence was entirely different. Ouspensky felt there was something in him, a bigger self, one that would be equal to any eventuality, any challenge. He had perhaps felt the beginning of this during "the miracle" and wisely held back from mentioning it to Gurdjieff. This new sense of "I" was not merely the result of a wide experience of life which Ouspensky undoubtedly possessed. It was something more than this. It was, he believed, the result of all the work he had put himself through in the last few years. With this in mind it may be easier to understand how he could reject Gurdjieff yet still hold fast to the system.

This "double-think" he tried to pass on to Zakharov and Petrov, both of whom he met later in Rostov, where he also started lecture groups. Both were thoroughly negative about Gurdjieff and the system, and it took some effort for Ouspensky to persuade them to reconsider. Zakharov eventually came around to his view, and tried to get to Tiflis and Gurdjieff. But fate was against him. Contracting smallpox on the way, he died in Novorossiysk—the first, perhaps, of a number of fatalities met in pursuit of the work.

Although early victories promised much, by the end of 1919, Denikin's White Army was routed and the revolution was complete. Along with thousands of other refugees, Ouspensky and his family made their way to Odessa, aiming to reach Constantinople. Although the more naïve among them believed the Soviet experiment would fail, or that life would somehow return to normal and they would again be able to live in Russia, Ouspensky had no such illusions. For him, Bolshevism *was* barbarism, a barbarism that in the West was finding much support among the very element it was pledged to destroy: the intelligentsia. St. Petersburg was gone, and with it, Russia. "To no place that I had left was it possible to return," a melancholy Ouspensky mused. When in late January 1920 Ouspensky arrived in Constantinople, he had closed a door on his past. He would never see Russia again and would remain an exile, a man without a country, for the rest of his life. Had he stayed, and had famine, looting, and indiscriminate murder not taken care of him, he would no doubt have been shot or, like other of the Stray Dogs, imprisoned.

Constantinople the second time around was a changed city. Twelve years before, Ouspensky had felt a vital, living spiritual tradition here. All that was gone. The Constantinople he met as he walked off the boat was already succumbing to Western drabness. When from the boat he spied the minarets of Stamboul and the Galata Tower, Ouspensky's first thought was of seeing the dervishes again. Soon after setting up home in a refugee camp on the island of Prinkipo, Ouspensky set out in search of them. He found them, as before, in the Tekke at Pera, the European part of the city, amidst the same tombstones, the same plane trees, and the same haunting music. He even thought he recognized some faces. But there was something different. It was not only that Constantinople itself had become a noisier but oddly empty city, in spite of the huge, thronging crowds. This time, watching the dervishes turn,

Ouspensky knew part of their secret. He had learned it, of course, from Gurdjieff, who had explained that the mysterious dance was in some way an exercise for the brain; this was related to the "Om" exercise he had given them in Essentuki. To see the dervishes now and to *know* must have been a vivid moment, full of powerful impressions. Ouspensky may very well have been one of the last people to witness them; fairly soon, with the rise of Kemal Attaturk, the dervishes, as well as astrologers, fortune-tellers, and all other such practitioners, would be banned.

As in Essentuki and Ekaterinodar, Ouspensky began giving lectures. It was almost a habit. Earning money by teaching English to his fellow refugees, as well as mathematics to children, in his spare time Ouspensky began to form a group. Their meeting place was the White Russian Club in Pera, and Ouspensky was helped in arranging things by his new friend, the academic Boris Mouravieff, another piece of human flotsam washed eastward by the revolutionary flood. Ouspensky's appeal was strong: in a city filled with people whose lives had been shattered, his strange new confidence, combined with the startling "system," must have seemed impressive. Soon his audience grew too large, and he needed another space. The fates were with him; in fact, at this point in his "octave," his personal branch of the Ray of Creation, Ouspensky hit a run of good luck. Through Mikhail Alexandrovitch Lvow, a former colonel of the Imperial Horse Guards—now a poverty-stricken shoemaker living under the stairs at the White Russian Club—Ouspensky met John Goldophin Bennett, a member of British Military Intelligence with an interest in other dimensions. Bennett's companion, Mrs. Beaumont,[5] had met Lvow and, taken by his plight, offered him a room in her flat. Not long after, Lvow had approached his benefactor and asked if she would allow him to use her drawing room, which was unoccupied, once a week for talks, assuring her that politics wouldn't be on the agenda. She agreed, even agreeing to the condition that, as the meetings were private, she would not be allowed to listen. Mrs. Beaumont knew no Russian, so this hardly mattered; but this is an early instance of the air of secrecy that would color Ouspensky's work from then on.

One afternoon, Bennett returned from work and heard a cacophony coming from the drawing room. "The meetings sounded like pandemonium," he said. Intrigued, Bennett was introduced to Ouspensky and asked what they were discussing. Ouspensky told him they were discussing the transformation of man.[6] He then explained that the difference between one man and another can be greater than the difference between a sheep and a cabbage. Understandably, Bennett was baffled. Ouspensky indicated a diagram depicting the different kinds of men, ranging from numbers one through seven, a categorization he had learned from Gurdjieff. Men number one, two, and three are dominated by their bodies, feelings, or thoughts, he explained. To reach Man Number Four required the coordination of all one's faculties. Bennett was deeply interested in a number of religious and mystical questions, but was strangely unimpressed by this account. Still, Bennett and Ouspensky became friends, and Bennett and Mrs. Beaumont would often visit Ouspensky and his family on Prinkipo.

Meanwhile, in Tiflis, Gurdjieff's institute had once again failed to materialize and Gurdjieff knew he had to get to the West. Ouspensky had not heard from him for some time, but had a strong sense that he would eventually turn up. He was right. In June, six months after Ouspensky, Gurdjieff and his band, which now included Alexandre and Jeanne de Salzmann (a teacher of the Dalcroze school of dance) as well as Major Frank Pinder, adrift in the collapse of the White Army, arrived.

Ouspensky hadn't seen Gurdjieff for nearly two years. The old attraction must have revived, for he began to think that, after all, it might be possible to work with him again. In any case, doing so might have been unavoidable. Unknown to Ouspensky, Bennett had already made the acquaintance of the de Hartmanns and was soon to meet Gurdjieff as well. Through a mutual acquaintance—the mystical seeker and sometime friend of Rudolf Steiner, Prince Sabaheddin— Bennett met the man who possessed "the strangest eyes [he] had ever seen."[7] Mrs. Beaumont, too, met Gurdjieff on this occasion, and while she agreed with Bennett about his eyes, she also noticed something else. Gurdjieff made her feel uneasy, "as if he knew some secret about us that we would pre- fer to keep hidden."[8] Later, throughout Bennett's long association with Ouspensky, Mrs. Beaumont would receive a less than warm welcome into the work.

In that first meeting, as he did with Ouspensky, Gurdjieff spoke with Bennett about the ideas that fascinated him: hypno- sis, paranormal experiences, and his own pet project, the fifth dimension—a step up, it seems, from Ouspensky. Like Ouspensky, Bennett felt that Gurdjieff was a man "who knows." "I had never before had the same feeling of being understood better than I understood myself,"[9] he said of speaking with Gurdjieff. And when it came to the fifth dimension, which Bennett believed was the source of freedom, Gurdjieff pre- dictably replied that while his speculations were more than likely correct, what good would five dimensions do him when he remained a slave in the ordinary three? Bennett was impressed, and when Gurdjieff invited him to a performance of sacred dances held the following Saturday evening, Bennett was certain he would go.

When he and Mrs. Beaumont entered the studio that evening, Bennett must have felt he had stumbled onto some kind of secret society. He had no idea that Gurdjieff, Ouspensky, and the de Hartmanns knew each other, let alone that they all practiced the same spiritual discipline. But here they were. The dancers were dressed in white, flowing costumes, each with a different colored sash. All were silent and seemed to pay no heed to each other. And then the man with the strange eyes entered the room. Dressed in black, Gurdjieff's sudden appearance commanded attention. The dancers arranged themselves in lines and stood stock still; to Bennett, their sashes formed a spectrum, a visual version of the "octave." De Hartmann began to play the piano, and the performers broke into a series of strangely impressive movements, the central one of which was called the Initiation of the Priestess. Bennett was moved by this but he and Mrs. Beaumont were totally unprepared for what followed. At the end, all the dancers lined up at the back of the hall. De Hartmann played a series of chords. Then Gurdjieff shouted a command, and at once the whole troupe leaped in the air and rushed toward the audience. Seconds from impact, Gurdjieff shouted "Stop!" and the group froze. Some, unable to check their momentum, tumbled over each other, hitting the floor. The audience gasped. It was a trick Gurdjieff put to good use a few years later, in Paris and during a performance tour of America.

Bennett was stunned and wanted to talk with Gurdjieff about the performance, but Gurdjieff left with Ouspensky immediately after. Bennett had by this time been warned by Army Intelligence that Gurdjieff might be a Russian spy, but by now this was irrelevant. What mattered was that Bennett had finally found the teacher he had been looking for. Oddly, Bennett did not ask to join the group. He did meet with Gurdjieff again, though. Through Bennett, Gurdjieff hoped to obtain the visas he needed to travel to England, but Gurdjieff's reputation as a possible spy prevented Bennett from being of any help. Ouspensky, however, would have better luck.

By this time, Ouspensky had handed over his groups to Gurdjieff, who hoped once again to open his institute, or at

least its Constantinople branch. They had even gotten to-geth-
er again to try to work on Gurdjieff's ballet—the cause of their
initial meeting and, by this time, a metaphor for their growing
estrangement. Ouspensky recalls with warmth an evening they
spent wrestling with a translation of some Persian songs that
Gurdjieff wanted to include in the scenario. That night
Ouspensky saw Gurdjieff, the artist and poet. Swimming in a
flood of images, symbols, forms, and metaphors, Gurdjieff told
a bewildered Ouspensky to turn a quarter-hour's worth of
recitation into *one* line. This went on for several hours. By
morning they were exhausted. "That was the real Gurdjieff,"
Ouspensky later enthused. But the next day, when they were
supposed to continue work, Gurdjieff refused and would do
nothing but tell dirty jokes, not even very good ones.
Ouspensky was disgusted. He was also disturbed that Gurdjieff
had taken to wearing black and seemed to make a point of
starting arguments and, once again, "acting" too much.

Nevertheless, as in Essentuki, Ouspensky helped
Gurdjieff as much as he could, introducing him to people—
like Mouravieff—and even stopping his own groups so they
wouldn't conflict with the institute. Gurdjieff invited him to
lecture at his "Constantinople branch," and Ouspensky did,
with Gurdjieff on hand to elucidate the more obscure elements. Gurdjieff visited the Ouspenskys at Prinkipo, bringing
delicacies, and in general a sense of renewed intimacy grew.
But Ouspensky was still aware of the difficulties, and any
understanding now, he knew, was only temporary. At the same
time, Gurdjieff's relationship with Madame Ouspensky, who
unlike her husband remained a devoted pupil, was strengthened, no doubt causing some estrangement between
Ouspensky and his wife. The central plot of "The Struggle of
the Magicians" is the battle between a white and black magus
over the allegiance of a virginal female adept. While Sophie
Grigorievna was certainly no virgin, there was clearly a tug of

war between her teacher and her husband. Having already lost Ouspensky as well as a sizable part of his flock, Gurdjieff couldn't absorb many more defections. There was little chance of that where Madame Ouspensky was concerned; one comes away feeling that she had little use for her husband's view of things.

Her real loyalty became clear when Ouspensky received the kind of news every writer dreams of. Unknown to him, a Russian émigré, Nicholas Bessaraboff, had arrived in America with a copy of *Tertium Organum*. He was deeply impressed by it—so much so that he turned up one morning with his copy at the home of Claude Bragdon, the writer, architect, and publisher. Bragdon himself had published some books on the fourth dimension and higher space, and, as he could read Russian, Bessaraboff was convinced that he must know of Ouspensky's book. Bragdon was as taken with *Tertium Organum* as Bessaraboff was and decided to translate and publish it. To his surprise, the book was a hit, selling more copies than he could print (he eventually had to turn the book over to Knopf). Important writers like Hart Crane were influenced by Ouspensky's book and joined in the praise. But neither Bragdon nor Bessaraboff knew of Ouspensky's whereabouts or even if he was still alive. They came across a copy of the *New Age* with Ouspensky's "Letters from Russia" and got in touch with Orage, but by this time he, too, had no idea where Ouspensky was. Yet Ouspensky's strange luck was still with him. While in London, an American Theosophist from Buffalo visited the Theosophical Society and asked if they had a copy of *Tertium Organum* for sale. A Russian woman overheard him (possibly Anna Butkovsky-Hewitt, which suggests she and Ouspensky remained in contact) and explained that she was Ouspensky's friend. She even gave him his address, and explained that Ouspensky was in Constantinople and was desperate to come to England. The Theosophist got this information back to Bragdon, who quickly sent Ouspensky three copies of the book as well as a hefty check for back royalties. Ouspensky was understandably pleased, although in his letter thanking Bragdon he refers to *Tertium Organum* as his "weakness."[10]

Bragdon was unable to help Ouspensky get to England. But Ouspensky's angel was working overtime. Soon after corresponding with Ouspensky, Bragdon received a telegram from an unexpected reader, Lady Mary Lillian Rothermere, wife of the newspaper baron and a passionate, if flighty, student of a variety of mystical interests. She had read *Tertium Organum* and was impressed and wanted very much to meet its publisher. She later showed up, as did Bessaraboff, at Bragdon's house in Rochester, New York. The result was a cable to Ouspensky: "Deeply impressed by your book *Tertium Organum*. Wish to meet you New York or London. Will pay all expenses."

Clearly Ouspensky had found the miraculous. His newfound devotee had even included a check.

Visas in Constantinople were highly sought and hard to come by. Even Gurdjieff, that master of every situation, had hit a wall trying to get one. But Ouspensky had no murky reputation behind him, and although it took time, he was again lucky in knowing the one person in town who could help: John Bennett. Bennett had already told him that he had practically struck gold with Lady Rothermere. Ouspensky was hoping his friends in the London Theosophical Society could help, but Lady Rothermere's telegram was almost as good as a visa itself. Bennett told him she had influence in high places. After waiting a few weeks, Bennett finally took matters in hand and explained to the British authorities that Ouspensky was an important figure and would be an asset as a visitor.

Bennett also suggested that Ouspensky's family should be welcome as well, but on this matter Madame Ouspensky had her own ideas. She preferred to stay where she was, in

Constantinople with Gurdjieff. His institute had once again closed. But she had no intention of going to England.

Ouspensky had been trapped once before. Yet not everything, he must have mused, need recur. Gurdjieff too was heading for Europe: the target, Berlin. Among his entourage was Ouspensky's family, including Ouspensky's step-grandson, Loyna, with whom Ouspensky had often played. Ouspensky would miss Loyna, we can assume, although his situation with the boy's grandmother was obscure.

Having once more waited for Gurdjieff to move, Ouspensky was free to depart. His new or forgotten road, it seems, was taking him to London.

LONDON CALLING

I F OUSPENSKY'S DAYS as a Stray Dog were the happiest of his life, his arrival in London in September 1921 must have run a close second. Lady Rothermere may not literally have been made of gold, but the plates on which she served Ouspensky's reception dinner were, as were the knives and forks.[1] She was also good at introductions and had an impressive guest list: on different occasions, at the dining table or in the lecture room, Ouspensky could find T. S. Eliot, Aldous Huxley, Gerald Heard, and a host of writers, journalists, psychologists, and doctors. Among this crowd numbered A. R. Orage, who had published Ouspensky's letters and had thrown him a life preserver in the form of Major Frank Pinder. They had, of course, met before, and the two had much in common. Both were renegade Theosophists, both were devotees of Nietzsche, both had written about cosmic consciousness, and both had a longing for the superman.[2] Yet although Orage was older by five years, meeting Ouspensky in his new guise as the teacher of Gurdjieff's system immediately established a difference between them. Orage was the student and Ouspensky, for the time being at least, was the master. Ouspensky's influence on Orage would be immense, but his presence was soon felt in other parts of the London literary world as well. Eliot and Huxley, as well as others who attended his talks, would incorporate Ouspenskian themes into their work. Ouspensky's influence on the London literary life of the 1920s and 1930s, like his effect on the Russian avant-garde, was considerable and still remains little known.

Ouspensky was right to think that his old Theosophical friends would be of help in his new home. Soon after his arrival, G. R. S. Mead, whom, like Orage, Ouspensky had met on his return from the East, arranged a series of lectures at the Quest Society, a Theosophical group Mead had founded in 1909. These followed the earlier lectures given in Lady Rothermere's Circus Road studio in St. John's Wood—about as far a cry from the refugee camp at Prinkipo as Ouspensky could get. It's curious to remember that no one who attended these lectures had heard of Gurdjieff or the work. Outside of the handful of people he had worked with personally, Gurdjieff was unknown. Ouspensky, however, was famous, almost an esoteric celebrity. *Tertium Organum* had received high praise and made impressive sales, and if the people who came to his lectures expected anything, it was heady talk about higher space and the fourth dimension. What they heard instead was a disappointment for some, a revelation for others.

For one thing, Ouspensky's manner was not designed to please. Given that in St. Petersburg and Moscow Ouspensky held the attention of a thousand people, one can assume, if not showmanship on his part, certainly some kind of charisma. If so, by the time Ouspensky arrived in London, he had sloughed this off. Anna, who met him again at this time, saw the change. He had, she said, "developed a hard outer shell," and she wondered why he had "crushed the gentle, poetic radiance of his St. Petersburg days."[3] It seems not to have occurred to her that Ouspensky's hard outer shell may have been formed by his experience with Gurdjieff. We don't know for certain, but as his biographer Colin Wilson suggests, the hard words from his master that Ouspensky had heard inside his chest very probably were about his "gentle, poetic radiance," which Gurdjieff no doubt saw as weakness.[4] Whatever

Gurdjieff had said, Ouspensky agreed with him. After three years of being told in a variety of ways that he was mechanical, it would be surprising if this indoctrination had no effect. Ouspensky seems to have arrived at a kind of compromise. He had enough belief in his own abilities, and enough exasperation with Gurdjieff's acting, to strike out on his own. Yet he adopted to the letter the whole of Gurdjieff's negative, if startling, doctrine. Ironically, it was precisely the most articulate expression of his "weakness," *Tertium Organum,* that established Ouspensky in the West—an irony surely not lost on him.

In any case, having been put through a spiritual, physical, and emotional wringer by both his teacher and "the history of crime," Ouspensky very probably determined that, for better or worse, it was time to lose his weakness. At forty-two, having lost everything else, he was making a fresh start in a strange land, armed with a few acquaintances and a glowing reputation. It was not the time for half measures. Certainly a good deal of his new taciturn self had to do with the fact that his spoken English, although improving, was still shaky. Also, Gurdjieff had taught that one of the principle means of leaking the energy needed for self-transformation was through useless talk. If this dictum was aimed at the loquacious Wraps Up the Thought, he certainly took it to heart. For the rest of his life, outside of a few close relationships, Ouspensky was known as a man of very few words. Years later, Count Hermann Keyserling—like Ouspensky, a philosophical traveler of the early twentieth century—remarked that Ouspensky was the most self-controlled individual he had ever met, having too firm of a grip on himself. Ouspensky made this impression on many who met him at this time. His new nickname could have been Sticks to the Point. For Rom Landau, who would meet Ouspensky years later, his reserve was "the outcome of an inner command not to talk, and, in fact, not to do more than was essential . . . Whatever Ouspensky had to say, was said in the shortest possible way, and was followed by silence." This made for some difficulties, as might be imagined. "Of course it was difficult . . . to carry on a conversation with a man who made no concessions to our habitual shortcomings or to social convention."[5]

London at the time of Ouspensky's arrival was still in the grip of a Slavic craze that had peaked just before the start of the First World War. Diaghilev's productions had been very successful; novels like Artsybashev's *Sanine,* a pagan-Nietzschean tract, and *The Breaking Point* (which Ouspensky had lectured on) were items of conversation. Given the temper of the post-war world, this is understandable. Europe and its humanist culture had been broken, and all the old values were shattered. T. S. Eliot would soon publish his most influential poem, *The Waste Land,* an account of the moral vacuum and loss of meaning later associated with the bleak philosophy of existentialism. Eliot's poem is filled with Eastern, esoteric, and occult references—Madame Blavatsky is the model for one character, Madame Sosostris—and indicates a yearning for some new teaching to fill the hole the war had punched through Western consciousness. In this landscape of emptiness and meaninglessness Ouspensky had arrived with his new, startling message.

His build-up was romantic and dramatic enough to pique a great deal of interest, even in the Jazz Age. A philosopher of higher dimensions and author of a very successful book who had escaped from the chaos of a collapsed Russia and against all odds had made his way to London: it was the kind of thing a publicity agent would die for. Yet by most accounts, it was the message, not the messenger, that impressed. To those not esoterically inclined, Ouspensky was not the most inspiring of figures. He seemed either to repel or to attract. To the writer David Garnett, Ouspensky was unfavorably reminiscent of Woodrow Wilson: "The same lavish display of false teeth, the same baffled, unseeing eye, the same aura of high thinking and patent medicines." Sharing a taxicab with Ouspensky in silence, Garnett surmised that his companion was "probably wondering what came next after OM MANI PADME HUM."[6] Paul Selver, a translator of Eastern European poetry, found Ouspensky "quite monumentally boorish. " He was an "exasperating Russian" who "sneered when I expressed the view that there were several Czech or Serbian poets of outstanding greatness."[7] Selver's real reason for disliking Ouspensky was the influence he would have on Orage, who Selver knew through the *New Age*—a feeling that most of Orage's old friends would come to share. For Roland Kenney, editor of the *Daily Herald,* Ouspensky "looked like a dejected bird huddling up in a rainstorm," although, unlike other birds, this one "was obviously a man of a dominant if not domineering type of character, with determination—or obstinacy—written over his every feature." Not taking kindly to competition, Dmitri Mitrinovic, the Serbian mystic who for a time had Orage under his spell, hated Ouspensky on sight. Others were disenchanted by his brusque practicality. The seeker of the miraculous now taught that there were no miracles. "Set yourself to do the possible and leave the impossible alone . . . Our lives can only be safely built on the foundation of the practical,"[8] a member of his audience recalled Ouspensky saying.

One reader of *Tertium Organum* who was deeply disappointed by Ouspensky the man, while maintaining admiration for the philosopher, was the writer Algernon Blackwood. When he started to attend Ouspensky's lectures Blackwood had been a devotee of higher space for some time, using the theme to great effect in his highly popular John Silence stories about a "psychic detective" at home in the fourth dimension. He had also had tenure in perhaps the most famous magical society of modern times, the Hermetic Order of the Golden Dawn, whose members included W. B. Yeats, the weird novelist Arthur

Machen, and the notorious Aleister Crowley. Bragdon had sent Blackwood a copy of *Tertium Organum,* and Blackwood was impressed; he was a great reader of Charles Hinton and knew the terrain well. Blackwood and Ouspensky even had mutual friends in Orage and G. R. S. Mead, and, oddly enough, Blackwood had spent a considerable time in the Caucasus, the setting for his mystical novel *The Centaur* (1911). So when Blackwood finally met the author of one of his favorite books, the experience was oddly flat. Speaking of the lectures, Blackwood remarked:

> Much wisdom, I am sure, was sprayed over us, many valuable hints offered, practical as well as theoretical, but the net result . . . was negligible. To get a straight intelligible answer to a straight question was almost impossible. I listened attentively, but I never heard an intelligible . . . question receive a satisfactory answer. The questioner was made to feel that his or her question was rather silly.[9]

This last remark refers to Ouspensky's often devastating replies and equally devastating silences. He was not prone to suffer fools gladly. When he felt that a question was asked out of mere curiosity or intellectual interest, he either waved it away or grunted a blunt rejoinder. ("Was the Buddha Man Number Seven?" "I don't know.") Added to his staccato English, the effect must have been disturbing. Blackwood's main criticism of Ouspensky was that he "shut down Wonder behind doors of common sense."[10] Blackwood's own work often exhibits a "gentle, poetic radiance," and like the early Ouspensky, he found Nature a source of mystical inspiration. That Ouspensky now considered such sentiments worthless more than likely turned away a potentially important convert, although Blackwood would continue to incorporate

Ouspensky's and Gurdjieff's ideas into his many short stories, even entitling a late collection *Shocks* (1935).[11]

Yet others were not put off by Ouspensky's stern demeanor. After hearing Ouspensky lecture, Orage wrote Claude Bragdon that his author was "the first teacher I have met who has impressed me with ever-increasing certainty that he knows and he can do."[12] It was through Orage that Ouspensky's main cadre would be formed. By the time he met Ouspensky, Orage had already been through a gamut of mystical and occult teachings, the most recent being the Psychosynthesis Group he had recently put together. Unlike psycho*analysis,* which aimed at taking the psyche apart, psychosynthesis was concerned with integrating psychology with religion and mysticism; understandably, it found more support in Jung's work than in Freud's. One psychosynthesizer Orage brought along was Maurice Nicoll; he would prove the most important of Ouspensky's London students and would also become one of his few friends. Nicoll was already slated by Jung to be his representative in England, and the two had formed a close relationship. When Freud later discovered that Nicoll had left Jung and had gone to work with Gurdjieff, he felt justified in his opinion of his ex-disciple, whose interest in occultism he had always disparaged. When informed that Nicoll had gone to Fontainebleu, Freud remarked to another devotee, "See what becomes of Jung's students?"

Nicoll, like Orage, was impressed. That August, while Ouspensky still languished at Prinkipo, Nicoll had written in his diary: "Prayer to Hermes. Teach me—instruct me—show me the Path, so that I may know certainty—help my great ignorance, illumine my darkness? I have asked a question."

Sitting in the audience at the Quest Society two months later, Nicoll thought he'd got an answer. That night he rushed home to his wife, who was still recovering from having their first child. Shaking her bed, he told her that she must come and hear Ouspensky. "He is the only man who has ever answered my questions," he informed her. So great was his excitement that he even forgot to ask about the baby. Ouspensky, he said, was like a kind of prophet. Nicoll's urgency must have been infectious; his wife took his advice and was soon as convinced as he.

Not all the faces were new. Bennett had returned to England from Turkey, and came to visit Ouspensky in his hotel room on Russell Square. Ouspensky told Bennett of his success, and Bennett asked to be able to attend some lectures. He was unsure if he would stay in London or not—he thought he might return to Turkey to pursue his studies. Unconcerned, Ouspensky informed Bennett that he could of course attend his lectures. As for Turkey: "You cannot decide," he said. "If you go to Turkey, it is not because you decide. You have no power to choose. No one has power to choose." It was a doctrine that many would hear in the years to come.

One of those who heard the message was Rosamund Sharp. Under the ironic pseudonym of Rosamund Bland, she wrote a series of letters to an unnamed friend during her first few months as one of Ouspensky's students. Married to the editor Clifford Sharp, the two were unhappy (she had already had an affair with H. G. Wells), and when Orage suggested she see Ouspensky, she assumed he was another psychologist, remembering Orage's most recent craze. Orage had told her he "had at last found a man [he] could believe in."[13] Coming from him, this was high praise.

Although at first she didn't know what to make of Ouspensky's teaching, something about it attracted her. It wasn't religion, philosophy, or psychology, but a combination of all three with a strangely practical side. She didn't care for the air of mystery that surrounded Ouspensky, nor for the atmosphere of Lady Rothermere's salon, where Ouspensky was

touted as "the latest thing"—an insight that proved correct, as
Lady Rothermere predictably soon lost interest and moved on
to other fads. But Ouspensky must have noted something in
her; as Gurdjieff often did with his students, he invited her to
meet with him alone. The place was a Chinese restaurant on
Oxford Street, one that over the years became a favorite of
Ouspensky's.

Rosamund was apprehensive, and when she arrived and
found Ouspensky waiting outside alone, she was surprised: she
had expected Orage to be there. They talked for two hours.
Ouspensky was obviously trying to gauge his effect, as he asked
her what she had got out of their last meeting. Soon her appre-
hension eased, and she found that behind the hard,
professorial exterior was a "wonderful person," who had the
"sweetest smile in the world"—his "only attraction from an
ordinary point of view, counting out his brains, of course."[14]
Ouspensky then asked her to formulate a desire, an *aim,* and
told her he could help her to attain it—a teaching strategy he
would employ in years to come. She admitted that this was a
bad time in her life; she was depressed, suffered headaches,
and felt at the end of her tether. Her life had become, as it had
for Anna, unbearable.

The theoretical material she had to absorb overwhelmed
her, but Rosamund soon felt a change. As Ouspensky and the
St. Petersburg group had found, she discovered that she was
losing many of her old interests, and that her friends felt she
was becoming different. She was afraid of this but already felt
that Ouspensky offered her something she could get nowhere
else; one tangible sign was that her headaches had already disappeared. Like Gurdjieff, Ouspensky gave his teaching out in
bits and pieces; Rosamund and the others had to put these
fragments together. It was hard work, and she admitted she was
no "brain," but the effort itself proved beneficial.

Her personal relationship with Ouspensky developed as

well; she discovered he was not always a cold, unemotional taskmaster. She visited him often at the Gwendyr Road flat that Lady Rothermere provided, a rather dreary affair, as another student, Kenneth Walker, would describe it. For Rosamund it was "a little dark underground room which is rather like a tomb."[15] There she discovered the cats that accompanied Ouspensky for the rest of his life. Cats were his favorite animal because they possessed an astral body, he said. (He would later tell Maurice Nicoll that they also remembered themselves, except when salmon was around.) Rosamund found Ouspensky's English charming—he had asked her to correct him when he made mistakes—and, finding him in this warm, friendly mode, wrote that "I felt him really human for the first time."[16] It was for Rosamund that, as mentioned earlier, Ouspensky bought cream buns and cakes and made tea, of which he was a connoisseur; each year Twinings, the famous tea merchants, invited him to their annual tasting.

Strangely, one of the friends from whom Rosamund began to feel distant was Orage himself. Ouspensky, too, was unhappy with him, and he remarked to Rosamund that Orage only played with his intellect and lacked real commitment. Already at one meeting, Ouspensky had taken Orage to task for his lack of seriousness. Orage would soon leave Ouspensky to sit at the feet of his real master; no doubt the charismatic, sparkling editor didn't care for being hauled on the carpet by a man he had practically saved from starvation.

Like Ouspensky in St. Petersburg, Rosamund became curious about her teacher's own aim: why was he doing this? Unlike Gurdjieff, Ouspensky was more forthcoming; he admitted to her that there was some "great work" involved in schools. Quite frankly, he confessed, the ultimate welfare of herself and the others didn't interest him very much. Whether people "wake up" or not for their own good didn't matter to him. (Years later Gurdjieff would be more abrupt: referring to

186

his students, he once told a shocked C. S. Nott that he "needed rats for my experiments," and to Claude Bragdon he spoke
of his "trained and freely-moving guinea pigs.")[17] What was
important for Ouspensky was finding people who could be of
use in the great work. Ouspensky was not too specific about
this great work, but this is clearly an early instance of what
would eventually become a kind of idée fixe: the need to make
contact with a "higher source," what he called the Inner Circle,
the esoteric masters of reality. Gurdjieff, he believed, had done
so. But as Ouspensky came to think, somewhere along the line
Gurdjieff had lost contact, had broken the initiatic chain, and
was now operating on his own. The system came from the
source; hence Ouspensky's determination to hold onto it.
Gurdjieff was only its messenger, and if Ouspensky could somehow show the Inner Circle that he understood the teaching
and was preparing people, perhaps *they* might get in touch with
him. He was once again looking for schools, only this time he
hoped to bring the mountain to Muhammad.

In any case, Ouspensky may have thought that Rosamund
was promising material. When she told him she had decided
not to have children, he approved, telling her it was a good
decision for women like herself, adding that such a decision
was "better for the work."[18] Yet by December of 1921, only a
few months after making his appearance, a depressed
Ouspensky told Rosamund that he was considering returning
to Constantinople. Things were not going well. His pupils were
not making much headway. No one was serious, least of all
Orage. It wasn't worth expending his energy for the results he
was getting.

Was this merely a show of irritableness? Or was it a
Gurdjieff-style ploy to get his London group to appreciate what
he was offering them? It's difficult to believe he really thought
of leaving. By this time his meetings had shifted from St. Johns
Wood to the Theosophical Hall at 38 Warwick Gardens, a larg-

er space in Earl's Court, closer to his own room in Baron's Court. Three evenings a week, forty to fifty people gathered to hear his lectures. What he told them was not cheery:

> You think you know who and what you are; but you do not know either what slaves you now are, or how free you might become. Man can do nothing: he is a machine controlled by external influences, not by his own will, which is an illusion. He is asleep. He has no permanent self that he can call "I." Because he is not one but many, his moods, his impulses, his very sense of his own existence are no more than a constant flux. You need not believe what I tell you, but if you will observe yourselves you will verify its truth . . . How can man, who cannot remember who and what he is, who does not know the forces that move him to action, pretend that he can do anything? . . . the first truth that must be grasped is that you and I and all men are nothing but machines.[19]

Many were won over, though not all. On one occasion the famous occultist and scholar A. E. Waite—himself, like Algernon Blackwood, a member of the Golden Dawn—stood up and announced to Ouspensky and his audience that there was "no love" in his system, and walked out. J. G. Bennett found this amusing. What Ouspensky thought of it is unknown, although it can be imagined. Although a decade earlier he had written that love is a "cosmic phenomenon," a great mystery and a creative force, in the system Ouspensky was developing it played no part. Like everything else, it was merely an expression of man's mechanicalness. Was there something more in this than Ouspensky's determination to stick to the letter of the doctrine he had learned at the hand of his remorseless master? Or did the fact that his wife had neither accompanied him on his journey nor shared in his triumph have anything to do with it? Ouspensky doesn't tell us. What we do know is that he worked hard, passing on to his students what he had learned, urging them to "remember themselves," explaining Gurdjieff's cosmology, demanding of them sacrifice. In one instance, this took the form of a precious tea service. Its owner thought that if she could break one of the cups—which had been in her family for generations—it would help her "self-remember." Ouspensky agreed, but she couldn't bring herself to do it.

When not separating the esoteric wheat from the everyday chaff—who, in New Testament fashion, Ouspensky informed his flock would be burned—he relaxed with Nicoll and his wife at their home in Chester Terrace, near Regent's Park. There Orage and Clifford Sharp often joined in. In Nicoll, Ouspensky found an intelligent and witty host. The two had much in common. Like Ouspensky, Nicoll had a deep interest in time, the Gospels, and psychology; under a pseudonym, he had also written several novels. For Ouspensky, who less than six months earlier was struggling to stay alive teaching English to his fellow refugees, it must have seemed that he had finally achieved some measure of stability.

He was due, however, for a shock.

THE RETURN OF MR. G.

G URDJIEFF'S GERMAN ADVENTURE wasn't successful. He gave some lectures in Berlin but once again failed to put his institute on sure footing. An attempt to purchase the Hellerau in Dresden, a former center of the Dalcroze Eurhythmics Institute, led to a legal battle and the sinister allegation that Gurdjieff had used hypnosis to get his way. The owner had already leased part of the building to other tenants, one of whom was the progressive educationalist A. S. Neill, but Gurdjieff wanted the whole space and somehow convinced the owner to agree. When Neill and the others angrily waved their leases, the owner relented, and Gurdjieff, uncharacteristically, took him to court. The owner told the judge that Gurdjieff had hypnotized him into breaking the lease, and Gurdjieff lost the case. For a man who could speak inside Ouspensky's chest, it was probably not difficult to convince a landlord that Gurdjieff's and his own best interests were identical.[1] Yet several years before, Gurdjieff had taken an oath never to use his powers for his own benefit—this "artificial life," as he later called it, would act as an "alarm clock," a permanent "wake up call" and stimulus to "self-remember."[2] If he did indeed use his powers in trying to secure the Hellerau, he either did not live up to his oath, or the oath, like so much else he said, was a story.

Ouspensky heard of Gurdjieff's difficulties but, with characteristic discretion, spoke of them vaguely, mentioning only "strange events . . . which ended in legal proceedings."[3] He had by this time begun to write the account of his years with Gurdjieff. Eventually, after much agonizing, indecision, and retitling, this would appear posthumously as *In Search of the Miraculous*.[4] We don't know if Ouspensky ever asked Gurdjieff exactly what had happened in Dresden, although it would be naïve to expect that if he did, he ever got a clear reply. He had the opportunity, though, because in February of 1922, Gurdjieff arrived in London.

Hearing of Ouspensky's success, Gurdjieff, who had already struck out several times with his institute, decided to pay his ex-lieutenant a call. Ouspensky invited Gurdjieff to his lectures and introduced him to his following. His attitude, he says, had become more "definite." As before, he still felt there was more to be gained from Gurdjieff's work, and he decided to once again help him with his institute and the ongoing "Struggle of the Magicians," still yet to see a performance. But Ouspensky was adamant: he, personally, could not work with Gurdjieff. Everything that had come between them before was still there.

His students felt otherwise. They were electrified by the master's visit. At Warwick Gardens, some sixty people gathered to hear the message straight from the source. Gurdjieff's presence was so impressive that for most of the time the audience sat in silence. On the platform, along with Gurdjieff and Ouspensky, were Olga de Hartmann and Frank Pinder, acting as Gurdjieff's translators. Gurdjieff launched into a talk on our many "I's" and on the impossibility of altering our emotions through mere decision. After several minutes of stunned silence, one brave soul ventured a question. "What would it be like to be conscious in essence?" "Everything more vivid," was the concise reply.

Almost at a stroke, Ouspensky had the rug pulled from under him. After hearing Gurdjieff, Orage, Ouspensky's main catch, changed allegiances. "I *knew* that Gurdjieff was the teacher," he declared. This was the general assessment, and when Gurdjieff announced that he was thinking of setting up his institute in London, we can imagine Ouspensky's chagrin; he tells us that if this was the case, he would go to Paris or America. Yet, faithful to his ex-teacher, Ouspensky did everything he could to assist him, and his students collected enough money to pay for all of Gurdjieff's troupe to come. No doubt thankful for this assistance, Gurdjieff himself was, however, not yet through with Ouspensky, and in a private meeting, he informed his renegade student that all his attempts to teach the system were worthless. His own development, too, was at risk. To save himself, he had to immediately and without reservation give up his pride and, as his wife currently was, once again become a student.

We can imagine Ouspensky's response. When he rejected Gurdjieff's advice, Gurdjieff took advantage of yet another lecture to announce to Ouspensky's group that their teacher was neither mandated nor qualified to teach *his*—Gurdjieff's—system, thus placing doubts on its source in the Sarmoung Brotherhood. Adding insult to injury, when Ouspensky noticed that Pinder's translation was incorrect and mentioned this, Gurdjieff openly rebuked him. "Pinder is interpreting for me—not you," Gurdjieff announced to the baffled group. The whole thing was clearly planned, and one can forgive Ouspensky for finding it difficult to not express some negative emotions that evening. It was one final "act" for which Ouspensky could never forgive Gurdjieff.

Gurdjieff later told Pinder that now Ouspensky's students would have to choose a teacher. The faithful, like Pinder, saw in this nothing but Gurdjieff's open-hearted concern that Ouspensky and his flock not be led astray. Less generous minds might see it otherwise: having failed in Tiflis, Constantinople, Berlin, and Dresden, Gurdjieff took advantage of Ouspensky's success to try to set up his own establishment in London. Yet once again it was not to be. The institute opened, but Gurdjieff was denied the necessary visa. When he decided that now he would try France, Ouspensky no doubt heaved a sigh of relief.

With money collected by Ouspensky's followers—mostly from Lady Rothermere and Ralph Philipson, a coal-mine millionaire—in July of 1922, Gurdjieff purchased a beautiful but run down chateau in Fontainebleau, about forty miles outside of Paris. The Prieure des Basses Loges had an interesting history, having been the home of Louis XIV's mistress, Madame de Maintenon; then later a Carmelite monastery; and more recently the property of Fernand Labori, the defense lawyer in the famous Dreyfus affair. After Gurdjieff got his hands on it, its reputation reached new proportions. Here, finally, the Institute for the Harmonious Development of Man would enjoy a solid base.

Almost immediately after the Prieure's opening in September there was a general exodus of Ouspensky's students across the English Channel. Orage, Nicoll, Bennett, and many others left gray London for the enchanted forest of Fontainebleau. To Ouspensky it seemed that "a very motley company" had gathered there. Some were from St. Petersburg, some from Tiflis, some from Constantinople, some from his own London groups. Ouspensky felt that many who scampered off had acted too hastily, but they had already made up their minds to go, and there was little he could do. He himself arrived for his first visit toward the beginning of November. Although he discovered very interesting and animated work underway, Ouspensky felt that the whole project was not correctly organized and would prove unstable. As in Essentuki, the inhabitants did the housekeeping, gardening, cooking, and general all-round chores, but here the grounds were immense and the upkeep considerable.

Gurdjieff lectured, and taught the movements, dances, and exercises.

The attraction of the Prieure, some of Ouspensky's students had remarked, was that it seemed to offer a kind of shortcut. It did, via the strenuous pass called "super effort." Having given up the *New Age* for Fontainebleau, the forty-nine-year-old Orage found himself digging a ditch and then filling it in again, several times. The "alarm clock" of not smoking, the hard labor, and Gurdjieff's frequent piquant remarks soon had the portly editor in tears. Nicoll abandoned a lucrative Harley Street practice and arrived with his wife and infant child. He was saddled with the job of "kitchen boy." Awaking at 5:00 AM, Nicoll lit the boilers and got the day started; by 11:00 PM he had washed hundreds of filthy, greasy dishes, cups, pots, and pans, without soap or hot water. His wife did the cooking. This went on for three months. For some reason, Gurdjieff singled Nicoll out as the general scapegoat and when, as often did, some mishap occurred, the master would shout "Nicoll!" and ape a gesture of despair. "More!" and "Quicker!" were the general commands, and Gurdjieff (to mix metaphors) was adept at shuffling the deck so that dozens of corns were stepped on each day, creating, as he believed, the necessary friction of "yes and no." But perhaps the greatest super effort was left for a child. The novelist Fritz Peters, brought to the Prieure as a young boy by his aunt Margaret Anderson, a member of the literary avant-garde, was required by Gurdjieff to mow the vast lawns of the grounds in increasingly less and less time, until at last the massive acreage was to be covered in one afternoon. It is a testament to the dedication Gurdjieff instilled—and to young Peters's stamina—that he was successful at his chore.

One visitor to the Prieure who was not required to work was the writer Katharine Mansfield. An ex-mistress of Orage, who had more or less discovered her, she was introduced to Ouspensky when it was clear that she was already dying from tuberculosis. When Ouspensky spoke with her, she was, he said, "halfway to death."[5] She was determined to make the best use of her time, and for her this meant going to the Prieure. Ouspensky himself gave her the address. Later, meeting her on another visit to Fontainebleau, he spoke with her about her spiritual longings. She felt that she and everyone else were like the survivors of a shipwreck, cast ashore on an inhospitable island unaware of their predicament—a sentiment that Ouspensky, with his sense of the absurdity of life, no doubt appreciated. Gurdjieff, well aware that Mansfield's last days were upon her, put her up in the Prieure's barn, where, he said, breathing the air of cows would have a salutary effect. Whether it did or not is unknown, but from her letters, Katharine Mansfield's last days seem to have been filled with a peculiar joy. Nevertheless, after her death at the beginning of 1923, Gurdjieff enjoyed the sinister reputation that colored much of his notoriety for the rest of his career. Around the same time, Ouspensky discovered that, in his absence, rumors had spread about Gurdjieff's predilection for seducing his female students. With typical loyalty, Ouspensky squashed these, although he may have had reason to give them second thought.

Ouspensky made several trips to Fontainebleau, and on most of them, Gurdjieff invited him to live at the Prieure. Ouspensky declined. It was, he admitted, tempting, but in the end Ouspensky said he could find no place there. Gurdjieff was not inclined to let Ouspensky go peaceably. One morning in London Ouspensky awoke to find a telegram from Sophie Grigorievna, requesting that he come to the Prieure immediately. When he did, Gurdjieff met him. He informed Ouspensky that he was not happy with many of his students and felt that the work was getting out of control. Assembling his pupils, Gurdjieff divided them into seven groups, the first of which included Orage, Dr. James Young (another psychosynthesizer), and Dr. Stoerneval. Gurdjieff then announced that only the first group could remain to work with him; all the others had to leave, including Ouspensky's wife and step-daughter. If this wasn't enough of a shock, he topped it off with another announcement: from that moment on he was breaking off all relations with Ouspensky. His dressing-down of his former student was now complete. It's unclear what prompted this action, but evidence sadly points to some in-group bickering between Orage and Ouspensky over Ouspensky's alleged "failure" to secure a British visa for Gurdjieff. There was also flak over remarks Ouspensky had made to a journalist. In an article about the Prieure in the *London Daily News* Ouspensky was quoted as saying, "Gurdjieff and I have reached our present state of knowledge by long hard work in many lands . . ." The journalist himself wrote that "In Gurdjieff he [Ouspensky] found a kindred spirit who had gone farther on the same road." For someone who had lectured much on the need not to identify with petty egoisms or to refrain from "inner considering"—basically, caring about what others might think of you—to be troubled by the loss of a little limelight seems baffling. Ouspensky had managed to raise the funds for the Prieure, and as a noted and respected author, his imprimatur in an article on Gurdjieff's work could only have been to its advantage.

The fracas was enough to cause much friction, and it sadly highlights that even on the road to the miraculous, petty vendettas and the desire to win the guru's approval were not absent. When Gurdjieff began to berate Ouspensky for not being more careful about the choice of people he allowed into the work—which was precisely Ouspensky's concern regarding Gurdjieff's own selection process—we can imagine Ouspensky had reached a limit. He continued to visit the Prieure, but every blandishment by Gurdjieff to tempt him to return and work was rejected.

Gurdjieff was, in any case, no longer banking everything on the possibility of drawing Ouspensky back. His ex-student had turned enough new material in his direction for him to consider other candidates for Ouspensky's position. One was J. G. Bennett. On one of Bennett's visits Gurdjieff invited him on a business trip to Melun—he was still, all the while, involved in several money-making schemes—and on the drive home (an initiation in itself, as Gurdjieff was an appalling driver) they turned onto a forest road. In a clearing they spoke in Turkish, and Gurdjieff informed Bennett of the vast plans he had in store. He intended to purchase more land on which he would build an observatory to study planetary movements. Gurdjieff told Bennett that he had great potential and that although the work was long, in his case, two years devoted to Gurdjieff's teaching would be sufficient for him to work alone—a contradiction of his dictum that alone a man could do nothing. Bennett was clearly attracted to the idea but also had some hesitation. Gurdjieff then suggested that Bennett accompany him on his coming trip to America and act as his interpreter. After that, the master continued, he could give lectures on his own. Bennett considered the idea but in the end declined. Gurdjieff may have known that he would; when Bennett tried to speak with him about his decision, his teacher ignored him. When leaving the Prieure for London, Bennett couldn't even find him to say goodbye.[6] Bennett would remain Ouspensky's student, and not until 1948, twenty-five years later, would he take up with Gurdjieff again.

Another target was Nicoll. Having lost interest in Bennett, Gurdjieff decided that Orage was his new man. But he evidently thought Orage could use some assistance, so he offered Nicoll the opportunity to accompany Orage to the New World. There is of course the possibility that Gurdjieff recognized the growing relationship between Nicoll and Ouspensky and thought it best to separate the two. As it happened, Nicoll, who had been at the Prieure for a year, had decided it was time to return to London and declined Gurdjieff's offer. Gurdjieff's reaction to this is unknown. In any case, in Orage he found an able and highly motivated exponent, and in December 1923, Orage and Dr. Stoerneval crossed the Atlantic, bringing the work to New York. Orage spent the next decade promoting Gurdjieff's ideas in the United States, only to break with him when he contravened his teacher's wishes and married Jessie Dwight, a young, strong-willed, independent woman who had no interest in Gurdjieff. At one point, when the tug-of-war between teacher and wife was at its height, Gurdjieff glared at the newlywed Jessie and warned, "If you keep my super-idiot from coming back to me, you boil in burning oil."[7] Most of Orage's mission in America consisted of attempts to drum up cash for the Prieure, demands for which became incessant and, by Orage's own admission, cost him much of the following he had diligently built up. It is to Orage's credit that he eventually cashed in his chips, returned to England, and threw himself again into literary and journalistic work. He died in 1934, after giving a speech on economics over the BBC.

CHAPTER SEVENTEEN

"HE COULD GO MAD"

O N HIS RETURN from Fontainebleau, Nicoll resumed his place at Ouspensky's lectures. At this time, Ouspensky was collecting the material that would eventually be published as *A New Model of the Universe*. On a visit to Ouspensky's basement flat, Nicoll found him at work. Ouspensky, he wrote,

> has the New Testament in German, French, Russian and English, and when he is speaking of a verse he looks at the translation in each of them and in the Greek version. He has a number of dictionaries in his room. He is fond of pencils sharpened to very fine points and always has several on his table. His mantelpiece is covered with old photographs, prints and packets of toning paper. He sits on a small uncomfortable chair. The walls are covered with a miscellaneous collection of pictures belonging to the landlord, all of which I have stared at many times without being able to remember any of them.[1]

Nicoll was responsible for bringing another important student into the fold. Resuming his Harley Street practice, Nicoll bumped into his old friend Kenneth Walker—like himself, a doctor who moonlighted as a writer. Walker had recently published a children's book about Noah's Ark, and, echoing

Ouspensky, Nicoll told him of a group of people in London who were in the process of building an Ark themselves. Walker knew that Nicoll had given up his practice and thrown himself into a strange life with a mysterious Asian guru, and was at first put off by his friend's remarks. Eventually he let himself be talked into going to one of Ouspensky's meetings. He was to attend them for the next twenty-four years.

Walker's account of the early days of Ouspensky's groups makes them sound like the clandestine meetings of a secret and illegal organization, a kind of modern-day Illuminati. Secret they may have been, but illegal they were not, and it's difficult to decide whether the cloak-and-dagger atmosphere Ouspensky created was an expression of some mild paranoia or a kind of acting of his own. When Walker arrived at Warwick Gardens, he found a woman at the door who checked that his name was on the list. He then entered a room, bare except for several small chairs that faced a blackboard and a small table. A few paintings graced the walls, and a vase holding some artificial cherry blossoms sat on a windowsill. People arrived in twos and threes and kept to a studious silence. The audience looked intelligent, Walker thought, but not particularly interesting. Ouspensky arrived well after the announced start of the lecture. Walker found the chairs uncomfortable, and the whole atmosphere reminded him of the Presbyterian churches of his youth.

At this point Ouspensky was a very solid man of medium height, whose closely cropped gray hair made Walker think he looked more like a scientist or lawyer than a mystic. Ouspensky sat at the table and, without looking at the audience, took a sheet of paper from his pocket. This he scrutinized for several seconds, holding it a few inches from his pince-nez. Finally he turned to the group and said "Well?" before beginning a staccato talk on our illusory sense of "I." It was, more or less, a routine he would maintain for the next seven years. He encouraged the group to test everything he said. "Faith," he told them, "is not wanted here . . . To accept something on trust, when you can prove it or disprove it, is laziness." When a woman asked about art, suggesting that Leonardo, Michelangelo, and other greats could not have been entirely mechanical, Ouspensky disagreed. There was no attempt to argue, convince, or cajole. To Walker, Ouspensky seemed "so detached from everything that I felt even an explosion would fail to shake him."[2] Then, abruptly, the talk was over.

At the end of the meeting, Walker asked if there would be another next week. He was advised to leave his telephone number; he would, perhaps, receive a call. Then, as he was leaving, he saw the secretary tell a group of people who were talking in front of the doorway to disperse. Walker was baffled by the need for secrecy; nevertheless, Ouspensky himself seemed impressive and Walker wanted to know more. After attending a few more meetings, Walker requested a personal interview.

When he arrived at Gwendyr Road, Walker had to wait, as Ouspensky was busy developing some photographs. Walker took the opportunity to examine the room. A bed ran along one wall, with two chairs opposite it, one on either side of a gas fire. On another wall was a low bookcase. On a table in the center of the room Walker found an assortment of things: books, papers, a typewriter, photographs, some old prints, letters, a camera, a galvanometer, and a scientific instrument of some unidentifiable kind. There was a half-empty tin of sardines on the mantelpiece, along with some bread and cheese and an unwashed plate, knife, and fork. To Walker all this suggested a "nice disregard for the inconveniences of which life is chiefly composed."[3] When Ouspensky returned, he turned on the gas fire and both men sat down. Walker then discovered how difficult it was to "have a conversation with a man who would answer questions, but initiate nothing himself." After a few general questions—one of which, "Why are you giving these lectures?," made Ouspensky laugh—the meeting ran out of steam. One nugget of wisdom did pass between them: "To have a clearly defined aim in life is of the very greatest importance," Ouspensky told his increasingly uncomfortable guest. Walker no doubt appreciated this, but his general impression was of Ouspensky's impersonality. Ouspensky was, he said, a man who remained far away.[4]

With the exception of Nicoll, Ouspensky's reticence was a character trait that most who came into close contact with him would experience. Bennett remarks that after returning to London from the Prieure, he wanted very much to speak with Ouspensky about a profound experience he had with "super efforts," when, like Ouspensky, he had broken through his resistance and reached the Great Accumulator. But when he tried, he found Ouspensky unresponsive. And when he did talk about Gurdjieff's remarks about different energies and their different speeds, Ouspensky showed little interest.

Chances are that Ouspensky wasn't interested; to his detriment, as the years went by, he showed less and less interest in any ideas outside of his own obsessions. But another factor was also at work. At one point Mrs. Beaumont had spoken of her misgivings about Gurdjieff to Ouspensky and asked if he thought he was a good man. At that time Ouspensky assured her that he was. Now he had had second thoughts.

In January 1924, at the apartment of Ralph Philipson, his main financial supporter, Ouspensky called together his key students and informed them that he was breaking off all contact with Gurdjieff. Although they knew that for several years relations between the two had not been cordial, the announcement was nevertheless a shock. Ouspensky asked for their ideas on how they should continue. After a few remarks he concluded that in the future, his groups would work independently of the Prieure; this meant that they would have to choose between working with him or with Gurdjieff. If they chose him, it meant they could have no contact with Gurdjieff. After several minutes of silence, it took Philipson, a no-nonsense Northumberland businessman, to ask the obvious question: why?

"Gurdjieff is a very extraordinary man," Ouspensky replied. "His possibilities are much greater than those of people like ourselves. But he can also go the wrong way. I believe that he is now passing through a crisis, the outcome of which no one can foresee. Most people have many 'I's'. . . But with Gurdjieff there are only two 'I's'; one very good and one very bad. I believe that in the end the good 'I' will conquer. But in the meantime it is very dangerous to be near him."[5]

And if the good "I" didn't win, someone asked?

"He could go mad. Or else he could attract to himself some disaster in which all those round him would be involved."[6]

Six months later it seemed that Ouspensky had been right.

Orage's American mission was a success, and after a celebrated performance of the "movements" at the Theatre des Champs Elysees in Paris, Gurdjieff headed across the Atlantic. He and his dance troupe were a hit in New York, and the charming and intellectually effervescent Orage introduced Gurdjieff to dozens of literary, artistic, and professional admirers, building up groups and a strong body of dedicated students. In June, Gurdjieff returned to France. Back at the Prieure, although he had broken ties with his master, Ouspensky once again paid a visit to Gurdjieff. About this occasion Margaret Anderson remarked that, sitting at Gurdjieff's left at a lavish dinner, Ouspensky acted like a small boy, flushed with the Armagnac forced upon him.[7] Knowing Ouspensky's fondness for spirits, it's difficult to conceive of drinks being "forced" on him, and Anderson's account suffers from the same considerations as those of others trying to earn points with the master. It's curious though that Ouspensky, having drawn a line in January, was again a guest of Gurdjieff. Perhaps he was investigating the reports he had heard about Gurdjieff's relations with his admiring female students. Or perhaps he was visiting his wife.

On July 8, Gurdjieff and Olga de Hartmann were in Paris, scheduled to return to the Prieure that afternoon. The two had made the trip together several times, and Olga showed great bravery riding with Gurdjieff, who, as Ouspensky remarked, drove a car as if he were riding a horse. On that day, before heading back, Gurdjieff asked Olga to take his Citroen to a mechanic and have the steering checked; he also signed over to her his power of attorney and, in a final odd decision, ordered her to take the train, leaving him to drive alone. Used to her master's strange requests, Olga complied, although it was a hot day and the train would be sweltering. At the intersection of the Paris-Fontainebleau and the N 168 roads from Versailles, traveling at around 70 mph, Gurdjieff's car swerved off the road and smashed head-on into a stone embankment, then came to a halt at a tree. The Citroen was wrecked. Gurdjieff was found by a passing policeman, his head resting gently on a car cushion. He was unconscious and covered in blood, and had suffered a massive concussion.

How his head got on the cushion remains a mystery. It's inconceivable that he and it were thrown out of the wreck in so neat a fashion. Yet how he could crawl out and arrange it himself, given the injuries he sustained, is equally baffling. Brought first to a hospital, and then to the Prieure, he remained unconscious for five days, kept alive by oxygen. It would take him months to recover. As Ouspensky had in Finland, Olga de Hartmann, in Paris waiting for her train, heard Gurdjieff's voice speaking to her. By all accounts this happened around the same time as the accident.

But was it an accident? Suspicion remains that Gurdjieff somehow arranged it; the precautions he took beforehand suggest as much. Yet he was also an abysmal driver, and the other factors could be coincidence. As one writer suggests, he may have wanted an excuse to close down the Prieure and relieve himself of his students—many of them, at least. In any case, from Ouspensky's perspective, the signs were all too clear. Gurdjieff had transgressed, lost contact with the Source, and, as Ouspensky had predicted, brought retribution upon his head. Gurdjieff's accident effectively put an end to the Institute for the Harmonious Development of Man. Visitors came, and he occupied the grounds for another decade, but for all intents and purposes, this phase of the work was over.

When Ouspensky heard about the accident, he was stunned. Although he had foreseen something like it, the fact that Gurdjieff had fallen victim to an *accident* was peculiarly upsetting. Gurdjieff was supposed to be outside "the law of accident." Having worked on himself, having achieved the level of Man Number Five—possibly more—he was supposed to be under "the law of fate," and to have rid himself of a few of the forty-eight laws under which man on the Earth is compelled to live. Yet he had now suffered something as mundane and stupid as a car crash.

Ouspensky confided his fears to his friend Boris Mouravieff. He, too, had succeeded in escaping Constantinople; unlike Ouspensky, he had found a home in Paris, where, he reports, Ouspensky visited him often. Mouravieff would also come to London, although for some reason Ouspensky never introduced him to his students. Mouravieff had met Gurdjieff in Constantinople and he visited him sometimes in Paris, but, by his own admission, he never came under his spell. He was in fact very critical of Ouspensky's relationship with his teacher. From his perspective,

Ouspensky's romantic "search" had left him open to abuse, a vulnerability that Gurdjieff took full advantage of; Gurdjieff's domination of Ouspensky was "calculated and perfectly established from the very beginning."[8] Mouravieff in fact found this to be true of most of Gurdjieff's students. Gurdjieff's whole system, he believed, was little more than a means of bringing people under his control. Gurdjieff's method of convincing his students that they were *merde* left them in a condition in which he could propose "any absurdity to his disciples, perhaps even a monstrosity, and be sure in advance that it would be accepted with . . . enthusiasm."[9] When Mouravieff brought this up, Gurdjieff's students would look at him with contempt, yet an anecdote told by Bennett suggests Mouravieff may have been right. Gurdjieff, Bennett said, had "ruthless methods of getting rid of those he did not want. He seemed to invite and yet to detest a kind of stupid adoration . . . One lady was particularly foolish about him, and he played a cruel trick on her that showed me how seriously we should take his warning to trust nothing and no one, and especially not himself."[10] At a formal tea one afternoon, Gurdjieff informed this particularly adoring follower that the best way to enjoy ice cream was with mustard. When she dutifully returned with the mustard pot he shouted, "You see what is round idiot. She all the time idiot. Why you here?" The poor woman burst into tears, packed her bags, and left.[11] She was of course foolish, but it's difficult not to suspect that Gurdjieff felt no qualms about making an example of her. Mouravieff may have only been taking Gurdjieff at his word when he warned he was not to be trusted.

Mouravieff was involved with editing and translating the manuscript of *Fragments of an Unknown Teaching* and so was privy to Ouspensky's account of his relationship with Gurdjieff, a subject about which the friends were prone to argue. At one point Mouravieff believed that Ouspensky, for all his criticisms, still remained under some kind of hypnotic spell. This came out particularly when Ouspensky came to Paris and, with Mouravieff, visited the site of Gurdjieff's crash. Inspecting the scene, Ouspensky fell into a deep silence, then turned to Mouravieff. "I am scared," he said. "It is frightful . . . The institute of Georges Ivanovitch was precisely created to escape from the law of accident . . . and now he has fallen under the power of the same law . . . I am still asking myself if it is really pure accident? Gurdjieff has always sold integrity, as well as the human personality in general, very cheaply. Has he not surpassed the measure? I tell you, I am terribly frightened!"

The two friends went on to Fontainebleau, where Ouspensky asked Mouravieff to telephone his step-daughter at the Prieure. Mouravieff was told she was not there. At lunch, Ouspensky kept returning to the question of integrity, linking this with Gurdjieff's accident. Then suddenly Ouspensky dropped the subject; Mouravieff prodded him several times, but he refused to speak about it. That evening, back in Paris at a bar in Montmartre, Mouravieff persisted and Ouspensky finally spoke his thoughts. "Suddenly," Mouravieff writes, "his expression changed. I had the impression then that before me existed another man—no longer the one with whom I had spent such an agreeable evening . . . He turned to me abruptly and said 'Imagine that a member of the family had committed a serious crime; nobody would want to talk about it.'"[12]

At that point, Mouravieff remarks, he felt afraid. Was Ouspensky's reluctance to talk about the affair a sign of Gurdjieff's hypnotic domination? Or was it more simple? Ouspensky believed in Gurdjieff and, through him, in the work. Now he saw that Gurdjieff was not awake, at least not all of the time. More than likely, all his doubts and the illicit rumors he had heard came to mind as well. It was at this point,

Mouravieff says, that Ouspensky's heavy drinking began. Their Paris evenings were habitually capped by long sessions in a variety of Montmartre bars. At this point a note of sadness enters the story. Later Ouspensky would say that after the accident Gurdjieff went insane. Others would make similar remarks. Gurdjieff himself provided some of the strongest reasons for their suspicions, mostly in the form of his books *Herald of Coming Good* and the monumental *Beelzebub's Tales to His Grandson,* two of the most unclassifiable works ever produced with a pen.[13]

CHAPTER EIGHTEEN

"THE SYSTEM IS WAITING FOR WORKERS"

T HE ACCIDENT CRYSTALLIZED Ouspensky's doubts about his teacher, but it also made clear his appreciation of the teaching. It was, in fact, all he had left, even if he wasn't absolutely certain about it. By this time, Bennett was taking a more prominent role in the meetings, and he remarked to Ouspensky one day at Gwendyr Road that he was convinced that their work would lead him to consciousness and even immortality. Ouspensky stood before the gas fire and looked at Bennett. Bennett may have been sure of achieving these aims, but not he. "I am not sure," he replied. "I am sure of nothing. But I do know that we have nothing, and therefore we have nothing to lose . . . I have tried too much and seen too much to believe in anything. But I will not give up the struggle. In principle I believe that it is possible to achieve what we seek— but I am not sure that we have yet found the way. But it is useless to wait. We know that we have something that has come from a Higher Source. It may be that something more will come from the same Source." [1] It was the same idea that he had subtly mentioned to Rosamund Sharp; until the last months of his life, it would be the central aim of his work.

The twenties were a relatively quiet time for Ouspensky. While Gurdjieff recovered from his accident, struggled with a failing institute, made trips to the United States, and began to write his impenetrable magnum opus, *Beelzebub's Tales,* in the Café de la Paix in Paris, Ouspensky gave lectures to a select group of forty to fifty students, worked on *Fragments,* and prepared *A New Model of the Universe* for publication. He seemed content in his small flat. Outside of accounts by Nicoll and Bennett, little is known of his personal life at this time, although his biographer James Webb suggests that he did have a mistress. Sophie Grigorievna wouldn't leave Gurdjieff and come to England until 1931, and even then she and Ouspensky did not really live together. He led, as his friend Mouravieff remarked, "a very lonely and isolated life," and this isolation began to tell in an increasing tetchiness and capacity to brood.

His relations with Bennett soured. The central cause was, once again, "the law of accident." During a business venture in Greece, Bennett was arrested on a charge of forging some title deeds; whether he did or not remains unclear. Hearing of this, Ouspensky sent him a telegram: "Sympathy to Bennett under 96 laws," suggesting that he had fallen to the level of the moon, the lowest rung on the Ray of Creation. It displayed a certain warmth and chiding humor. But when Bennett's room was searched, letters from Ouspensky were found. His Russian name made the Greek police suspicious, and they passed on the information to the British Home Office. Ouspensky was always mildly paranoid about the police—Nicoll had even admitted as much to Kenneth Walker—but to find that he was under suspicion of being a Communist spy was insufferable. Ouspensky became enraged with Bennett and dropped him, cutting off all contact. Bennett proved resourceful and started groups of his own, sending written reports of his activities regularly to Ouspensky. In retrospect it seems clear that Bennett and Ouspensky would never hit it off; Bennett's overzealous and pushy ambition to evolve probably struck the aristocratic Ouspensky as a bit oafish, while Bennett's own intelligence and independence made him chomp at the bit as a student.

Aside from Mouravieff, Ouspensky's only close relationship at the time was with Nicoll, who comes across as an altogether warmer and more sensitive character than Bennett. He was evidently the only one of his students who could make Ouspensky laugh, more than likely no easy task. In 1927, Nicoll purchased a cottage by the sea in Sidlesham, and Ouspensky would come there for weekends. He enjoyed the rest, and Nicoll proved an excellent host, serving freshly caught lobster and Southdown mutton. Ouspensky said he slept better there than he did in London, and at one point he remarked that "One can almost feel the world turning here." He liked walking by the sea, carrying a variety of cameras and binoculars, and would often peer through them at some item for several minutes at a time. He spoke to Nicoll about his cat, Vashka, who fed on asparagus, olives, and fish, and played with Nicoll's dog.

Sometimes he would spend an entire morning reading a novel, not speaking at all, admitting to Nicoll that often when he read he was thinking of something else. He enjoyed visiting the local pub and told Nicoll that his fondness for taverns was in his bones. Recounting his early travels, he informed Nicoll that in the Caucasus there was an Ouspensky Mountain, named after one of his ancestors, who had defeated a bandit tribe on the site. He generally ate very little, although he enjoyed food, and was for the most part vegetarian, although he did eat some meat—something, he said, the English ate far too much of. He wasn't fond of whiskey, preferred gin, and told Nicoll that drinking was like "borrowing from tomorrow." By all accounts, Ouspensky racked up some heavy debts in this way, yet he never seemed drunk and always made a point of eating something while he drank. He also made a point of being courteous to waiters and waitresses and had a profound dislike of people who weren't. Like most visitors to England, Ouspensky also complained to Nicoll about the climate.

Winters, he said, were something to recover from. It must have been a great sacrifice for him not to be able to live in Paris, and at times he may have wished that Gurdjieff had got that British visa after all.

Ouspensky may have seemed to be marking time, but his lectures were having good effect. He did not, as Gurdjieff did, work with haida yoga, the "quick method" of shock and disruption that the master used to such unsettling effect. ("Haida" is a Russian term for "quick".) His slow-but-sure approach to grasping the ideas and practicing self-remembering and self-observation produced results nonetheless. Kenneth Walker discovered that the work even helped his bedside manner. "The more I put into practice the psychological principles of the system," he wrote,

> the more convinced I became of their value. I found, for example, that with their help I was able to overcome certain difficulties in my professional life, difficulties resulting from negative imagination. I no longer lay awake at night . . . listening for the telephone to ring and for the night-sister to tell me that the patient on whom I had operated had suddenly collapsed. I ceased to wonder during the small hours of the morning whether it would not have been better for me to have done this rather than that, for by now I had fully realized the futility of such thoughts. And as the wastage of energy through worry and identification lessened I found myself able to do more and with steadily increasing efficiency.[2]

Walker was among the few who in these years listened to readings from *Fragments of an Unknown Teaching*. Ouspensky had completed the manuscript of his book about his time with Gurdjieff by 1925, yet he continued to revise it for many years.

Although as early as 1923 he announced that it would be published soon, until his death in 1947 it wasn't released for publication. Aside from the short lectures he revised for *The Psychology of Man's Possible Evolution,* it was his last piece of writing. He wrote practically nothing for the next twenty-two years. For a man who was "before everything else" a writer, this was odd; more than anything else, it marks his greatest sacrifice to the work. It's difficult not to feel that after encountering the system, he more or less abandoned any creative thought.

He was never happy with *Fragments.* In an unpublished introduction written in 1927, Ouspensky summed up his feelings at the time of entering Gurdjieff's work. The predominant emotion in him, he said, was fear—

> fear to lose myself, fear to disappear into something unknown. I remember a phrase in a letter I wrote at that time: "I am writing this letter to you, but who will write the next letter, signing it with my name, and what he will say I do not know." This was the fear. But there were many other elements in it as well: the fear of taking a wrong way, the fear of making an irretrievable mistake, the fear of losing some other possibilities. All this left me later on, when on the one hand I began to gain confidence in myself and on the other to have practical faith in the system.[3]

Some of this fear seemed to remain, however, and it made Ouspensky reluctant to let the work reach a wider audience. He was concerned that the essence of the work could not be transmitted through a book, and that, once published, *Fragments* would become a kind a textbook on Gurdjieff's ideas, which is exactly what happened. The purist in Ouspensky wanted to keep the ideas from profane hands;

perhaps he thought that if he published it, the Higher Source would not be amused, seeing their ideas cast into the melee of the Outer Circle. Until 1949 it remained a kind of secret text, available to only the few. Had Ouspensky had his way, it would never have seen printers' ink.

Yet even though people like Walker and other students benefited from his lectures, Ouspensky's own goal seemed as far away as ever. Their spiritual self-development was all well and good, but as Ouspensky had told Rosamund Sharp, as far as he was concerned it was only a side effect of the real issue. "The system," he wrote in 1926, "is waiting for workers." By 1930, he had been in contact with Gurdjieff and the system for fifteen years. He had been operating on his own for seven, a central number in the work cosmology. He had waited patiently. He wanted to see what Gurdjieff would do. Now it was time to act. Gurdjieff's efforts had not achieved the results he had wished. Indeed, by 1930, Gurdjieff's relationship with Orage was about to rupture. His finances were minimal, his reputation ambiguous, and he had cast off many of his closest students, like the de Hartmanns. Wall Street had crashed, and *Beelzebub's Tales* could not find a publisher. Ouspensky, on the other hand, had slowly but persistently established himself in London and worked diligently with his core of students. He could continue this way or he could try something else.

He opted for a new octave. In October 1930, Ouspensky announced that he was giving a series of public lectures on "The Search for Objective Consciousness." He hoped in this way to attract more attention to his work. His optimism prompted a largess of spirit; he even asked his secretary, Madame Kadloubovksy (who would later translate a revised edition of *Tertium Organum*) to invite Bennett, who was welcomed back into the fold. When the two men met, Ouspensky explained his reasoning:

I waited for all these years . . . because I wanted to see what Gurdjieff would do . . . I am still as certain as ever that there is a Great Source from which our system has come. Gurdjieff must have had contact with that source, but I do not believe it was a complete contact. Something is missing, and he has not been able to find it. If we cannot find it through him, then our only hope is to have a direct contact with the source. But there is no chance for us to find it by looking, of that I have been convinced for nearly twenty years. It is much better hidden than people suppose. Therefore, our only hope is that the source will seek us out. That is why I am giving these lectures in London. If those who have the real knowledge see that we can be useful to them, they may send someone. We can only show them what we can do, and wait.[4]

It was not an encouraging prospect, more or less a kind of mystical whistling in the dark; by this time Ouspensky had been searching for schools for almost twenty years. For better or worse, he was convinced that neither he nor anyone else could do anything on their own, although he had already gleaned everything he could from Gurdjieff's system and had already had a few bites of higher consciousness through his own efforts. He had, it seemed, thought himself into a corner. Gurdjieff was a dead end; his own efforts were useless; his pessimism and world-rejection led him to ignore or disparage any other ideas or avenues; he had practically given up writing; and, to his seasoned eye, the situation in Europe suggested that another war was on the drawing board. He could either stick to his present course or toss aside everything and embark on a complete rethink. But that would mean abandoning the system he had struggled so hard to grasp and had gone through so much to preserve.

Ouspensky decided to include a series of hints and slight-ly camouflaged code words relating to the work in his book *A New Model of the Universe*, edited, translated, and finally pub-lished in 1931. At almost 600 pages, it was an odd collection of philosophical, scientific, and mathematical speculation cou-pled with ideas about esotericism, his account of his nitrous oxide experiments and study of dreams, colorful pen-portraits from his search in the East, and reflections on sex, eternal recurrence, and the true meaning of the Gospels. Practically all of it had been written several years earlier in Russia.

A New Model of the Universe was well-received and reestab-lished Ouspensky as a central metaphysical figure of the twentieth century. Once again, Ouspensky was becoming the intellectual flavor of the month through a book that made no mention of Gurdjieff or the work. The book became wide-ly influential, and over the years writers as disparate as J. B. Priestley, Jorge Luis Borges, Malcolm Lowry, and Aldous Huxley would mine it for ideas. On the strength of it, Ouspensky could very easily have come back into the world and continued with a literary career. But years of self-reliance, coupled with an authoritarian streak, prevented Ouspensky from having any interest in new ideas. And in any case, Ouspensky emphatically forbade his students to write anything about the teaching, a constraint that rubbed some the wrong way. He had found the truth, insofar as it could be found, and all that remained was to teach it. Although he himself had made notes during his years with Gurdjieff, we know he wrote nothing after completing the manuscript of *Fragments*.

In any event, with his new lecture series and a new book, Ouspensky's public profile increased. There was renewed interest in his work. Attendance at the lectures rose; soon the number of talks had to increase to meet the demand. The Inner Circle had yet to make contact, but there were many oth-ers who wanted to hear what Ouspensky had to say. There were other developments as well. In September of that year Ouspensky informed a shocked Maurice Nicoll that he "had better go away," pausing before he added "and teach the system." Until his death in 1953 this is exactly what Nicoll did. His profound interest in Christian esotericism is evident in the several volumes of his *Psychological Commentaries on the Teaching of Gurdjieff and Ouspensky,* now a standard text. Now that Nicoll had gone, Ouspensky delegated more responsibilities to Bennett and another student, Francis Roles. With his work expanding and the assistance of able lieutenants, he may have felt life was becoming easier. If so, he was due for a surprise. After nearly a decade of living apart from her husband, Madame Ouspensky came to England. She had made previous visits and, like Ouspensky himself, never liked the English. But this time it was different. Gurdjieff, it seemed, had sent her— exactly why is unknown—and this time she would stay.

The two men themselves had met that summer for the last time. Ouspensky rang the bell at the Prieure's gates but was not granted admission. He and his former teacher met on the terrace of the Café Henri IV in Fontainebleau. It would be churlish to infer that Ouspensky came to gloat. But to all intents and purposes, his work had been successful, while Gurdjieff had seen better days. The Prieure's doors were soon to close, and his best pupils were gone. His debts were considerable, his health was in question—he had gained much weight—and his reputation as an author was nil. It's unclear why Ouspensky came or what the two had to say to each other. But from then on, master and pupil moved in parallel octaves.

By 1933 Ouspensky's groups had grown so large that he needed to expand; Madame Ouspensky's presence no doubt added to his considerations. A house was found in Gadsden, Kent, on the Great West Road out of London. A large Victorian mansion with seven acres, Hayes House was Ouspensky's first attempt at setting up his own Prieure. The decision probably had more to do with Sophie Grigorievna than with Ouspensky, who had been content to live in his small basement flat with his cat for ten years. In any case, the situation did not change much. Ouspensky lived most of the time in London, while Madame, as she was called, quickly came to rule the roost in Kent. Here eight or ten students lived full time under her unnerving eye, with more students visiting on the weekends.

Madame's years with Gurdjieff had been profitable. She acquired from the master a penchant for revealing pupils' flaws, a practice that no doubt went well with her already prepossessing character. Work at Hayes House was more physical than sitting on a hard chair in a London hall listening to Ouspensky lecture. There was gardening, housework, cooking, and cleaning, all with the aim of "super effort" and aiding "self-observation." But Madame's real specialty was her devastating observations on "false personalities." She likened these to a "hot air pie," which looks impressive but crumbles at the slightest touch. She seemed to instill a kind of fear in her charges. Gurdjieff had done the same. But for all her presence, Madame lacked the master's charm and warmth. Kenneth Walker recalls, "Although most of us feared her we realized how valuable was her help . . . She was an expert in the stripping off of masks, in the detection of hypocrisy and fraud, and in separating the real from the counterfeit."[5] A later student, Irmis B. Popoff, recalls "the sensation that crept along my spine when I heard Madame Ouspensky approaching, her cane announcing her as she came closer and closer." Many students thought of her as a "monster."[6]

Although Madame's English was poor, she shared Gurdjieff's talent for pithy one-liners. Philosophical chatter, of the kind she no doubt often heard from old Wraps Up the Thought, was "the pouring of emptiness into the void." Talk about the system without effort was merely "singing about the work." One student was simply "a piece of meat"; another was "completely devoid of mind." No doubt these barbs could help a student gain insight. But they could also be abused, as could the assumption that one's personality was invariably false, or that Madame's diagnoses were infallible. Yet mature, accomplished individuals like Walker found the ragging beneficial. "How dumbfounded my friends would be," he nevertheless mused, "if they were suddenly to be transported here! What would they make of it all? How puzzled they would be to explain that we, reasonably intelligent people, were sitting here at the close of a hard day's work at the feet of a woman who seemingly did nothing but insult us."[7]

How much Ouspensky himself joined in or approved of Madame's "method" is debatable; although he was authoritarian and could, when needed, shout "Moscow fashion," he was an altogether gentler soul. On one occasion in wintertime, when an earnest student asked for an interview, he replied "Oh, I think it too cold today. No one can remember themselves in this cold."[8] Not immune to Madame's bite himself, more than likely on most occasions he stood aside. He was, in any case, prone to stay in the background, either in his room or in London. Perhaps he felt that such buffetings would separate the weak from the strong, and held back. Walker recalls summer meals held outside in the garden. He and the other students would sit in rows, holding their plates on their knees like children; Madame, however, had a table to herself in front of them from which she held forth. Often on these occasions, newcomers would be assigned seats in the crossfire; from her vantage point, Madame unerringly pinned the "false personality" of people she had practically just met. Ouspensky, Walker observed, was sometimes present, but on most occasions would dine in his room.

For Bennett, by default Ouspensky's closest male associate, Madame Ouspensky was a great lady. His admiration was powerful enough for him to abandon his wife, Mrs. Beaumont, on Sundays, the one day of the week they could have time together, so he could spend a "work day" in Kent. On one occasion he brought Mrs. Beaumont along, but for reasons unknown she was not invited back. The fact that she was another grand dame may have had something to do with it. Faced with the choice between working with Madame or enjoying a day with his wife, Bennett decided that his spiritual development took precedence, and for the next three years he and Mrs. Beaumont only saw each other in passing. Bennett found the condition harsh and unreasonable yet seemed not to question it. Understandably, Mrs. Beaumont was distressed. Her depression would increase over the years, yet Bennett, his sights set on attaining consciousness, seemed unaware of her feelings.

Bennett rationalized his behavior as an expression of "the resolve I had taken to do without question anything that Ouspensky might ask of me," forgetting, it seems, Gurdjieff's lesson concerning ice cream and mustard. "The first duty of a pupil," he believed, was "implicit and unquestioning acceptance."[9] With this in view Bennett saw in every one of Ouspensky's actions a test of some kind, effectively nullifying any attempt Ouspensky made to loosen up and be friends. This undoubtedly got on Ouspensky's nerves. On one occasion, Ouspensky mentioned his hobby of collecting old prints and remarked that he would like to find some of Moscow and St. Petersburg. He then asked Bennett to find a shop. On Oxford Street Bennett discovered a large collection of prints at a Mr. Spencer's establishment, and Ouspensky was delighted. He invited Bennett to go with him one afternoon, but on the day Ouspensky suggested, Bennett had an important business meeting. Thinking he was faced with a test, Bennett cancelled the meeting and spent the day with Ouspensky. Ouspensky loved the shop, bought several prints, and then invited

Bennett back to his apartment for tea, which he prepared from a special selection he had made for Twinings. The whole while Bennett was stiff and formal, on the alert to be awake and remember himself, and completely missed that Ouspensky, a lonely man, merely wanted some congenial company.

Bennett, however, was the wrong man to choose; he had, it seems, a streak of spiritual masochism. He loathed his weakness and made inordinate and unreasonable demands on himself. Adopting Ouspensky's exercise of repeating the Lord's Prayer inwardly, after five years Bennett had got to the point of reciting it simultaneously in Greek, Latin, Russian, and German hundreds of times a day. He seemed unable to enjoy simple pleasures. Taking pride in his wretchedness, he wrote in his diary: "There is something so revolting and humiliating in one's enjoyment of pleasant things."[10] He was not a good candidate to help an already reserved man relax.

Yet it has to be said that Ouspensky didn't make things easier for himself. On one occasion, Bennett had a vision of the fifth dimension and managed to capture its essence in a formula: "In eternity the laws of thermodynamics are reversed." Excited by his insight, he spoke of it to Ouspensky. But Ouspensky had covered all the dimensions years ago and was not impressed, calling Bennett's vision mere "formatory thinking," a product of mechanical mental associations. It was reminiscent of Gurdjieff's handling of Ouspensky's own insights, and it made Bennett realize that during the ten years he had worked with Ouspensky, he had found it impossible to speak with him about his deepest experiences or, if he did try to share his ideas, Ouspensky would simply reject them. He also realized that after a decade of doing the work, he was no better off than when he started.

There were some exceptional moments. One occurred in the wee hours one night in 1933, by which time, Bennett remarks, Ouspensky had adopted the habit of staying up half the night drinking. He would enjoy a few bottles of wine, fortifying himself with a variety of hors d'oeuvres, reminiscing about Moscow and St. Petersburg, or delivering impromptu lectures on Russian poetry to the stalwarts who joined him. Bennett believed Ouspensky was trying to put himself back to a time before he had met Gurdjieff. On this occasion, however, it was Bennett who enjoyed a kind of trip, having an out-of-the-body experience after the two men had polished off four or five bottles. Bennett "saw" and "heard" himself as if he were another person, and even "watched" his thoughts. When he told Ouspensky what had happened, Ouspensky asked if it was worth sitting up all night for and remarked that only if he remembered what he had just seen would he be able to work. No one, he said, could show it to him; he had to see it for himself—an admission, perhaps, that the system was not as foolproof as Ouspensky had believed.

Ouspensky's lectures continued, and as the work expanded, he drew more attention. One new arrival was the journalist Rom Landau, who interviewed Ouspensky and included him in his best-selling book *God Is My Adventure*, a collection of articles on the major spiritual figures of the day. Ouspensky featured prominently next to Rudolf Steiner, Count Keyserling, Krishnamurti, and others, including Gurdjieff, whom Landau had met and was immediately put off by. After attending one of Ouspensky's talks, Landau remarked on his peculiar English, consisting of "soft melting vowels" and "distinct brisk consonants," whose "soft cadences" and "sudden stops" made it seem that Ouspensky was really speaking Russian, using English words.[11] This lilting speech was complemented by Ouspensky's habit of breaking off a sentence if he couldn't find the right word. Then he would throw out "or something else," "anything you want," or "whatever you like." Landau says it gave the impression that as far as Ouspensky was concerned, his audience could take what he had to say or leave it, but after ten years of lecturing on the same subjects, he may have developed a touch of impatience.

Interviewing Ouspensky at Kent, Landau encountered the formidable reserve mentioned earlier, but his journalist's expertise managed to get around it. During the interview, Ouspensky answered the questions that for the rest of his life would arise with what must have become an irritating persistence. "Everything that I had been hunting for in the East, in occult literature, in secret doctrines, was in that system which I found in Moscow among a small group of people, instructed by a certain Gurdjieff," his host told Landau. That system, he continued—perhaps hoping that the Higher Source was one of Landau's readers—was only "propagated by Gurdjieff—for it was not Gurdjieff's own discovery but an esoteric system which had been entrusted to him by others." But then, he explained, something happened. "I had begun to feel somehow out of touch with Gurdjieff. It seemed to me as though he were changing, but whatever the cause I could no longer understand him, and it appeared to me that he had drifted away from his original idea."[12] Of his relations with Gurdjieff himself, Ouspensky remarked that after breaking with him in 1924 he hadn't seen him, forgetting for some reason his visits to the Prieure or that last meeting at the Café Henri IV seven years later. It's unclear whether Landau mentioned his own meeting with Gurdjieff, during which, he believed, Ouspensky's old teacher had tried to hypnotize him. Gurdjieff had told Landau that he spoke "pre-Shakespearian English." He called Americans "half-Turks, half-Turks" and tried to foist a special brand of cigarettes on Landau, who was a nonsmoker. Landau found himself questioning Gurdjieff's sanity, convinced that "Evasiveness, contradiction and bluff . . . seemed to have become part of Gurdjieff's very nature."[13]

Other visitors to Kent were on better terms with Ouspensky's old teacher. In 1934 the de Hartmanns visited

C. S. Nott, one of Orage's New York students. After the death of his teacher, Nott had moved to England and kept up relations with Gurdjieff, now living in Paris. During a visit to Hayes House, the de Hartmanns spoke to Ouspensky about Nott, who was anxious to find anyone with whom he could talk about the work. Ouspensky was interested in acquiring students who already had a background in the system, and more than likely he was curious to know more about Orage's activities, as well as those of Gurdjieff. He told the de Hartmanns he'd be happy to see Nott, and on their next visit they brought him along.

As a student of Gurdjieff, Nott was off-limits to Ouspensky's groups, and this had already caused him considerable trouble. Nott's wife was very close to Nicoll, but the edict made it impossible for them to associate. A few years earlier, Nott had tried to speak with Ouspensky and had written him a letter, asking to meet. Ouspensky had replied by sending one of his lieutenants to check Nott out. He must have failed the test, as he never heard from Ouspensky or the lieutenant again.

At Kent, Nott took in the large drawing rooms filled with Russian prints, ornaments, and icons; it seemed to him that the Ouspenskys were trying to re-create Old Russia. He was surprised to discover that instead of the cold, austere intellectual he was prepared to meet, Ouspensky turned out to be warm, friendly, and easy to talk with—when he spoke, that is. On this first meeting, it was Madame who did most of the talking, assailing Nott with a barrage of questions, aiming to gauge his understanding of the work. When he began to tell them about Orage's group, Madame cut him short and announced: "There were many things Orage did not understand or understood wrongly. Mr. Orage was too formatory for one thing."[14]

"Formatory" was one of Gurdjieff's favorite words for Ouspensky, Nott recalled, and, as Orage's favorite student, he may have remembered Orage's quip concerning Ouspensky's latest book: Orage had called it "A New *Muddle* of the Universe." Nott satisfied himself with informing Madame that he had come for a friendly chat, not a catechism. Ouspensky agreed, and on this occasion at least he reined in the dragon, signaling her to pipe down. Ouspensky then spoke casually with Nott about self-remembering, self-observation, and other work terms. Nott informed Ouspensky that after his accident, Gurdjieff never used those terms, but instead employed a whole battery of new ones, like "Being-Parktdolg-duty," and that all of them came out of *Beelzebub's Tales*. Madame pricked up her ears. "We do not have this," she admitted. Nott must have smiled. It was, he informed her, the bible of the work, and, oddly enough, he happened to have a typescript copy with him, one of the hundred copies that Orage had sold at ten dollars apiece.

Before Nott left, Ouspensky asked if he could borrow his bible. Nott agreed, and when Ouspensky asked what he could do for him in return, Nott asked to come to his meetings. Ouspensky consented, on the condition that he asked no questions and made no mention of Gurdjieff or *Beelzebub's Tales*.

CHAPTER NINETEEN

NIRVANA AND STRAWBERRY JAM

I N 1936 OUSPENSKY decided that Hayes House was no longer suitable, and he acquired a larger and more impressive headquarters in Virginia Water, twenty miles out of London. With a hundred acres, Lyne Place was a formidable center for Ouspensky's work. An eighteenth-century mansion in bad repair, it came with an English garden, rhododendron walks, a boathouse, and a small lake. There was also a farm, a greenhouse, pigsties, barns, stables, and a vegetable garden, all within a short walk of a wooded area. The grounds needed much work, but then so did Ouspensky's students; as at the Prieure, all of the physical labor was a pretext for self-remembering and self-observation. It was also Ouspensky's intention to develop a self-sufficient community. Hitler was on the rise, and Ouspensky was certain another war was inevitable; neither he nor Madame wanted a replay of Ekaterinodar. Ouspensky had also made some changes in his lectures, bringing in more material from his own investigations, blending ideas about recurrence, the Devil, and higher dimensions into the system. There were also some disturbing developments. Bennett recalls that Ouspensky would introduce a new idea or exercise, talk about it for a time, and then, when the students had become quite excited by it, drop it suddenly with no explanation. This could of course have been a milder version of Gurdjieff's own tactic of moving the goal posts as often as possible. But it could also have indicated a certain loss of direction.

In three months Ouspensky's groups got Lyne Place into good enough shape for Ouspensky and Madame to move in. A cadre of students lived there, and on the weekends a hundred more came. It was a matter of prestige to be invited, and by this time Ouspensky's "school" had about a thousand students—so many that he had to find a larger London meeting place, Colet House in Baron's Court. At Lyne Place, Madame had more room to operate. The students grew their own wheat, milled the flour, and baked bread. The gardens and orchards provided sufficient vegetables and fruit. Timber was felled, a sawmill constructed, sheep kept, and fields ploughed. It seemed that, in England at least, the work was establishing itself very securely. But as so often happens, while the community grew and the work developed, the leaders grew more aloof and the intimacy dissolved. Ouspensky and Madame became more and more withdrawn, delegating most of the hands-on work to their lieutenants. For Ouspensky this meant that the isolation he was already experiencing increased. He must have enjoyed riding his horse Jingles around the grounds, seated on the Cossack saddle a student had given him. But something was missing.

More than likely, this was why he became friendly with Nott. At Lyne Place, he often invited Nott to his study, where he invariably opened a bottle of wine. The topic of discussion was Gurdjieff. By now Ouspensky's assessment of his old teacher was fixed, and receiving a copy of Gurdjieff's first publication, *Herald of Coming Good,* did nothing to change it. The book's outrageous and megalomaniacal advertisements for future books convinced Ouspensky that it was the work of a paranoiac. Gurdjieff's mind, he believed, was unhinged. He requested that his students hand in their copies—Gurdjieff had sent one to each of them. They did so, and Ouspensky destroyed them. Soon after, Gurdjieff himself recalled the book, perhaps realizing that it did his reputation no good.

Nott didn't share Ouspensky's opinion of Gurdjieff, yet he felt himself drawn to the apostate. Ouspensky, too, appreciated the growing intimacy. It must have been a relief at times to relax and open up. "You know," he told Nott, "when Gurdjieff started his Institute in Paris, I did everything I could for him. I raised money for him and sent pupils, many of them influential people. When he bought the Prieure I went there myself and Madame stayed for some time. But I found that he had changed . . . He did many things that I did not like, but it wasn't what he did that upset me, it was the stupid way he did them. He came to London to my group and made things very unpleasant for me. After this I saw that I must break with him."[1]

Nott offered a polite disagreement, but Ouspensky only continued.

"You see," he said, "Gurdjieff's mind never recovered from his accident."

Nott couldn't accept this. And when he explained to Ouspensky that Gurdjieff's actions couldn't be judged on the same level as other people's, Ouspensky must have shaken his head.

"No," he said. "He lost contact with the source after Essentuki. His behaviour goes contrary to the teaching. Then the accident."[2]

When Nott replied that, for him, Gurdjieff *was* the source, Ouspensky must have smiled. Nott continued to visit Ouspensky, however, finding him a warm and sympathetic man. Ouspensky's relations with Bennett had soured again—it is unclear why—and although he must have felt Nott's uncritical devotion to Gurdjieff betrayed a simple mind, he had no one else to speak with and was more than likely glad of a little human contact. He certainly wasn't getting it from Madame, and his own students were becoming more and more rigid. Nott himself had remarked on the groups' artificiality, and Kenneth Walker, too, had spoken of too many people turning up at lectures wearing their "meeting faces." It was almost as if working on oneself was becoming mechanical.

Ouspensky must have felt that something more was needed. In one conversation with Nott, he remarked that they must make contact with an esoteric school. Nott was surprised: hadn't he already done that, years ago, when he met Gurdjieff? Nott must have sensed that Ouspensky was looking for a new stimulus, and he made a suggestion: "Why don't you let me read *Beelzebub's Tales* to a small group of your older pupils."

Ouspensky declined. When Nott asked why, Ouspensky tried to put him off, saying that the book needed much "mental preparation." Nott persisted and explained that the needed preparation wasn't mental; all that was required was patience and perseverance. And in any case, Ouspensky himself had read it, hadn't he?

He had not. When Nott asked why, Ouspensky said, "It sticks in my throat."[3]

Beelzebub's Tales is admittedly a difficult book, but it must have been doubly so for Ouspensky. Nott was astonished at Ouspensky's remark, and perhaps to make up for not reading Nott's bible, Ouspensky handed him a typescript of *Fragments*. Nott read a few pages and was impressed.

Later, on a visit to Paris, Nott spoke with Gurdjieff about Ouspensky. When Gurdjieff made some unflattering remark, Nott came to Ouspensky's defense. He liked Ouspensky, he told Gurdjieff, and he enjoyed talking with him. "Oh yes," Gurdjieff replied. "Ouspensky very nice man to talk to and drink vodka with, but he is weak man."[4]

Nevertheless, when he returned to Lyne Place, Nott took with him a ten-pound parcel of delicacies for Madame, straight from Gurdjieff's fabled Paris pantry. He was to do so several times in the years to come. And after suggesting the idea to Ouspensky, Nott and his wife were allowed to teach some of Gurdjieff's movements to a select group of Ouspensky's students, another indication that Ouspensky recognized the need to infuse new vitality into his work.

One of the students to benefit from Nott's input was Bennett. Although estranged from Ouspensky, he remained on good terms—as much as one could—with Madame. Bennett must have been trying; when one of Ouspensky's students, Francis Roles, an authority on tuberculosis, diagnosed Bennett with the disease, Ouspensky offered a treatment, suggesting that Bennett drink an extract of aloes. Yet after he recovered, Ouspensky seemed to lose interest. He allowed him, however, to study the movements. Yet Bennett's delight in being given a new task was dimmed by a crisis with Mrs. Beaumont. After years of accommodating Bennett's spiritual needs, his wife was beginning to feel the strain. Studying the movements meant spending more time at Lyne Place, and Bennett asked Madame if the ban on Mrs. Beaumont's presence could be lifted. Madame agreed, yet Mrs. Beaumont herself had other plans. She was, she thought, simply in the way, and in any case was by this time an elderly woman. When Bennett responded to a sudden intuition that something was wrong and returned to their flat, he found her unconscious and breathing heavily. She had taken a large dose of sleeping pills—a possible dig at the work. She recovered, but it was a close call. She told Bennett she had had a remarkable experience: she had entered heaven and felt the presence of Christ. She asked him not to speak of it but she wanted to talk about it with Ouspensky.

When they met, Ouspensky told her that he knew something important had happened to her. Mrs. Beaumont said she wanted to wait some time before describing it in detail, to make sure that it was not simply imagination—a critical reserve that Ouspensky must have appreciated. She suggested a year, and he agreed, and after that both he and Madame treated her with more consideration. When the year had passed, Ouspensky reminded her of her promise; they met again, and she related her near-death experience. Afterward, telling Bennett of her meeting, she wept. "I am deeply sad for him," she said. "I had not understood how much he suffered. When I told him all that had happened to me, he was on the verge of tears, and said that since a young man he had been waiting and hoping to have for himself the experience which proves the reality of the other world, but it had never come to him." "He is a great man," she continued, "and I have always respected him, but now I feel differently . . . I am sad for him . . . I do not believe he will get what he is looking for." "He is," she added, "terribly lonely."[5]

Another visitor to Lyne Place who recognized Ouspensky's loneliness was Robert S. de Ropp, a biochemist who in the 1960s became a counterculture figure with his books *Drugs and the Mind* and *The Master Game*. In the 1930s de Ropp was involved in a pacifist group, the Peace Pledge Union, and through it became acquainted with two of its central figures, Aldous Huxley and Gerald Heard. An intelligent, perceptive mind with a no-nonsense sensibility, de Ropp himself was an extraordinary catch, but it's clear Ouspensky was also interested in him because of his connection to Huxley and Heard. Like Gurdjieff in Ouspensky's own case, he knew that if someone like Huxley wrote about his work, word would get around.

As it happened, Huxley did write about Ouspensky, but not the way Ouspensky would have liked. In 1939 Huxley published a novel, *After Many a Summer,* in which the character of Mr. Propter, who spoke of personality as a trap and of living on the mechanical level, was based on Ouspensky. By the time the book was published Ouspensky's paranoia had increased, and at his meetings he often remarked on how others had "stolen" his ideas. Another "thief" was the novelist and playwright J. B. Priestley, whose play *I Have Been Here Before* (1937) dealt with the question of recurrence and featured the enigmatic Dr. Görtler, a character based on Ouspensky. Priestley couldn't be accused of theft: in the playbill and in book form he acknowledged his debt to the Russian metaphysician. Yet as in the case of Huxley, Ouspensky's secrecy had been breached, and his followers were indignant. On the other hand, the success of the play carried over to *New Model*, sales of which increased. Priestley tried hard to meet Ouspensky, but with no luck; Ouspensky must have considered him a security risk. This was unfortunate. Like Ouspensky, Priestley was a "time-haunted man," and his conversation might have lessened Ouspensky's loneliness.

De Ropp, however, was positively pursued. After meeting one of Ouspensky's students and reading *New Model*, de Ropp attended a few lectures but was not impressed. Ouspensky's students seemed stiff and formal, and Ouspensky himself seemed to lack compassion. After listening to six lectures, he dropped out. Ouspensky, however, was determined, and as de Ropp remarks, he sent a doctor out to speak with him, possibly Kenneth Walker. The doctor must have been persuasive; de Ropp agreed to visit Ouspensky at Lyne Place. When Ouspensky asked him why he had stopped attending the lectures, de Ropp said that he saw no compassion in Ouspensky's approach. And in any case, his followers did not work for peace.

Ouspensky peered at him. "Work for peace?" he asked. "What is work for peace?" They were passing by the pigsties, where a young man, his face taut with the effort of self-remembering, was shoveling manure. Ouspensky then answered his own question. Gesturing toward his student, he turned to de Ropp and chuckled: "Work for peace."

De Ropp was unsure of the connection, but as he himself was becoming disenchanted with Huxley's and Heard's belief that meditation would stop Hitler, Ouspensky's joke must have seemed symbolic. In any case, he decided to listen to the lectures again. This time he was convinced; Ouspensky was the teacher he had been looking for.

For de Ropp, Ouspensky, at fifty-eight, was at the height of his powers. He seemed massive and "moved with the ponderous intentionality that at times reminded me of an elephant."[6] De Ropp and the others attributed this deliberate movement to Ouspensky's self-remembering, although de Ropp admitted that this may not have been true. Like others, he recognized Ouspensky's authoritarian streak. Ouspensky's face was that of an emperor-scholar, he said, who could also be a tyrant. He was also Russian to the core, and de Ropp found it necessary to distinguish between what was the teaching and what was just Ouspensky.

De Ropp quickly fell into the routine—lectures in London, with Bennett reading the material and Ouspensky answering questions, then the drive to Lyne, most times in silence, Ouspensky chauffeured by a former member of the Royal Corps of Engineers. At Lyne, Ouspensky relaxed over food and drink in the kitchen—long sessions that often lasted till morning, when the master and whoever had gone the limit with him were shooed out by the cook before she prepared breakfast. De Ropp points out that Ouspensky's company was always male, Madame making sure no female students joined him in his cups. For some, these marathons were a kind of teaching ploy, "an acid test whereby those weaker members who had fallen by the wayside through over-indulgence . . . lived to regret it."[7] For de Ropp, however, they were often simply boring. "How many times have I sat up with Ouspensky in the kitchen drinking far more than was good for me, losing sleep in vain waiting for him to let fall some pearls of wisdom.

But the pearls rarely fell."[8] Instead, de Ropp and the others were transported to Ouspensky's past—Moscow, St. Petersburg, The Stray Dog. Ouspensky favored *zoubrovka,* a fiery peppered vodka, of which he could accommodate quite a bit without showing much effect. But there was at least one night when a pearl hit the floor. Once, after Ouspensky had related his remarkable experiences in Finland, when he heard Gurdjieff's voice inside his chest, de Ropp replied rather lamely that Gurdjieff must have been a strange man.

"Strange!" Ouspensky replied. "He was extraordinary! You cannot possibly imagine how extraordinary Gurdjieff was."

Ouspensky's words, spoken with that emotion, in that voice—*extraordinary*—made de Ropp believe for a moment that he *could* imagine. Like practically all of Ouspensky's students, he had no idea if Gurdjieff was alive or dead or exactly what had caused Ouspensky to break with a man he so obviously loved. "I had the feeling," de Ropp remarked, "that in his relationship with Gurdjieff Ouspensky had confronted a problem that was absolutely beyond his power to solve."[9]

As time went on, Ouspensky spoke increasingly about the need to make direct contact with the Higher Source. At one point Bennett provided a possible lead; he had corresponded with the Bash Chelebi, the hereditary chief of the Mevlevi dervishes, then in exile in Aleppo, Syria, and had arranged a visit. Ouspensky was delighted with the prospect—a trip probably would have done him good. But events once again overtook him and nothing came of it. He then became convinced that it was important to give his own groups more of a public profile. By the late 1930s his personal contact with his students had dwindled, though he continued to give lectures and answer questions. But in the years leading up to World War II, Ouspensky became preoccupied with establishing his own connection to the esoteric center. Since he thought giving his work a greater public profile could do this, one plan was to give his own school a formal identity. To this end he drew up a prospectus for something he called the Historico-Psychological Society. The idea seemed to serve two ends: the society would hold public lectures, publish a journal, and engage in other "respectable" activities, through which it would draw interested people, among whom might be found suitable workers for the system. But it would also satisfy Ouspensky's own growing paranoia and unreasonable need for secrecy. With a "brass plate" on the door and an impressive name, he believed, his society need not fear unwanted scrutiny by the police. (Ironically, unknown to Ouspensky, during the Dirty Thirties he was already under surveillance by the British Home Office, who saw every Russian as a potential spy.) As it was, his students were subject to a battery of rules. They were not, for example, allowed to speak about the ideas with anyone outside the system, nor were they to acknowledge each other if they happened to meet in a public place. Perhaps absurd, the rules did serve two purposes. They imposed a measure of self-discipline, beneficial in itself; and they prevented loose talk which might have attracted unwanted attention. Many chaffed at them, but others saw them as a means of self-remembering.

Ouspensky's Historico-Psychological Society, however, found few supporters and at least one very vocal critic. When Ouspensky read out the prospectus, which included the study of "psycho-transformism," comparative religion, and a historical approach to different psychological schools, Madame indicated her opinion by laughing. Madame laughed "till she wept, dabbing her eyes with a tiny lace handkerchief."[10] Understandably, Ouspensky was less than pleased. Considering the kind of assistance he would have received from his wife, it was almost a blessing that World War II arrived and put an end to his idea.

Madame, meanwhile, was making preparations of her own. Determined not to starve again, she was stockpiling supplies of dried fruit in the cellar. When de Ropp finally managed to get his friends Huxley and Heard to Lyne, they were shown around the grounds, including Madame's secret cache of food. Both Huxley and Heard were convinced that war was inevitable and that the only thing an intelligent person could do was to leave England and head to America, which was their intention. They advised the Ouspenskys to do the same, but at this point Ouspensky wasn't convinced that England would fall to Hitler. In any case, the idea of exiling himself again was probably distasteful. Ouspensky enjoyed meeting Huxley and Heard, although both declined to join any of his groups. He told de Ropp that his friends were the kind of people he had known in Russia, the intelligentsia. He was happy to meet them, but when it came to work, they were, he said, useless. For Huxley's part, when asked about what he had found at Lyne, he quipped that Madame's teaching was a mixture of nirvana and strawberry jam.

Another friend who de Ropp introduced to the Ouspenskys was Rodney Collin, who would become an important figure in Ouspensky's last years. "Large and genial," de Ropp wrote, Collin "exuded a certain fervour which I later associated with all true believers."[11] A writer, journalist, and traveler, Collin too had been in the Peace Pledge Union and, like the young Ouspensky, was a seeker. He had read *New Model* when it was published and was impressed, but at that time he believed that he wasn't yet ready for its message. In 1935, however, with his wife, Janet—eight years his senior and independently wealthy—he attended some of Nicoll's groups, and at that point Ouspensky's ideas stuck. After visiting Lyne and being introduced to Ouspensky, the two became devoted students, and Janet's wealth enabled them to buy a house in the vicinity. They became central fixtures in Virginia Water, and until Ouspensky's death a great deal of the maintenance of Lyne Place as well as other ventures would depend considerably on Janet's finances.

In 1939 Madame was stricken with Parkinson's disease. For some reason, one of her students was convinced that only Gurdjieff could cure her, although to many in Ouspensky's groups, Gurdjieff was only a name—and one rarely mentioned, at that. On a visit to Paris, C. S. Nott conveyed the message to Gurdjieff. He agreed to come to England if necessary, but he emphasized that Madame herself would have to make an effort.

For some years Gurdjieff had been teaching a small group of students in Paris, many of them women, as well as supervising other groups, like the one led by Jeanne de Salzmann, Alexandre de Salzmann's wife. Although he made little impact on the French—their innate rationality worked against him, and with Hitler at their doorstep they may have had other things on their minds—his ideas had reached a few important individuals, one of whom was the surrealist poet and Hindu scholar René Daumal. A precocious youth, in his teens Daumal had experimented with a variety of drugs and, like Ouspensky, achieved a breakthrough into another form of consciousness. But by the time he met Alexandre de Salzmann, his health had declined, and his belief in poetry had diminished. Daumal, who was close to madness and on the brink of death, saw de Salzmann as a powerful father figure; he remained close to him until de Salzmann's death from tuberculosis in 1933. A decade later, on the run from the Nazis because of his Jewish wife, Daumal himself would follow, leaving the manuscript of his metaphysical novel, *Mount Analogue*, unfinished.

Aware that Gurdjieff possessed healing powers, Ouspensky was nevertheless not anxious for him to come to

Lyne Place. Although each night he regaled his drinking partners with tales of the "extraordinary man," the thought of meeting him again and what might come of it more than likely prompted a powerful inhibition. Madame herself may have felt ambivalent about receiving treatment; against all expectation, she began to recover. It was a provident development, as the outbreak of war made travel across the English Channel difficult. Ouspensky hated violence and war, but he may have breathed a sigh of relief at that thought that even Gurdjieff would find it hard to get through a U-boat blockade.

Once again, the history of crime had caught up with Ouspensky. When the first air raid sirens began to blare, the several children at Lyne were huddled into a well-timbered room in the basement. Madame made arrangements for as many of the London women and children as possible to get out of the city and come to the house, where they would be safe and, if need be, could survive on the food she had presciently stashed away. Ouspensky, too, took part in preparations. On one occasion, seeing that de Ropp and Kenneth Walker were building "bomb shelters"—basically a kind of covered ditch—he ordered them to fill them in. This was one time when filling in a hole one had just dug was not a work tactic; Ouspensky had the wit to see that the ditches would become traps when the rain got to them. Although Walker and de Ropp put up a fight, Ouspensky's "Moscow shout" convinced them, and later, when similar shelters across England were flooded, they saw that he was right. The London groups were cancelled; blackouts made meetings impossible, and Ouspensky must have mused that now it would become, if such were possible, even harder to make contact with Higher Source. Once again events were against him.

On September 6, 1940, the Germans bombed the London docks. Twenty miles away at Lyne, the blaze was still spectacular. Ouspensky, de Ropp, and others stood on the roof and watched. De Ropp heard Ouspensky say, "This I cannot remember." He was trying to remember if it had happened "last time," and he was unsure.

What he and Madame did remember was 1917, the end of St. Petersburg, and all that had followed. A basement filled with smoked hams and dried fruit was some security, but they were both in their sixties and had been through a lot. Huxley and Heard had warned them that a new Dark Age was on its way. By now, both of them were safe in Southern California, pursuing their own paths to enlightenment with the help of Swami Prabhavananda. Others, like Krishnamurti and Christopher Isherwood, were there too. It's somehow difficult to think of Ouspensky basking in the California sun, but the general idea must have seemed logical. He now believed that Hitler would win the war, but the real terror would follow, when a backlash of Communism would sweep across Europe. Fascism or Communism: it made little difference. In either case, the culture of barbarism would gain the upper hand. Under those conditions, work would be impossible. At one point Ouspensky had told his students that he had never sought out the opportunity to start a school; the responsibility had been thrust upon him. All things considered, he had not done badly. Watching the train of pupils walk past from the top of the long staircase at Colet House one evening, he had mur-mured to himself in Russian, *vse ya sam*, "All this I did myself." Indeed he had. But now this phase of his work was over.

In the autumn of 1940, Ouspensky told his students that in January he and Madame were leaving for America.

CHAPTER TWENTY

THE JOURNEY TO THE WEST

S OON AFTER OUSPENSKY announced that he and Madame
were leaving for America, Janet Collin and her daughter
left for the United States to help prepare for their arrival.
While Madame, who left a few weeks ahead of Ouspensky,
found her first port of call in Rumson, New Jersey, Ouspensky
was setting guidelines for those who remained. They were to
carry on as before. The work must be maintained at the highest possible level. "All in London should make sure to avoid
the smallest departure from the letter of the System as contained in the writings I have left." Ouspensky, who once
believed that the meaning of life was in the pursuit of knowledge and had rebelled against both positivism and Theosophy
because both had hardened into doctrines, was now taking
steps against revisionism.

Most tried to follow his orders, but others thought differently. Bennett reflected that when he first met Ouspensky, he
had taught that one must grow or die. To Bennett, rigid adher-
ence to the writings of an absent teacher did not seem like
growth. Mrs. Beaumont agreed. Witnessing the dismay that
Ouspensky's departure was causing his students, she asked
what was the point of "working on yourself" for twenty years—
as many of Ouspensky's older students had—if you were still as
dependent on your teacher as ever? De Ropp was even more
frank. He was baffled by Ouspensky's decision to leave, much
as Ouspensky had been years before by Gurdjieff's decision to

stop work at Essentuki. He couldn't believe that Ouspensky and Madame, with whom he had developed a very strong relationship, would run from danger. "Was it really right," he asked himself, "for the Ouspenskys to desert their followers, who had, after all, provided them with every creature comfort? . . . Slowly, sadly, I began to realize that my teachers were not superhuman . . . They were not particularly heroic. They wanted peace and quiet."[1] De Ropp was disgusted. Had he known, he could have pointed out that Gurdjieff himself, advised by his American followers to come to the United States, declined and remained in Paris, his shutters drawn, carrying on his small, fugitive groups, all throughout the occupation.

De Ropp remained and continued to work at Lyne, insofar as that was possible. But he soon had cause for more misgivings. Like Mrs. Beaumont, de Ropp's wife was never really taken into the fold; she especially aroused the wrath of Madame, who had advised against the marriage. Madame didn't think much of the younger female students, "toward whom she seemed to feel a certain dislike."[2] Sensitive, withdrawn, and not particularly brilliant—de Ropp admits the marriage was one of necessity—de Ropp's wife was out of her depth and everyone knew it. Madame, de Ropp remarked, didn't know her strength and used it unstintingly. De Ropp's wife received nothing but disapproval, and her diary later revealed the extent to which she was affected by Madame's unerring perspicacity. When de Ropp returned after a weekend away, he found his wife rocking herself in a chair, repeating over and over, "I must try to remember myself."[3] Gurdjieff had said it was easier to die from laziness than from making efforts, but he hadn't said anything about going mad. De Ropp's wife was diagnosed as schizophrenic and ended her days in an asylum.

On January 29, 1941, Ouspensky sailed out of Liverpool for New York. Shortly before he left, Bennett buttonholed him and asked some questions about his own lack of development. Ouspensky replied that Bennett's problem was that he always made false starts. "If you keep returning to the starting point," Ouspensky said, "how can you hope to make progress?" Bennett asked if he could be allowed to write about the system. Ouspensky replied that writing was useless. Even if he did write about the system, it would only be to convince himself that it was impossible to do so, something which Ouspensky knew from first-hand experience, having whittled away at the impossible for years. Nevertheless, he added, he had no intention of publishing *Fragments*.[4] It was not the most inspiring of send-offs.

Had Ouspensky reflected on how apt his words were to his own situation? He was once again going into exile, once again having to start from scratch, and once again disappointed in his search for schools: if anyone was going back to the starting point, he was. Although Colet House had been a success, no one from the Inner Circle had knocked on his door, and now, with another war raging, the possibility of meeting one of their representatives in New York seemed minimal. He had once written that some members of esoteric schools "live among ordinary people . . . often belonging even to the uncultured classes and engaged in insignificant and perhaps, from the ordinary point of view, even vulgar professions."[5] For all he knew, he may have passed an agent of the Higher Source walking out his door. Indeed, the possibility that they had sent someone to his lectures and then *decided not to contact him* may have crossed his mind, although he seems not to have committed this to print. Was the war an opportunity to rethink things, or should he persevere with the routine he had adopted for so long?

It is possible, but not likely, that Ouspensky discussed these questions with an unexpected travel companion. On board the SS *Georgic*, Ouspensky discovered that Rodney Collin would be with him for the long voyage; he, too, was heading to New York, from there to leave for a new job with the British government in Bermuda. Although Janet Collin would later say that Rodney had become for Ouspensky a kind of adopted son, it's unclear how reciprocal their affections were. Collin had a background in "causes": along with the Peace Pledge Union, he had been a member of Toc H, a society of comradeship formed after World War I, as well as the Youth Hostel Association—he had even written for their journal, *The Rucksack*. Although never a member of the Theosophical Society, he had leanings in its direction and was deeply attracted to the notions of schools and esotericism. Collin was one of the few Ouspensky followers who showed little interest in Gurdjieff, seeing in Ouspensky the archetypal teacher. (It was a role that Collin, like Bennett, aspired to and would eventually adopt.) Ironically, when Collin first met Ouspensky, he had told him, as Ouspensky had Gurdjieff, that he was a writer. Ouspensky's reply was much the same as he had recently given Bennett: writing was useless. Collin took this to heart and for ten years wrote nothing. But while Collin would continue with Ouspensky until the end, Bennett had decided that it was time to go his own way. His bon voyage meeting with Ouspensky was his last. From then on, the only contact between the two men was by correspondence, and most of this was acrimonious.

One of Madame's first visitors in the New World was C. S. Nott, who found her a changed woman. Outside her domain at Lyne and again a refugee like himself, Madame was less formidable, altogether warmer, more sympathetic, and more understanding than he had known her to be in England. He also visited Ouspensky, who was staying at a hotel in New York City; as in England, in America Ouspensky and Madame would continue to lead separate lives. On Ouspensky's arrival, a lavish party had been thrown for him. When Nott met with him, he mentioned that the members of Orage's old group were thinking of inviting Gurdjieff to New York. Characteristically, Ouspensky replied that if that were so, he would go to California. Nott then suggested that Ouspensky meet with this group; Ouspensky agreed, and a meeting was arranged at the Madison Avenue apartment of Muriel Draper. It was perhaps a mistake. Nott was nervous and Ouspensky seemed ill at ease, either from the trip, his drinking, a growing kidney condition, or possibly fear of a hostile reception. Whatever the reason, the meeting was not a success. Ouspensky failed to impress. Orage's group found him too intellectual, too cold, and too eager to inform them that in London he had a thousand students. "No authority" was one verdict. "He speaks from his mind," another. Nott nevertheless helped to form a new group for Ouspensky, but most of the members agreed that he lacked both Gurdjieff's charisma and Orage's warmth.

They may also have got wind of remarks Ouspensky was making about his old teacher. Meeting with Claude Bragdon, Nott was informed that "Ouspensky tells me that Gurdjieff is suffering from paranoia and that this accounts for his strange behaviour."[6] Nott of course denied this, and remarked that for him, Ouspensky himself seemed a bit "touched" on the subject of Gurdjieff. In any case, how could the author of *Beelzebub's Tales* be paranoid? It was a rhetorical question, alas; Bragdon declined the copy Nott offered him, telling Nott that he was quite happy with the system of yoga he was working with.

Nott felt sympathetic toward Ouspensky, regardless if he was touched or not. After they spent an evening together he felt that Ouspensky was " a sick man, suffering from the lawful infirmities of age," although he was only sixty-three. But he knew there was something more. Along with the ravages of time, Ouspensky was suffering from "some specific disease" and was drinking "strong concoctions that I could not take."[7] When Nott remarked on this, Ouspensky replied, "It's the only thing that relieves the boredom and depression that comes over me at times."[8] Compassionate, Nott realized there was little he could do.

Nott was also privy to Ouspensky's growing tetchiness. When a new edition of *New Model* appeared, Ouspensky noticed that the dust jacket mistakenly reported that he was working with Gurdjieff in a community in London. Enraged, Ouspensky called Nott and unleashed his fury. He would demand the book be recalled or, failing that, he would refuse to accept any royalties from it—a peculiarly self-defeating strategy. Nott sympathized with Ouspensky but saw little point in getting upset. Ouspensky, however, was adamant. Nott had been a publisher and had connections with the press, and Ouspensky asked him to arrange a press conference so that he could clarify the mistake. But without a new book or anything newsworthy, Ouspensky was not a hot topic. No one was interested. This only increased his sense of wounded pride.

Perhaps fearing that without his presence Lyne Place would fall apart, or at least that its octave might develop in a direction he wouldn't like, Ouspensky inaugurated a system of informants, Fourth Way tattletales who kept an eye on things and made sure everyone toed the party line. Inevitably Bennett fell victim; he had started his own groups and—like Ouspensky himself—followed his own lead in working with them. Ouspensky reached out with a transatlantic wrist slap; he also reminded Bennett of his rule about not writing about the system. Bennett replied that Ouspensky had said it was *impossible* to write about the system, not *forbidden*. A rupture was due.

Nevertheless, Ouspensky got on with business, setting up groups in New York, one of which met in his studio apartment on 79th Street. The lectures followed London procedure: if there were no questions, there were no answers. "You must pay by asking questions," he told his new students.[9] If there were none, he would sit in silence. He also seemed to grow dismissive of anything smacking of mysticism or spirituality, although

at Lyne he had turned a deaf ear when Madame began reading from the great religious books, something that Kenneth
Walker had found rewarding and which "imparted to the ideas
a certain warmth which they previously lacked."[10] Here, however, whenever a student spoke of hearing angels, feeling a
sense of mystical oneness, or any other "fuzzy" sensations,
Ouspensky would reply, "Inspirazzione, intuizzione, imaginazz-
ione!"[11] He denied ever having mystical experiences himself,
either forgetting or lying about his trips on nitrous oxide or
that brief moment on the Sea of Marmora. Some students
found this difficult to take and challenged him; more often
they left, calling him a vain old man and a materialist.[12] To the
sixty-something ex-Symbolist, it is difficult to guess which criticism hit harder.

By this time it was not only the Ouspenskys who had relo-
cated; Lyne Place seemed to have been as well. Its new name
was Franklin Farms, in Mendham, New Jersey. Its purchase was
for the most part made possible by Janet Collin, who acted as
a kind of *aide-de-camp* for Madame. Once the residence of the
governor of New Jersey, the large granite house sat amidst
rolling hills. As at Lyne, the impressive grounds had fallen into
disrepair—a double asset, as the condition no doubt brought
down the price and provided its inhabitants with an opportunity to work. There were barns and empty silos, disused
outbuildings and rusting aviaries, once the home of exotic
birds. Again as in Lyne, here Madame ruled the roost. In fact,
as Ouspensky's health began to decline, aggravated by his
Herculean drinking, she became the focal point of the work.
Although crippled and walking with a cane, her presence was
electrifying; even from her bed, where she spent more and
more time, she was able to send out shocks to her students'
emotional centers. Her effect was disorienting, and students
couldn't tell whether they loved her or hated her, wanted her
attention or wished to escape. She created, as Bennett said of

Gurdjieff, an "atmosphere . . . impregnated with a feverish excitement that made it hard to tell what was right and what was wrong."[13]

Some were not as susceptible as others. Marie Seton, Ouspensky's secretary, remarked that Madame could be seen as a "dominating woman who . . . lived in very comfortable circumstances with all her housework done on a grand scale by mostly sincere men and women who were under her spell." Marie herself was immune; she was unsure if Madame was "genuine or a charlatan; or whether she was simply a commanding type of neurotic." For Marie, Madame "had great power over people whose imagination was captured by her." Those who had "long been under Madame's discipline were drab in clothes, joyless and strangely close-up people . . . fearful of her displeasure."[14]

One individual who clearly felt Madame's power was Nott. Nott had been invited to visit Franklin Farms, and as at Lyne, his relations with the Ouspenskys were cordial, although he admitted that he never felt as close to Madame as he did to Ouspensky. On one occasion at Lyne, after Nott had introduced Gurdjieff's movements to Ouspensky's students, Madame arranged a gala performance of the dances. Nott, however, wasn't invited—punishment, perhaps, for his refusal to join the work under Madame's supervision. (After Gurdjieff, working at Lyne he said "would have been like going back to school after having been at University.")[15] Now, in America, Nott had grown friendly with a couple who were working with Madame in Mendham. They invited him to dinner, and the conversation naturally turned toward the work. Nott had promised Madame that while at Franklin Farms he wouldn't mention Gurdjieff or say anything about *Beelzebub's Tales*. Nott may have been splitting hairs, but to his mind the edict held while he was at Mendham, nowhere else. Feeling it would be dishonest to withhold, and more than likely indulging in a bit of proselytizing, Nott spoke to the couple about his bible. They were of course interested. But when Madame found out, she was enraged and told him he had broken his promise. She then declared that he could no longer have any contact with her students. Nott thought this was absurd, and the two argued. Realizing there was no place for him at Mendham, he left. Nott was immediately ostracized, especially by the couple he had spoken to about *Beelzebub's Tales*. He never saw the Ouspenskys again.

Ouspensky, too, was capable of meting out punishments. More often than not, Bennett was the usual recipient. Ouspensky's informants had filed a considerable report on Bennett's intransigence. It has to be said that Bennett tried his best to maintain direct contact. He had even sent Ouspensky a long paper on the fifth dimension, hoping to get some creative feedback. But as he should have expected, Ouspensky dismissed it, saying it was only a new theory of thermodynamics. Nothing new, Ouspensky declared, could be found through the intellect. The only hope was to make contact with the higher emotional center—a refrain that cropped up repeatedly throughout his talks in these years. Sadly, he added, "we do not know how this is to be done." Bennett, like Ouspensky, had a mind of his own and, after twenty years of following Ouspensky's lead, decided it was time to use it. Like many students, he had fallen into the trap of imitating his teacher, eschewing initiative in favor of securing his approval. Even Madame had chided him for copying Ouspensky's bad English. It was time for this to stop. Bennett ignored Ouspensky's orders, and Ouspensky responded by having his solicitor write Bennett and demand the return of all Ouspensky's papers, including his lectures. All Bennett could quote from was the published material. Ouspensky also instructed the people left at Lyne to break off all contact with Bennett. But even this was not enough. A naval officer who attended Bennett's lectures confronted Bennett one day about a letter he had received from a friend in America, who informed him that Bennett had stolen all of Ouspensky's ideas. He was informed that if he hoped to ever join any of Ouspensky's groups, the officer had to break with Bennett immediately; he did. For someone who had been accused of "stealing" Gurdjieff's ideas, Ouspensky himself seemed an especially proprietary man.

One of the people outraged by Bennett's excommunication was de Ropp. With his wife in an asylum and their children with relatives, de Ropp had found a job in New York and, although disillusioned by his teachers, was nevertheless drawn to working with them again. He knew Bennett, was friends with him, and was one of the people left at Lyne who had been advised against maintaining contact with him. Ouspensky had accused Bennett of operating a "psychological black-market"; his excommunication reminded de Ropp of the paranoiac purges of Joseph Stalin. Ouspensky seemed apt to throw people out of the work for the flimsiest of reasons. But the "super effort bug" had bitten deep, and, being at loose ends in his life, de Ropp thought he would give his teacher another chance.

De Ropp looked up Rodney Collin, who was then living at Mendham and working for the British government in an office at the Rockefeller Center. By this time Collin's own relationship with Ouspensky had taken a curious turn. Commuting between New York and Mendham was tiring, and after a long day, Collin found himself too exhausted to attend Ouspensky's evening lectures. Yet one night he realized that something more than exhaustion was keeping him away. Jumping out of bed in the early hours, he discovered Ouspensky, as was his custom, alone in the kitchen drinking. "Why am I afraid of you?" Collin shouted. Ouspensky looked up from his glass and calmly replied, "Why do you say I?" Collin was stunned, and from then on he spent every free moment with Ouspensky.

Whether Ouspensky himself appreciated this is another question.

Collin invited de Ropp to Franklin Farms, and de Ropp was surprised to discover that it was like returning to Lyne. Many of Ouspensky's students had made the crossing, and with Madame once again in charge, the whole atmosphere had an eerily dreamlike quality. The place was larger and showier than Lyne; de Ropp noted that the stone had been shipped out from Italy by its previous owner. But what really struck him was the change in his teachers.

The East Coast had not been kind to them. "Neither Ouspensky nor Madame Ouspensky had ever been really healthy even in England," he reflected. "Both had the pale flabby faces of those who spend too much time indoors." "At least in England," he remarked, "Ouspensky had his horse and his Cossack saddle . . . but he seemed to have lost all interest in physical activity. He gave lectures in New York, so dull that after hearing a few I absolutely refused to attend any more. Between lectures he sat in his study." De Ropp said, "[I] sat up with him on several occasions but was saddened by what I found. He was quite obviously ill, drinking far too much, and still wandering in imagination through the streets of Moscow and St. Petersburg."[16]

Commenting on Ouspensky's increasing paranoia, de Ropp felt that "here was a man who had one of the best minds of anyone I had ever met indulging in really ridiculous fantasies." It was clear to him what was happening. "Ouspensky," he saw, "was no longer a teacher. He had lost his power and had wrecked his health . . . The only honest thing for him to do . . . was to face his own weakness, send all his disciples packing, close down that ostentatious house, and either die or, by a supreme effort, recover his lost power."[17]

Ouspensky did neither. The situation was out of his control, possibly more than even de Ropp realized. De Ropp doesn't mention it, but at one point Ouspensky may have suffered a stroke and was, for a period, helpless, quite literally a prisoner in his own home. Madame, too, had withdrawn, and according to de Ropp was trying to run a Fourth Way school by remote control. She was helped in this by a brother-and-sister-team that de Ropp called "the archangels." Rarely bearers of glad tidings, they were very young and very cruel. "It was one thing," he said, "to receive direct from Madame those often withering comments on one's weaknesses that she was so fond of making. It was quite another to receive them publicly and with a note of satisfaction from the archangels."[18] De Ropp received one himself at a particularly trying time. Back in England, his insane wife's diary had been found, and within it her detailed account of Madame's harsh treatment. De Ropp's relatives were up in arms, claiming Madame had brainwashed the girl; they found it hard to understand why de Ropp was carrying on with the Ouspenskys again. They were not the only ones. "I could no longer maintain," de Ropp admitted, ". . . that my teachers could not make mistakes."[19]

Like de Ropp, in the early 1940s Marie Seton found herself in New York. She admits that between 1936 and 1938 she had been "absolutely nobody in 'the System.'" She did, however, have the advantage of speaking fluent Russian; at the time she got involved in the work she was translating Chekhov's *The Cherry Orchard*. This naturally attracted her to Ouspensky. The two got to know each other. Ouspensky was always glad to find intelligent people he could speak with outside the work, and if the person was a young, attractive female, all the better. Now, when she met one of Ouspensky's students and discovered that he was in New York, she was happy to get back in touch. Ouspensky, too, was glad to see her and asked her to be his secretary again. Uprooted for the second time, he more than likely appreciated someone other than Madame who could speak his native language.

Marie noticed that there was a "young married couple with money who were so deeply involved that they paid the major bills." This was Rodney and Janet Collin. That Ouspensky's New York operations were maintained by well-heeled students wasn't unusual—in London, Ralph Philipson and Lady Rothermere had footed many bills. Ouspensky, after all, was providing a teaching and an environment found nowhere else. No one was forcing them to be his students. Yet Marie noticed something odd. "I cannot say there was an exact day when it struck me that P. D. Ouspensky was strangely extravagant considering the young couple were paying the bulk of the bills. But he would direct me to buy the most lavishly expensive fruit, cheese and delicacies for his personal consumption." She also noticed that "the people who actually paid the bills were not asked to share these expensive foods." She, however, was.

After his lectures, Marie recalled, Ouspensky would ask some students, including the Collins, to a restaurant—more than likely Longchamps, where he was well-liked by the waiters. There the party would break up later and later, and during the evening Ouspensky would grow sarcastic, oftentimes getting quite harsh with Rodney and Janet, who, more often than not, picked up the check. Knowing Rodney Collin's appreciation of Ouspensky, he probably saw these evenings as a "test." Ouspensky, however, was only more irritated by what he probably saw as a sign of stupidity, although his irritation was often really aimed at himself for spending time with "sheep." As Marie wrote, the Collins "lived to gain his approval and the more they hoped for it the less they got it." The situation had uncomfortable echoes of Ouspensky's own times with Gurdjieff. Perhaps to cloud this, Ouspensky drank. Sometimes he refused to leave the restaurant, talking to Marie about his life, and inevitably, the years before he met his teacher.

Although Marie respected Ouspensky, she began to question his judgment. His anger and increasingly frequent outbursts also disturbed her. One afternoon he mentioned a good restaurant he had heard of and requested her to cancel that evening's lecture so the two of them could have dinner there. Marie did but couldn't refrain from asking how he could justify canceling a lecture simply to go to a restaurant, or what the meaning of his bad temper was.

"They are such fools," Ouspensky replied. Then he added: "I've lost control of my temper." "I took over the leadership to save the System. But I took it over before I had gained enough control over myself. I was not ready. I have lost control over myself. It is a long time since I could control my state of mind."

Couldn't he try to gain control over himself, she asked. As it was, his students believed he was teaching when he flew into his rages.

"They are fools!" he said with contempt. Then he told her that she was the only one who had gained anything from his work—something he had also told Rosamund Sharp. The others, he said, were just deluding themselves.

Marie then asked the obvious question: "Why don't you give up the lectures and try to gain control of yourself again?"

"The System," Ouspensky replied, "has become a profession with me."

The work, it seemed, had become a job.

Other things kept Ouspensky fixed in place. He had, he told Marie, become dependent on the comfort and the luxury that the Collins provided. Given that he had been transplanted twice and had faced starvation and possible death in those years in the Caucasus, this could be excused. But it was in fact a poor substitute for what was really lacking. The problem was not even that he had failed to achieve the "psycho-transformation" that was the aim of the system, although his reaction to

Mrs. Beaumont's near-death experience showed how deeply he missed that. Like everyone else, Ouspensky wanted to feel he had been a success at his work. It's difficult to escape the sense that somewhere back in the thirties, when he first expanded his operation, he began to feel that something had gone wrong. Although he was always fond of drink, his abuse of it seems to have begun then. He was not really cut out to be a teacher. But his years of writing were behind him, and he must have known it.

Perhaps the octave had shifted in a way he had not anticipated. As Ivan Osokin so often did, he had made a mistake. Just when it was difficult to say, although a certain meeting with a certain extraordinary man is more than likely a good bet. Each evening, powered by alcohol, he traveled through time—the fourth dimension—to the days before that meeting. In those days, he told Marie, "a thousand or two thousand people" came to his lectures. Now, thirty years later, there were only a hundred—"too few."

CHAPTER TWENTY-ONE

THE END OF THE SYSTEM

I N THE SUMMER of 1946, in the Grand Ballroom at New York's Steinway Hall, Ouspensky announced to his shocked students that he was leaving the United States and returning to England. Madame would remain, and those of his people who worked at Mendham would continue with her. His New York people who were not a part of Franklin Farms would have to fend for themselves. "Grief, astonishment, disbelief, despera- tion . . . we wriggled, panted and gasped for air in a frantic effort to save ourselves from despair" was one reaction to this declaration.[1] Ouspensky's people had been "pushed, verbally lashed, abused, annoyed [and] banged about." They "respect- ed, loved and tried to understand him."[2] But now he was leaving them. Some, like Irmis B. Popoff, tried to find a place in Mendham, but Madame wouldn't have it. Irmis, Madame said, was "the emotional Mrs. P with nothing in her head." Yet, like many others, Irmis didn't take offense, although she admitted that Madame didn't evoke the same admiration as Ouspensky did. The two, she knew, were "so different from anyone else I had ever met, so far above and beyond the aver- age person that they must have sound reasons . . . for everything they said or did."[3] It was evident to Irmis that "[t]hey were far more conscious than I was." Yet at the same time she admitted that she "hated them . . . loved them . . . [and] questioned their sanity."[4] Now, having lost her teacher, Irmis had to find her own bearings. At one point this brought her to a reading of *Beelzebub's Tales*. There, she said, we "sat on our hard backless wooden benches for three or more hours at a time, listening to dull voices read in a dull monotone from a book that made no sense . . . depriving ourselves of cigarettes . . . struggling against sleep [literally], against cold, against hunger, against bodily needs, since we could not excuse ourselves . . . while the reading was in progress."[5] She may have felt she had left the frying pan for the fire.

Madame was not happy with Ouspensky's decision, but he was determined. If there was ever a time for super efforts, it had come. Against the advice of his doctor and Madame's urgent pleas, on January 18, 1947, a pale, weak, and unmistakably ill Peter Ouspensky forced his recalcitrant body to walk slowly across the hall at Mendham, step outside, and get into the waiting car. Although only sixty-eight, his body was physically much older, and each step cost him a tremendous amount of will power—something that, ages ago, his teacher had told him he didn't possess. Gurdjieff had once said that a sure way to build up "force" was to make the body do something it didn't want to. Those evenings at Longchamps and the rich, expensive foods were behind him, and with each agonizing movement Ouspensky was adding considerably to his reservoir of "force." He must have known he was dying.

Years earlier Gurdjieff had told Ouspensky that the Earth was in a very bad place in the universe. In the winter of 1947, one of the worst places on the planet was England. The war had gutted the economy, much of London was in ruins, food and electricity were rationed, and to top it off, the first months of the new year saw one of the coldest spells in recorded history. Ouspensky's predictions about the war hadn't come to pass, but he was not excited about the kind of Europe the Allies would construct. Western democracy seemed another name for soulless materialism. But England had one thing that

America did not. It had the only past he could return to. Arriving in Constantinople all those years before, Ouspensky had looked back at his homeland with the sad realization that it had ceased to exist. *There was no Russia.* "To no place that I had left was it possible to return."[6] To a man for whom the past was always important, this must have been a dreadful loss. He had never felt quite at home in England, but it was all he had left.

Ouspensky's students were excited when they received the letter announcing his return. Many of them had believed that once the war had ended he would come back to them. Now the Ark had hit dry land, they said, and it was time to work again.

Among those who met Ouspensky at the dock at Southampton was Kenneth Walker. Like the others, he had heard that Ouspensky was unwell, and there were rumors that his return to England was not, as it seemed to many at Mendham, a sudden decision but part of a long and carefully conceived plan. Speculations as to what this entailed were rife, but the name of Ouspensky's old teacher was often whispered: one rumor suggested that Madame had invited Gurdjieff to Franklin Farms, and this, they knew, would be enough to make Ouspensky cross the ocean. In truth, they did not know what to expect, but they were certainly not ready for what they saw. Ouspensky had returned, "but not the Ouspensky of old." As he stood on the dock, Walker saw stepping onto English soil "a man whom we hardly recognized, a man who had aged by twenty years since we had last seen him, a man on whom Death had already set its mark."[7] Ouspensky, Walker realized, had lost all of his former enthusiasm and drive, and it was clear that whatever his intentions, it was doubtful that he would be able to carry them out. Walker learned later that up until the last moment, it was uncertain whether Ouspensky would be able to make the trip at all.

Months before, Ouspensky had asked two students who had made their way with great difficulty from Lyne to Mendham to derequisition Colet House from the navy—which had occupied the building during the war—and prepare it for his arrival. This eventually happened, but Ouspensky's first port of call was Lyne Place. Driven to Lyne from Southampton, Ouspensky settled into his old room. As had become increasingly his habit, he spoke to no one. To Walker, however, it was clear he was preoccupied with something. Two months later, he emerged from his seclusion and made his last public appearances. At Colet House, in a series of six momentous meetings, Ouspensky gave his students—as well as anyone else interested in the work—the biggest shock the system ever received.

Francis Roles—along with the excommunicated Bennett, one of Ouspensky's chief lieutenants—had gathered together three hundred of the faithful. If the intimate circle was startled at Ouspensky's health and appearance, this larger group felt an equal dismay. But what they saw on the platform at Colet House was nothing compared with what they heard. Ouspensky had always been brusque and was never one to suffer fools gladly. Those who had waited six years for his return were used to short, practical answers, when there were answers at all. But now, through the intermediary of a Miss Quinn, who had accompanied him from Mendham, Ouspensky outstonewalled even himself. His English was difficult, his speech somewhat slurred, but the general gist was clear. Every mention of the teaching, every remark about sleep, mechanicalness, self-remembering, every question couched in the jargon of the system was thrown back at the questioners with the absurd and unbelievable reply that Ouspensky had no teaching, that he had never taught them anything, and that, in any case, why should they believe anyone who told them they were mechanical? Who said they were asleep? It must have been an excruciating experience, and Ouspensky did not make it easy. He had nothing to teach them, he said. When one student asked, how he could find harmony, Ouspensky replied, "This is your question? It is my question now, and I have no answer." Later he said it was a "musical term, nothing more." When another asked if he wished them to continue with the program he had given them in 1940, he answered that he had given no program. When one asked what was the aim and purpose of esoteric schools, he replied, "Oh, that is a very big thing," and then added, "Maybe not." When one student remarked that he had chosen the Fourth Way and asked Ouspensky's advice on how to get on with it, he replied, "I don't know." Another asked if it was possible to establish contact with a school. Ouspensky said, "No." To the question "What is reality?" he responded, "Nothing, probably." And when someone said, "I want to escape from mechanicalness and sleep," he commented, "Probably impossible." When one student remarked that she wanted to become different than what she was, Ouspensky replied that this meant change, and he no longer believed in it. When another insisted that some people *do* change, he said, "Lucky people." It took Kenneth Walker to ask the question that everyone else was too afraid to ask: "Do you mean, Mr. Ouspensky, that you have abandoned the System?" To this his teacher simply replied: "There is no System."[8] In his final trump, Ouspensky had out-shocked even his master.

Ouspensky did leave them a few guidelines. It was up to them to decide what they wanted from life. An aim—an ordinary, everyday aim—was essential. And they could rely only on themselves. If Ouspensky's students came away from these meetings in February, March, May, and June with anything more than disillusionment and confusion, it was the sense that it was up to them to make a fresh start. When one student asked if it was possible to make efforts by oneself, he answered:

263

"Yes, certainly. Only by yourself. Only possible. No other way possible." And when one asked, "How is it possible to start work?," he replied, "One must know what one wants." It was, it seemed, as easy as that. But Ouspensky had learned that knowing what one wanted was perhaps the most difficult task of all.

In private meetings, Ouspensky's disappointment was clear. Somewhere along the octave, something had gone wrong. But who exactly had failed was unknown. Many students believed that Ouspensky's volte-face was prompted by their inability to grasp his teaching. Given that students like Walker had spent twenty-four years following Ouspensky, it's understandable they'd have difficulty accepting the fact that their teacher had publicly admitted his life's work was a mistake. It meant that those who had followed him were mistaken too. Some held on to the thought that Ouspensky's last meetings were a kind of shock, shaking them out of a set pattern and opening them to the new phase of work he had prepared. But one question asked during those last meetings seems to argue against this. "Are you going to publish *Fragments*," one student asked, "or are you going to be content to go down to those yet unborn as having broken your promise and worked against esotericism?" Ouspensky at first seemed not to understand, but when the question was repeated, he simply answered, "No." Not only had he given up the system, he had abandoned the single most eloquent and exhaustive presentation of it—which was also his last piece of writing.

Back at Lyne, Ouspensky turned inward and reflected on his life. If he had any teaching left, it was that people should look over their past. They should find the crossroads where they might have made a different decision, taken a different route, and had a different life. As in the beginning, recurrence filled his thoughts, and it's little wonder which of his own crossroads drew his attention. In *Four Quartets*, T. S. Eliot, who had learned much at Lady Rothermere's, wrote, "In my end is my beginning." Ouspensky believed this, and now, as his end was approaching, he was preparing to begin again. *Fragments* would not be published. But he retitled his sole novel *Strange Life of Ivan Osokin* and hoped to see its English publication before he died. He did not, but the wheel was coming full circle.

Certainly one student who believed preparing for his next life was his teacher's dying aim was Rodney Collin. Collin had followed his teacher to England in April and had attended his last meetings. Unlike Walker, he was one of the few who didn't believe Ouspensky had abandoned the work, or if he had, it was only to open himself and others to the possibility of even greater work. Like the young Ouspensky, Collin had a thirst for the miraculous, and this, as well as his deep belief in his teacher, may have colored his perception. But if Collin's account is to be believed, in his last days Ouspensky had not only found the miraculous but became a source of it himself.

At first the miracles seemed more an Ouspenskian version of Gurdjieff's acting. Deciding that England was after all too inhospitable for a man in his condition—or perhaps deciding to give his New York groups the same shock he had delivered in London—Ouspensky announced that he was returning to the United States. On September 4 Ouspensky's group went to Southampton, put their luggage on board, and had even arranged for Ouspensky's car to drive up to the dock. Then shortly before the boat was due to sail, Ouspensky announced in a quiet voice, "I am not going to America this time." This time? Did he mean his last trip, or his last life? Was Ouspensky taking a different step at a crossroads, leaving, as it were, a temporal bookmark in the pages of his life, or was this merely one of the "vagaries of an old man who had lost his mind"?[9] For Rodney Collin, the change in plans was "like the 'stop' exercise on the scale of the whole Work . . . . Everyone's personal plans were turned upside down, and a space made in the momentum of time when something quite new could be done."[10] For others, it may have seemed that a tired and cranky invalid had shown an appalling lack of consideration.

Collin had no doubts. For him, all of Ouspensky's actions in the last months of his life were charged with terrific meaning. "All that Ouspensky did and said at that time seemed to have exactly this purpose and effect—to sort out the people who could respond to the miraculous from those who could not."[11] Part of this process involved a series of bizarre journeys around England that the dying Ouspensky undertook, accompanied by Collin, other students, and, very often, his cats. Driving at night and without food, Ouspensky returned to places he had known: West Wickham, Sevenoaks, and Nicoll's old cottage in Sidlesham (55a Gwendyr Road was not on the itinerary, having been destroyed by a bomb in the Blitz). At the end of one trip, returning to Lyne, Ouspensky didn't leave the car with the others, but remained seated there overnight, surrounded by his cats. One devoted female follower stood outside by the window, her arm raised in a kind of salute. Ouspensky was either oblivious of this or too weak to respond, otherwise he more than likely would have chided the woman for her foolishness.

Ouspensky was apparently returning to important places in his past in order to fix them in his consciousness so that *next time* he would remember. According to Kenneth Walker, it seemed clear that there was something he wanted to change. To alter the past had always been an obsession for Ouspensky, and now it seemed that he was making every effort to give himself as good a chance as possible of doing that. He was, according to witnesses, literally forcing his body to stay alive. He ate little and had no care for comfort. Collin wrote: "After having spent a whole night forcing his dying body to walk, and waking us in order to make experiments, Ouspensky said 'Now do you understand that everything has to be done by effort?'"[12] Collin believed that everything Ouspensky did now was part of a supreme effort with one goal: to die consciously. This, Collin believed, was the final "super-effort" in his long search for the miraculous.

Memory had always been important for Ouspensky. In his last talks in New York the theme had surfaced again and again, along with that of recurrence. Since he had covered the topic in theory and in literary presentation years before, the new interest now seems puzzling. More than likely, the feeling that he had come to a dead end with the system had been with him for some time. In 1943, one night at Longchamps, Rodney Collin had asked Ouspensky why everything had come to a dead stop. Ouspensky replied with an insight he had learned years before in St. Petersburg: "You forget one thing; many people forget it—to learn, you have to teach."[13] Was he talking more about recurrence now to gain a greater insight into it for himself? Standing on the roof at Lyne seven years earlier, watching the London docks burn, Ouspensky had said he did not remember this. Now, as he willed his decrepit physical form to go on, was he taking steps to make sure that next time he would?

If so, it seemed to many that his efforts were having an effect. For Rodney Collin, Ouspensky's last days took on the character of a mystery play, and the events surrounding it were all a part of the great "miracle of change" that he and the others were privy to. New knowledge, and a new understanding and certainty, were released in the weeks leading up to his death. This was because Ouspensky was no longer *talking* about the possibility of living outside of time. He was, in his actions and in his determination to accept every suffering, actually accomplishing it. Everything was "strange, new, unreasonable."[14] Ouspensky had made a "terrible crack into heaven"[15] through his efforts to "turn every unfavourable trick of fate . . . into advantages." By relinquishing his normal powers and faculties, he "was enabled to achieve supernormal ones."[16] In this way Ouspensky became a living force, a "permanent intermediary between ourselves and the highest powers."[17]

At the end of his car journeys, Ouspensky retired to his room at Lyne and became even more silent. Yet even then his teaching did not stop. "He would have two or three people sit with him," Collin records, "not doing anything, just sitting, smoking . . . drinking a glass of wine, for hours on end . . . One racked one's brain what to say, how to start a conversation . . . Many people could never bear it. But after a while, these became the most interesting times of all . . . One began to feel—everything is possible in *this* moment."[18]

What exactly happened during Ouspensky's last few weeks remains unclear. Even Collin admits that without faith, or, in Ouspensky's words, positive attitude, everything their dying teacher was going through could be seen as the sad demise of a broken, disappointed man. Joyce Collin-Smith, Rodney's sister-in-law, has even suggested that Ouspensky was suffering from Alzheimer's disease and was no longer accountable for his actions.[19] By now, however, everything is conjecture, and we may never know the truth. But for the people who witnessed it, the strange death of Peter Ouspensky must have been an extraordinary time indeed.

For one student, Ouspensky performed the miracle Gurdjieff had managed years before: she heard his thoughts. Terrified, she asked him to communicate normally. Ouspensky understood her fear and agreed. Another felt the presence of a tremendous power, some "Christ-like being, as far above Ouspensky, as Ouspensky was above us."[20] Ouspensky felt the presence too and asked his pupils, "You notice?"[21] They did. Another believed he had reached the level of the angels; another, that, after all, Ouspensky finally did achieve the cosmic consciousness he had sought for so long. He became a changed man. Years before, a student, one of many, asked if he ever regretted having met Gurdjieff and pointed out that even

before meeting him he had written "two very brilliant books."
Ouspensky replied: "They were only books. I wanted something more. I wanted something for myself."[22] More than
thirty years later, many believed he was finally getting what he
wanted and, in the process, was creating a kind of "mystical
body" that those who were strong enough in faith could participate in. As Ouspensky was moving "outside time," he would be
there for them for all eternity as well.

Or so it seemed to Rodney Collin. Others saw things differently and were distressed by the influence Ouspensky's
eager pupil had over his failing teacher. To them, the long car
journeys and repeated super efforts were Collin's idea, not
Ouspensky's, and it has to be said that Collin's efforts to write
himself into the script of Ouspensky's life offer some support
for this view. If we accept Marie Seton's report on Ouspensky's
assessment of the Collins ("They are fools!"), the intimacy with
his teacher that Collin believed he enjoyed may have been one-
sided. For all his patience, there must have been times when
Ouspensky found Collin's puppy-eagerness and efforts to gain
approval annoying. Sick, in pain, and disappointed, at one
point his irritation got the better of him and he slapped Collin
in the face. Rodney, thinking this a teaching strategy, followed
suit and did the same to Francis Roles, shattering his ear
drum. Almost immediately after, during a sudden flight back
to America, Collin believed that "lying in his bed in Surrey,"
Ouspensky "possessed with his own mind a young man flying
over the Atlantic."[23] The young man was Collin. When he
arrived at Mendham, Collin frightened Madame by assuming, literally, Ouspensky's identity, taking on his gestures and
voice. When he returned to Lyne, he was determined to
assist Ouspensky in his conscious death, a death in which he
would die not as ordinary men do but at a level at which he
would become immortal.[24] For Collin, Ouspensky's death had
taken on the character of Christ's crucifixion, and Ouspensky

himself, when he crossed that final threshold, would become a kind of spiritual being, available to all those who needed him and sought his help with sufficient urgency and faith.

Shortly before his death, Ouspensky assembled his group and reiterated the message of his last meetings: they must, he told them, reconstruct *everything* for themselves. On what turned out to be the last day of his life he woke, dressed, and, refusing all help, made a final effort to address his students. The content of that last briefing is unknown. At dawn on October 2, 1947, Peter Demian Ouspensky died.

"I will always be with you," Collin believed his teacher could say, "but lightly and smoking a cigarette." Collin took this to heart, and as he crossed London Bridge that day, he believed Ouspensky was in someway beside him. For many, Ouspensky's death marked an end: of his work, of the system, and of their tutelage under him. But for Collin, Ouspensky's death was "the new beginning of everything," just as his last months had been "the happiest and most vivid period" of his life.[25]

The strange events had not ceased. After Ouspensky's body was removed for burial at Lyne Church, Collin locked himself inside his master's bedroom and for six days refused to leave, even pushing aside a ladder that had been raised against the window. Finally, after his wife had arrived from Mendham, the bell from Ouspensky's room rang, and Janet went to see her husband. He sat cross-legged on Ouspensky's bed, unshaven, dirty, and emaciated from lack of food. He had an "angelic" air about him and claimed that during his vigil he had been in telepathic contact with Ouspensky, who, he believed, had finally escaped from recurrence. A new phase of the work was starting, and Collin would be the head of it. It involved schools, self-remembering, and other familiar themes; but to these was added a strong religious sense and a belief in a new age about to dawn on mankind.

Years later, in Lima, Peru, after setting up several work groups in Mexico and South America, converting to Roman Catholicism, and becoming involved with a questionable spirit medium, Rodney Collin fell to his death from a cathedral tower under mysterious circumstances. His major work, *The Theory of Celestial Influence*, was dedicated to Ouspensky: "MAGISTRO MEO Qui Sol Fuit Est Et Erit," "My Master, who was, is, and will be the Sun."

EPILOGUE

THE REQUIEM SERVICE for Peter Demian Ouspensky was held at the Russian Church in Pimlico, London. The service's closing verse seemed peculiarly apt for its recipient:

> Give rest eternal in the blessed falling asleep, O Lord,
> To the soul thy servant departed this life,
> And make his memory eternal.
> Memory eternal!
> Memory eternal!
> Memory eternal!

Once, during a stay in Paris, Madame and Ouspensky sat at a café with some students, and though the students tried their best to communicate, Ouspensky seemed peculiarly withdrawn. Perhaps speaking to both her husband and her pupils, Madame remarked that it was "very hard to make a friend of Mr. Ouspensky." This was a verdict that some of his oldest students shared at the end of their teacher's life. For Kenneth Walker, Ouspensky had been linked in his mind with his parents: "As I had always respected, but never really known, my father, so had I always respected but never really knew Ouspensky . . . As human being and human being we two had never met."[1] This from a man who had been Ouspensky's pupil for twenty-four years. J. G. Bennett felt much the same. Hearing of Ouspensky's death, Bennett "felt a great love towards him, such as I had never known while he was alive." A "great cycle" of his own life had closed, spanning twenty-seven years, and Bennett felt "love and gratitude" toward his ex-teacher. But he "felt no nearer to him than [he] had before."[2] C. S. Nott was also saddened by the news. He had liked Ouspensky and believed he was a good man. But he could not forgive him one mistake, that "kink in him [that] had caused him to reject Gurdjieff as a teacher."

And what did Gurdjieff think? According to one report, after their break Gurdjieff "nearly always spoke of Ouspensky in scathing terms as one who exploited his ideas; brought many of his pupils grief . . . even caused their death; and who, if he had not left Gurdjieff to set up on his own, need not have 'perished like a dog.'"[3] To "perish like a dog" was the reward one earned for not working on oneself, a fate Gurdjieff used as a favorite threat to put the fear of the Lord—or himself—into his students. But had Ouspensky "perished like a dog"? Gurdjieff was not known for sentimentality, and in the Fourth Way there is, at least according to Bennett, a peculiar custom known as the "way of blame," part of which entails speaking less than kindly about the dead. When Alexandre de Salzmann, one of Gurdjieff's closest pupils, was dying of tuberculosis, Gurdjieff refused to visit him. When de Salzmann finally summoned the strength to see Gurdjieff at the Café Henri IV, the master was, according to one witness, "not very kind."[4] De Salzmann died a few days later. Yet when he heard of the death of Orage, Gurdjieff shed tears and whispered, "I loved Orage like a brother." Clearly the master's response to the demise of his students was unpredictable and, like everything else about him, open to many interpretations.

Then again, perhaps some students of Ouspensky's received final words about their teacher that have not come down to us, since after Ouspensky's death, many of them found their way to Gurdjieff.

"You are sheep without a shepherd. Come to me." This was the telegram that Gurdjieff sent to Lyne after hearing of his ex-pupil's demise. Until Ouspensky's death, many there knew Gurdjieff only as a name, and one hardly spoken at that. He may have been dead, he may have been mad, he may have been a black magician. Now, with the loss of their own teacher, they had an opportunity to find out. Ouspensky's death, the strange circumstances surrounding it, and his last, startling meetings had thrown his London students into chaos. Some gathered around Rodney Collin; others followed Francis Roles. And others took Madame's advice when she told them there was only one thing to do: go to Gurdjieff. He was neither dead nor mad and was still teaching in Paris. He was, as he said, a shepherd, and was always open to increasing his flock.

Some went, but not all. Maurice Nicoll declined the invitation and carried on with his groups until his death in 1953. Rodney Collin followed his own star. Francis Roles carried on Ouspensky's teaching "according to the letter of the System" as best he could; eventually he would align himself with Alan McLaren of the School of Economic Science and, in the early 1960s, the Maharishi Mahesh Yogi. Others did go, but not for long. Disgusted with Mendham, in 1948 de Ropp met Wym Nyland, then Gurdjieff's US representative, and through him was led to the master. For de Ropp, Gurdjieff was "the most extraordinary human being" he had ever met. He practiced the movements and got used to being told that he and his companions moved "like worms in shit." But de Ropp, fond of nature and wholesome living, quickly grew to loath the ambience of Gurdjieff's late years: crowded, smoky hotel rooms, the many disciples, the endless lunches, and, most of all, the famous "toasts to the idiots." He had already seen enough alcohol around Ouspensky. Gurdjieff seemed old and sad, and in any case, remembering Gurdjieff's remark about guinea pigs, de Ropp reflected on his own experiments with those animals and concluded that they were stupid creatures. He soon left. Kenneth Walker led a brigade of Ouspensky's followers to Gurdjieff's Paris apartment, where he and his wife, both teetotalers, were also subjected to the toasts. Although he too recognized Gurdjieff's power and wrote a few books on the work, he seems to have quietly withdrawn from the scene. He died in 1966.

The one student of Ouspensky's who remained with Gurdjieff was Bennett. Following Madame's advice, in 1948 Bennett went to Gurdjieff's apartment on the Rue de Colonels Renard and, twenty-five years to the month, tried to pick up their conversation where they had left it, back at the Prieure in 1923. For many years after, in the English-speaking world, aside from Gurdjieff and Ouspensky themselves, Bennett's name was the one most associated with the work. Yet he, like Rodney Collin, found himself moving in other directions, becoming a devotee of Subud, Hinduism, and, finally, Roman Catholicism. At one point he was convinced by Idries Shah, the writer on Sufism, to hand over the ownership of Coombe Springs, a spiritual community along the lines of the Prieure and Lyne. Shah had convinced Bennett that he was a representative of the Masters of Wisdom (another name for the Inner Circle) and that by donating Coombe Springs he would be helping them in their work. After Bennett agreed, Shah promptly sold the property for a considerable sum.

Gurdjieff survived Ouspensky by two years and twenty-seven days, dying on October 29, 1949, also in strange circumstances. The coroner who performed the autopsy allegedly remarked that Gurdjieff should have been dead years before, as all his internal organs were nearly destroyed. Against her husband's wishes, Madame had sent her master the manuscript of *Fragments*, asking if he thought it should be published. Legend has it that Gurdjieff said, "Before I hate Ouspensky, now I love him. This very exact, he tell what I say." *In Search of the Miraculous,* the account of his life with Gurdjieff that Ouspensky had refused to publish, is now the most widely read book on the work.

• • •

Throughout this book I've tried to keep my own remarks to a minimum, contenting myself with providing the "evidence" and wanting the story of Gurdjieff and Ouspensky to more or less tell itself. Yet having "lived" with Ouspensky during the months of research and writing—vicariously, it's true, yet nonetheless intensely—I can't come away without asking a question, one, I suspect, most readers will find themselves asking as well: what went wrong? For clearly something had. How did the author of one of the most exhilarating and optimistic books on philosophy and metaphysics, *Tertium Organum,* end his days in sadness, depression, self-abuse, and a complete rejection of his life's work? For myself, it's clear that Ouspensky's final meetings, when he denied even the existence of the system he had taught for more than twenty-five years, put an end to his life in the work and were not, as some of his followers believed, the beginning of a new phase of it. Through a supreme effort of will and with blistering honesty, Ouspensky publicly announced that he had made a mistake. The system didn't work—or, at least, it didn't achieve the goal he had believed it would. Had he suspected this earlier? More than likely. The fact that he considered some of his closest students "fools," as well as the fact that he no longer saw himself as an explorer of man's "possible evolution" but felt he was merely going through the motions of a job, suggest that he had had misgivings for some time before his final, liberating confession. He had banked everything on the methods and ideas he had learned from Gurdjieff. And he was wrong.

277

But perhaps there were other mistakes as well. For me, it's not an exaggeration to suggest it was a mistake for Ouspensky to abandon his own creativity and ideas to become an exponent of Gurdjieff's teaching. That teaching was new, formidable, intellectually impressive and, with Gurdjieff himself as an example of the possibilities it offered, very attractive, especially for a scrupulously honest man like Ouspensky, who had the courage to admit that his own efforts at securing the miraculous were not successful. And yet, as Colin Wilson points out, there was a streak of pessimism in Ouspensky that prevented him from seeing how successful his efforts really were. Although he felt he had not profited by them, during his nitrous oxide experiments Ouspensky *had* glimpsed the deeper reality underlying our world of space and time. If nothing else, a reading of *Tertium Organum* alone confirms this. For my taste, nothing Gurdjieff wrote, nor any other Fourth Way book, approaches Ouspensky's first work in its enthusiasm, insight, brilliance, and ability to convey difficult ideas with seemingly effortless clarity. Yet some lack of confidence, some sense perhaps of his own weakness, led him to reject his early work and instead devote himself to a search for people who *were* successful at grasping the miraculous and could perhaps show him how it could be done. His romanticism prompted him to believe that *somewhere* there existed a different life, a world without *byt,* without the boring necessities of the wooden world he returned to after his nitrous oxide excursions, a world devoted solely to the miraculous. Hence his readiness for Gurdjieff.

Here, I believe, Ouspensky's own thoroughness and dedication worked against him. For once having accepted the system, he stuck to it with an admirable but ultimately counterproductive tenacity. And here, perhaps, Gurdjieff is to blame. Gurdjieff's insistence on our mechanicalness, our sleep, our utter lack of will, freedom, or ability to *do*, led Ouspensky to believe that without the system there was no hope. His pessimism about his efforts, combined with his insight into human folly, suggested that, unpalatable as it was, Gurdjieff's grim assessment of mankind was correct. Peter may have believed in the transformative power of art, poetry, nature, and love, but Demian was too aware of humankind's perennial predilection for self-deception.

Demian, it seems, won out, but clearly he was helped by the efforts of his teacher, Gurdjieff. If Ouspensky had doubted himself less, or if his hunger to find the miraculous had been less urgent, he might have shrugged off his master's endless chiding, reprimands, criticisms, and rebukes and much sooner gone his own way, assimilating what he had learned and synthesizing it with his own insights. But as we saw at the outset, Ouspensky was prime material for the struggle between "yes and no." His intellect and drive were powerful enough for him to recognize that he was an exceptional man. Yet his very honesty prevented him from lying to himself about his success in finding the miraculous. And then, to meet a man who *knew*, a man whose very presence spoke of mastery and power—to the romantic intellectual, aware of his own shortcomings, such a man must have made an extraordinary impression. The fact, too, that Ouspensky had lost both his father and grandfather when very young must be brought into the equation. One part of him, the fiercely independent philosopher, wanted to scale the heights of higher consciousness on his own; another, self-conscious, self-doubting, wanted no doubt to win the magician's approval. "Yes and no" pulled at him from the start, and it was not until his last days that the tug of war ended and Peter emerged once again, sadly, with little time left to do more than regret his mistake.

It is clear to me that Gurdjieff was wrong to hammer away at Ouspensky, and this suggests that the infallible master had his blind spots. Either Gurdjieff was unable to see Ouspensky's own powers and abilities, or his need to dominate was too great. It is true, Ouspensky could have left whenever he wanted to. Some need, some weakness prevented him from cutting the ties earlier or, indeed, ever: although physically separated from Gurdjieff, it's clear that Ouspensky was never very far from him in his mind or heart. Was it a salutary lesson to continually and without remorse hold Ouspensky's weakness up to him and to others as well? Clearly, Ouspensky loved Gurdjieff and wanted his approval. Yet Gurdjieff had learned the virtues of separating his inner life from the world outside, and no doubt he saw Ouspensky's affection as just another manifestation of mechanicalness. And if the object was to get Ouspensky to stand on his own two feet, then why did Gurdjieff undermine all of Ouspensky's efforts to do that, why did he go out of his way to humiliate him? Gurdjieff, too, perhaps had a weakness, a need to dominate and master the people around him. Like some sadly dysfunctional relationships, in many ways the two were made for each other.

It is no mystery, then, what had happened to turn the poetic author of *Ivan Osokin* and *Tertium Organum* into an often humorless, dour, and unapproachable teacher, a position he was not truly suited for. Gurdjieff had happened. In the presence of the great master, poetic, life-loving Peter felt somehow childish and immature, all his philosophy and love of beauty and goodness were made to seem mere adolescent romanticism. So he changed himself, "worked on himself," until that weakness disappeared and he became hard. This is why in later life he dismissed his students' remarks about higher consciousness, mysticism, and the miraculous. His dismissals were, no doubt, directed at himself as much as at them: no one is as rigorous in rejecting a former self than the converted. But Peter never really disappeared. He was only hidden, and over time he gradually returned—regrettably, too late. It was unkind of Madame Ouspensky to laugh at her husband's attempts to reach the Inner Circle, but in a way she was right. Ouspensky did not need to find the source of Gurdjieff's ideas, which in any case was more than likely Gurdjieff's own fertile mind. He did not need to find an esoteric school. He did not, perhaps, even need to find the miraculous. It was only at the end of his life that he realized what the real goal of his journey was: himself. One hopes that the next time around, this insight, perhaps the most valuable of the many he passed on to his students, comes to him sooner.

AFTERWORD

Since the cloth edition of this book was first published in 2004, it has attracted two radically different types of response. Some readers have seen it as a cheap attack on Gurdjieff, a gossipy account adding nothing new. Others have appreciated it as a fresh, liberating way of looking at his work and at his relationship with his most famous pupil. But of the many letters and reviews the book has provoked, none has meant as much to me as the one I received from Ouspensky's granddaughter, Tatiana Nagro. After thanking me for sending her a copy and commenting on the book's beautiful and professional presentation, Ms. Nagro added a comment that deserves to be quoted in full. She wrote: "As a child I loved my grandfather, and personally I think he needs and wanted to be separated from Gurdjieff. Without my grandfather's work, few people today would have any detailed knowledge of the system." I couldn't have asked for a better vindication of my own work.

Many of the book's readers have asked about my own involvement with Gurdjieff's system. I originally intended to include a chapter on my time "in the work," but later felt it didn't fit with the rest of the book. I include it now in the hope that this brief account will answer the questions of those who are curious.

I first came across the names of G. I. Gurdjieff and P. D. Ouspensky in 1975, in Colin Wilson's *The Occult*. At the time, I was nineteen and living in New York City, playing bass guitar with the then-unknown pop group Blondie. I had just become interested in books about magic, the occult, and esotericism, and I have to admit that in my first exposure to Gurdjieff, I was more interested in the reports of his remarkable powers than in his austere doctrine. He was as fascinating as the many other figures in Wilson's book—such as Aleister Crowley, Rasputin, and Madame Blavatsky—but I wasn't drawn to his teaching. Two years and many books later, I had changed my mind.

I had read Ouspensky's early work *Tertium Organum* as well as *A New Model of the Universe* and was impressed by both. I then read his account of his time with Gurdjieff, *In Search of the Miraculous,* which had a seriousness and an urgency unlike most of the occult literature I was devouring. Gurdjieff's doctrine—that human beings have enormous powers of consciousness, which are obscured by a mechanical habit of sleep—struck me as self-evident. I believed that we experience only a fraction of what our consciousness is capable of and that the aim of all occult or spiritual practice is to tap this hidden reservoir of power. I had made some attempts to do this on my own, with interesting results. But after covering a lot of fascinating ground, after a while I had to admit I wasn't really getting anywhere.

It was then that I wondered about Gurdjieff. I still had some resistance. I'm not much of a joiner, and Gurdjieff's "Fourth Way" was based on the idea that one can do nothing on one's own; according to him, being in a group was absolutely necessary. This made me hesitate. Other elements put me off, too. For example, I love books and music and found it difficult to accept Gurdjieff's assertion that my favorite poets and composers were just as asleep as everybody else. Nevertheless, there was something about his teaching that attracted me. It certainly struck me as the most demanding and rigorous I had come across. As presented by Ouspensky, it was lucid and almost scientifically precise, although I quickly discovered that this was not the case with Gurdjieff's own books. Most importantly, it was based on experience and knowledge, and this meant that it was honest. In a realm where wishful thinking and self-deception are commonplace, this seemed important.

By the early 1980s, interest in Gurdjieff, who had died in Paris in 1949, was undergoing a kind of revival. New memoirs and accounts by his students seemed to appear overnight. James Webb's definitive study, *The Harmonious Circle,* appeared then, too. Gurdjieff's name was in the air. Yet, unlike now, it was difficult to find a school that practiced his teaching. When you pick up a Fourth Way book at a bookshop today, you'll more than likely find a bookmark inside advertising a Gurdjieff and Ouspensky center. There are dozens of websites dedicated to "the work," the homely name given to Gurdjieff's system. Many of these are bogus, having no connection with Gurdjieff's original groups in Russia. Nevertheless, they show that Gurdjieff and his teaching have a much higher profile today than when I first became involved.

My first encounter with people actually practicing the system was at a public lecture at the Barbizon Hotel on Sixty-third Street. I was surprised at the number of people who attended; apparently, I wasn't the only person in New York who wanted to wake up. One speaker made a point of emphasizing the difference between "I" and "it"; he repeated a certain phrase several times throughout his talk: "Like what it does not like." I took this to mean that "it" is our mechanical, habit-ridden self, which we mistakenly believe is awake, while "I" is our true self, submerged beneath layers of sleep and automatism. At present, "it" dominates us, and a brief period of self-observation shows how little free will we really possess. The aim of the work is to study "it," to learn its habits and character, while at the same time gradually making the "I" stronger. After the lecture, I returned to my apartment excited by what I had heard, wondering if I should call the telephone number on the flyer that had been handed out.

The irony was that my entry into the work was much more close at hand than I realized. A friend who was interested in spiritual ideas knew I was reading a lot about Gurdjieff. We had talked about a variety of things—Jung, Kabbalah, Hinduism, Buddhism—and when I mentioned the lecture to him, he showed great interest. A few days later he asked if I were really interested in getting involved in the work. I said yes. "In that case," he said, "call this number." Then he handed me a piece of paper. On it was a telephone number, but not the one on the flyer. "It's my teacher. I mentioned you to him," he went on. "He's expecting you to call. I've been working with him for about a year, but I wanted to see how serious you were before telling you about it. If you are serious, I'd recommend you call soon."

I did. The man's voice on the other end was steady, deep, and to the point. Would I like to come next week and have a chat? Then he gave me the address.

The meeting place was a small apartment on the Upper East Side. A woman answered the door, and I was ushered into a small room and asked to sit down. The apartment was decorated in an Eastern fashion, with Persian carpets and wall hangings, Oriental ornaments, and *objets d'art*. There were also many paintings; these, I later found, were the work of my host. After a few minutes the man I had spoken with came in and introduced himself. His name was Paul, and I later discovered that he was one of the principal teachers of the Gurdjieff "movements," the extremely difficult sacred dances that Gurdjieff claimed he had learned at the mysterious monastery of the Sarmoung Brotherhood. Whether or not this was true remains an open question, but a few years later, when I began practicing the movements myself, where they came from seemed irrelevant. What was clear was their ability to evoke unusual states of consciousness.

Paul was the most composed person I had ever met. I was impressed by his movements; he seemed relaxed yet alert and carried himself with an economy of action. He had presence. After introducing himself, he sat there for a few moments, untroubled by the nervousness most people feel in such situations and usually relieve through talk. Then he asked me about myself—what did I do, and why was I interested in the work?

Although I was only twenty-four, I already had a few achievements under my belt. By that time I had left Blondie and started my own group. One of my songs had been a top-ten hit. I had been on television and radio and had been interviewed for magazines and newspapers. I was playing to large crowds and making a comfortable living.

All this meant very little to Paul. He took it all in, nodded, and then asked why I was interested in joining his group. It was an unexpectedly difficult question. In the end I fumbled and lamely said that I wanted to wake up. "Yes," Paul remarked, "but that will take time." He told me how the work required seriousness and commitment, and he wondered if I could make that kind of commitment. I said I could. "Well," he said, "I have a beginners' group that meets once a week. You can come to that and we will see." He wrote down the address and handed it to me, then said, "Please come on time."

Paul's group met in a basement apartment on a side street between Lexington and Park Avenues. That first meeting set the pattern for the rest. The group sat on hard wooden chairs in a bare room, the only other furnishing being a wooden table on which rested a vase of flowers, a pitcher of water, and some glasses. Paul sat in front of us; occasionally at the meetings, there was another chair beside his and another teacher would join him. There was no lecture. We sat in an uncomfortable silence until someone found the courage to speak. General questions were frowned upon; remarks had to be focused on practical matters relating to the exercises Paul had given.

The group had been given an exercise; after that first meeting, Paul taught it to me as well. It was called "sensing your body." The instructions were to sit in a chair with your legs slightly apart and your hands on your knees. Then you were to sense your right arm, starting at the shoulder and working down to your fingers. You were to continue with the right leg, then with the left leg and left arm, and then start again, this time with the right leg, then the left leg, and so on. After completing a cycle and returning to the beginning, you were to sense the top of the head, then the face, then the neck. Finally, you were to sense your whole body. It was difficult at first to understand what was meant by "sensing," but after a time I experienced a curious tingling, as if a slight drizzle were falling on me. After some weeks, I was told to end the exercise by standing up and taking a few steps, while maintaining my sensation.

Although Paul tried to keep us focused on the exercise, people would invariably bring up personal matters during the discussions. One of the reasons Gurdjieff emphasized the need for groups is that he knew different personalities would grate on each other, creating the friction he believed was necessary for work. I was often impatient when people brought up some personal crisis and subjected the group to a long monologue about it. I realize now that this was probably why Paul let them do it: It provided an opportunity for us to see our own short-comings. After one such meeting, my displeasure must have been very evident because Paul took me aside and in true Gurdjieffian fashion gave me a brisk talking-to, informing me that I would never get anywhere as long as I thought I knew better than anyone else. Sadly, I've failed to profit from this advice as much as I might have.

I practiced sitting in the morning and "self-remembering" during the day, making "appointments" with myself when, no matter what I was doing, I would try to feel a full self-awareness.

This may sound easy, but it wasn't. In the midst of going about your affairs, suddenly to pull yourself out of the stream of events and remember that you are "here" requires considerable effort. Indeed, Gurdjieff's basic idea was that we do not "remember ourselves"; instead, we are habitually sunk into a kind of half-dream state we mistake for consciousness. This surely seemed to be the case, it being difficult enough for me just to remember my appointments with myself, let alone to work up a real sense of my being, especially when I was with someone else.

People in the work celebrate Gurdjieff's birthday on January 13; for my first celebration, I was invited to a gathering in a house outside the city. Along with a few other people, I drove out with my friend who had introduced me to Paul. I was impressed by the house—it was more a mansion—and by the number of people there. It was an odd gathering; despite the many in attendance, the atmosphere wasn't festive. Nor was it solemn, although there was certainly an air of seriousness.

After someone took our coats, we were invited to move into a large room and take a seat. Then I was introduced to Gurdjieff's ritual of toasts, accomplished with powerful vodka. We were each given a tumbler and, after an appropriate toast, obliged to empty it. This happened several times. I hadn't eaten yet, and the effects came on quickly. They added to the oddness of what happened next. Someone announced that, in honor of the occasion, we would be treated to a special performance of the Babylonian epic *Gilgamesh*. That in itself was unusual, but it was no preparation for what followed. I looked to the center of the room where a small stage had been erected and recognized the actor Bill Murray, from *Saturday Night Live*. I had no idea that he was also interested in Gurdjieff's ideas, or that he was involved in the same organization that I was. I enjoyed the performance, but it was difficult after my toasts to keep a straight face whenever I heard him say "Enkidu."

In 1982 I left New York and moved to Los Angeles, where my involvement with the work became deeper and more intense. I joined a group and also started attending "ideas meetings," where sections of *In Search of the Miraculous* or Gurdjieff's jawbreaker of a book, *Beelzebub's Tales to His Grandson,* were read and discussed. My friends and I were reading as much literature on the work as we could find —fascinating books by Maurice Nicoll, J. G. Bennett, Rodney Collin, and other Fourth Way writers.

I also started attending work weekends. At a large house north of the Hollywood Hills, people from different groups would gather for intensive "work days." These would begin with a morning talk, followed by a new exercise, which we were asked to perform throughout the day. As Gurdjieff had done at his Prieure in Fontainebleau, the leader would give students physical tasks to perform: gardening, cleaning, preparing meals, carpentry. The task itself and how well it was performed wasn't the aim of the exercise; rather, the idea was to remember oneself, to focus on the work at hand, and to perform what Gurdjieff called "conscious labor."

A famous story about Gurdjieff's Prieure involved the editor A. R. Orage, who arrived there in 1923 expecting to receive words of wisdom from the master and was instead handed a shovel and told to dig. Orage dug until his back ached and he was in tears; then he was told to fill the hole in again. He wondered what madness he had gotten into until one day he found himself enjoying the digging and feeling no pain at all: He had forced himself beyond his artificial limits and broken through to his hidden reservoirs of energy.

I experienced a milder version of the Orage treatment when, after spending an afternoon painting a long wooden fence, I was informed that it wasn't the right color and I had to paint it all over again. I was indignant until I realized that the painting wasn't the point; instead, it was the insights that came to me while doing it. On another occasion, while raking leaves, I had what I believe to be an unalloyed moment of wakefulness. Reaching down to scoop a batch of wet leaves into a trash bag, I found myself staring at them in amazement, as if I had never really seen a leaf before. I remembered how fresh and clean the world had seemed as a child, and for a few moments I enjoyed that same clarity. It was then that the whole idea of sleep and mechanicalness became real to me and not just an idea.

It was also around this time that I started practicing the movements. At first they were impossible: The old game of trying to rub your stomach with one hand while patting your head with the other gives some idea of what's involved, but that is a hundred times easier. About a dozen students would line up in rows and, to the accompaniment of a piano, throw themselves into contortions, like puppets with their strings cut. Often I would drop out in disgust with myself. But one evening I persevered, and after ignoring my dismay I found myself doing the movements with ease and confidence. I experienced a sudden rush of power. At the end, I was so full of energy that I wanted to get in my car and drive nonstop to San Francisco— eight hours away—just for the fun of it.

In the summer of 1983, a friend and I decided to set out on our own mini "search for the miraculous" by taking a trip to Europe. Along with visiting Stonehenge, Avebury, Chartres Cathedral, and other sacred sites, we visited Gurdjieff's Prieure in Fontainebleau, which by then was an abandoned château. In Paris we also tracked down the apartment on the Rue des Colonels Renards, near the Etoile, where, during the German occupation, Gurdjieff had conducted his secret groups. He also spent his last days there. A year later, with the same friend I visited Franklin Farms in New Jersey, the site of Ouspensky's own "prieure."

It was on my return from Europe that my doubts about my place in the work began. I have always had an eclectic mind, and while absorbing all I could about Gurdjieff's ideas, I was also taking in a great deal of other material. Making comparisons was frowned upon, but I found it difficult not to put Gurdjieff's system in context with the work of other thinkers. I saw no point in denying that many of his ideas had parallels in the work of other philosophers and psychologists and that, although his presentation and practice were startling and very different, his basic ideas were not as unique as his more convinced students believed. Many people in the work viewed Gurdjieff as something of a superman, and, although he was without doubt one of the most remarkable men ever to live, he was not, I believed, infallible. More to the point, it struck me as dangerous to consider *any* teacher infallible, whether it be Gurdjieff or anyone else.

Other issues, too, led me to feel less eager to continue. For one thing, I found it difficult to understand why Gurdjieff treated Ouspensky, his best pupil, in the questionable way he had; in fact, the mystery of his behavior remained with me long after I had dropped out of the work. Twenty years later, it was what inspired me to write this book. It was difficult not to be impressed with Gurdjieff, but I began to wonder about his motives. Also, I was less than unequivocal in my appreciation of *Beelzebub's Tales,* the bible of the work. Although I ploughed through it, and found much of value, I also found it almost unreadable and couldn't fathom why he would purposely make his ideas difficult to grasp. Then, too, my other reading was raising many questions. Although at first I had been scornful of any criticism about the work, I now could see why many people whom I considered intelligent and insightful would be repelled by it. Moreover, although I had attained some results, I felt that after four years I was pretty much where I had started. This seemed to be the case for other people as well, although it struck me that, for many, the work had become more a lifestyle than a means to achieve an end, as it had originally been for me. Finally, the teaching itself, for all of its rigor and discipline, seemed curiously lacking in *positive* content. The impetus behind "working" seemed to be the negative motivation of escaping from sleep. In the work of other writers—for example, that of Colin Wilson—I found more optimistic goals, but when I brought this point up during meetings, I was advised that both the lack of positive goals and the particular goals Wilson proposed were only ideas, simply another form of sleep.

These ideas, however, were giving me much more incentive than the now-routine work repertoire. They provided a needed carrot to complement the Gurdjieffian stick, and I was not about to drop them. I stuck with it for a while and experienced some profound soul searching, but in the end I thought it was dishonest to continue with so many reservations. After some weeks of indecisiveness, I announced to my teacher that I would be leaving. At first I felt a bit at loose ends, but soon a feeling of freshness and freedom surfaced, and to this day I consider it the right decision. I had learned a lot from the work, and I have a lot of respect for its practitioners. But, in the end, it was not for me. It was not for Ouspensky, either, at least in the form in which it was taught by his master; and in this book, *In Search of P. D. Ouspensky: The Genius in the Shadow of Gurdjieff,* I have tried to understand why.

Editor's note: Gary Lachman's account of his involvement with Gurdjieff's esoteric system of thought was first published in the November-December 2004 issue of Quest Magazine, *under the title "In the Work."*

NOTES

Introduction. The Seeker and the Sly Man

1. Throughout this book, "work" is used both in the specific sense of Gurdjieff and Ouspensky's teaching, and in the generic sense of "the business at hand." Gurdjieff's Work is here capitalized to make this distinction, but for the remainder of the book, both uses will be in lowercase, in the faith that context will make the difference clear.

2. Denis Saurat, quoted in C. S. Nott, *Journey through This World* (London: Routledge & Kegan Paul, 1969), p. 47.

3. Frank Pinder, quoted in ibid., p. 91.

4. G. I. Gurdjieff, quoted in ibid., p. 107.

Chapter 1. Childhood of the Magician

1. P. D. Ouspensky, *A Further Record* (London: Arkana, 1986), p. 1.

2. Rom Landau, *God Is My Adventure* (London: Faber and Faber, 1939), p. 175.

3. For an account of my own experiences with precognitive dreams, see my article "Dreaming Ahead" in the winter 1997 issue of *The Quest.*

4. P. D. Ouspensky, *In Search of the Miraculous* (London: Routledge & Kegan Paul, 1983), p. 3.

5. P. D. Ouspensky, *A New Model of the Universe* (New York: Alfred Knopf, 1969), p. 3.

6. Ibid.

7. Ouspensky, *A Further Record,* p. 300.

8. Boris Mouravieff, *Ouspensky, Gurdjieff, and the Work: "Fragments of an Unknown Teaching"* (Chicago: Praxis Research Institute, 1997), p. 11.

9. Colin Wilson, *The Strange Life of P. D. Ouspensky* (London: Aquarian Press, 1993), p. 15.

10. Later, in 1913, Ouspensky would give a lecture on Mikhail Artzybasheff's novel *The Breaking Point,* which deals with the question of suicide; Ivan Osokin's sad fate suggests that Ouspensky may have had a more than literary interest in the theme.

11. P. D. Ouspensky, *Strange Life of Ivan Osokin* (London: Arkana, 1987), pp. 10–11.

12. Ouspensky, *A New Model of the Universe,* p. 433.

13. Ouspensky, *Strange Life of Ivan Osokin,* p. 13.

14. Rosamund Bland, *Extracts from Nine Letters at the Beginning of P. D. Ouspensky's Work in 1921* (Cape Town: Stourton Press, 1952); Marie Seton, "The Case Of P. D. Ouspensky," *Quest* no. 34, Bombay, India, 1962.

15. Ouspensky, *Strange Life of Ivan Osokin,* pp. 123–24.

16. Ibid. p. 125. Note: Italics in quotations are in the original unless otherwise identified.

17. Ibid.

18. Ouspensky, *A New Model of the Universe,* pp. 474–75.

19. Ouspensky, *Strange Life of Ivan Osokin,* p. 82.

20. Ibid.

21. Ibid., p. 84.

22. Ibid., p. 87.

23. Ibid., p. 88.

24. Ibid., pp. 100–101.

25. Ibid., pp. 106–12.

26. Ibid., p. 99.

Chapter 2. Dreams of Hidden Knowledge

1. Carl Bechhofer-Roberts, in P. D. Ouspensky, *Letters from Russia 1919* (London: Arkana, 1991), pp. 56–58, excerpted from Carl Bechhofer-Roberts, *In Denikin's Russia* (London: Collins, 1921).

2. Like all of the material in *A New Model of the Universe,* Ouspensky's chapter on dreams was begun at an earlier time, in this case 1905, and completed at a later date. Not having access to his original manuscript and, more significantly, not reading Russian, it is unclear to me how much Ouspensky altered his initial writings in view of his work with Gurdjieff. A close reading of the book does reveal some very obvious work ideas. It's possible that, in my account, what I see as Ouspensky's "prescience" regarding some of Gurdjieff's ideas may indeed merely be material added to the text after the fact.

3. For a brief survey on the history of hypnagogia, see my article "Waking Dreams" in *Fortean Times* no. 163, October 2002; also the chapter "Hypnagogia" in my book *A Secret History of Consciousness* (Great Barrington, Mass.: Lindisfarne Press, 2003).

4. Ouspensky, *A New Model of the Universe,* p. 243.

5. For Daumal's experiments in lucid dreaming and other altered states of consciousness see his essay "A Fundamental Experience" in *The Power of Words* (San Francisco: City Lights, 1993). For an account of Daumal's relationship with Gurdjieff, see my article "Climbing Mount Analogue" in *The Quest* vol. 89, no. 5, September/October 2001. Two good popular accounts of lucid dreaming and the dream state in general are Stephen LaBerge's *Lucid Dreaming* (New York: Ballantine Books, 1985) and *Creative Dreaming* (New York: Ballantine Books, 1974) by Patricia Garfield. A short but highly informative academic study is *Lucid Dreaming: The Paradox of Consciousness during Sleep* (London: Routledge, 1994) by Celia Green and Charles McCreery. Fredrick Van Eeden's early essay "A Study of Dreams" can be found in *Altered States of Consciousness,* edited by Charles Tart (New York: Anchor Books, 1969).

6. Ouspensky, *A New Model of the Universe,* p. 245.

7. Ibid., p. 252.

8. Ibid., p. 6.

9. Ibid., p. 252. It is curious that Ouspensky speaks of "golden dots, sparks and tiny stars" appearing before his eyes. This experience of what are called "entopic lights," or *eigenlicht,* is a kind of prelude to the hypnagogic state. In his little-known work *An Essay on the Origin of Thought* (1973), the Danish philosopher Jurij Moskvitin gives an account of his own investigation into the roots of human perception, which he sees as intimately related to this fascinating form of optical fireworks. For a brief account of Moskvitin's ideas see "Thinking about Thinking: Jurij Moskvitin and the Anthroposphere" in my book *A Secret History of Consciousness.*

10. Ouspensky seems to have missed an important aspect of both hypnagogic experiences as well as dreams: that they are both highly self-symbolic. Around the same time that Ouspensky was making his observations, another dream researcher, the psychologist Herbert Silberer, stumbled upon this curious discovery. Silberer found that his hypnagogic visions corresponded to his thoughts just before drifting into sleep, and also to his emotional state, or, as Ouspensky also observed, to his physical condition. Ouspensky, it seems, was aware of how dreams and hypnagogic phenomena "symbolized" his physical state—his feet caught in the blankets—but apparently missed Silberer's other two categories. Another dream researcher aware of this self-symbolic capacity was the Swedish religious philosopher Emanuel Swedenborg. For a brief account of Silberer's work see my *Fortean Times* article "Waking Dreams" (see note 3, this chapter), which also touches on Swedenborg's ideas. The most thorough study of hypnagogia to date is Andreas Mavromatis's exhaustive study *Hypnagogia: The Unique State of Consciousness between Wakefulness and Sleep* (London: Routledge, 1987).

11. P. D. Ouspensky, *Talks with a Devil* (Wellingborough, England: Turnstone Press, 1972), p. 93.

12. Ouspensky, *A New Model of the Universe,* pp. 248–49.

13. Ibid., pp. 263–64. Curiously, although Ouspensky didn't live to know it, his insight has in recent years gained strong scientific support. Recognizing that the brain's "forty-hertz oscillations," associated with consciousness, also occur during REM sleep— i.e., sleep typically linked to dream states—the neuroscientists Denis Pare and Rudolfo Llinas concluded that the only difference between our dreaming and waking states is that in waking states the "closed system that generates oscillatory states" is modulated by stimuli from the outside world. The external world we perceive through our senses while awake, then, may really be a kind of waking dream, or at least a kind of continuous dream state onto which is added a waking-state topping, which is exactly what Ouspensky is saying.

14. Ibid., p. 255.

15. Ibid.

16. Ibid., p. 261.

17. Held in 1899 and 1907, The Hague Peace Conferences (they were also known as simply The Hague Conferences) were a forerunner of both the League of Nations and the United Nations. Held in The Hague, Netherlands, these international conferences lasting several months were generally aimed at codifying the rules of warfare and limiting arms development.

18. Peter Washington, *Madame Blavatsky's Baboon* (London: Secker & Warburg, 1993), p. 160.

19. For a full account of the satanic world of the Russian *fin de siècle* see Kristi A. Groberg's essay "The Shade of Lucifer's Dark Wing: Satanism in Silver Age Russia," in *The Occult in Russian and Soviet Culture*, edited by Bernice Glatzer Rosenthal (Ithaca and London: Cornell University Press, 1997), pp. 99–133.

20. Ouspensky, *A New Model of the Universe*, p. 114.

21. Ibid., p. 6.

22. J. G. Bennett, introduction to *Talks with a Devil*, p. 12. Even here Ouspensky's links with Theosophy prove crucial. The two stories making up *Talks with a Devil* were written during Ouspensky's

visit to India and Ceylon in 1914. Originally published in a St. Petersburg newspaper, they were collected and issued as a book in 1916. In the 1920s, Ouspensky, then in London, began collecting the material that would eventually be published as *A New Model of the Universe*. He initially thought to include one of the stories, "The Benevolent Devil," but changed his mind. But the idea of translating the stories remained. J. G. Bennett remarks that he and Ouspensky discussed publishing an edition in the 1930s. All of Ouspensky's copies of the 1916 edition, along with the rest of his library, were lost during the Bolshevik revolution, but Ouspensky suggested to Bennett that he might be able to locate a copy through the Theosophical Society. According to Bennett, Maud Hoffman, a friend of Annie Besant and C. W. Leadbeater, found a copy at the Reading Room of the British Library. It was from this copy that the English translation was finally made.

23. Ouspensky, *A New Model of the Universe*, p. 338.

24. Gurdjieff, too, expressed the belief that the Sphinx was much older than official Egyptology recognizes, as his remarks about "pre-sand Egypt" in *Meetings with Remarkable Men* suggest.

25. Hinton's feats of memory have a long occult heritage, going back to the fabled "art of memory" first practiced by the ancients and later revived by Renaissance magicians like Giordano Bruno. See Frances Yates, *The Art of Memory* (London: Routledge & Kegan Paul, 1966). Memorization of "tattwa" symbols and "god forms" was also standard practice among members of the Hermetic Order of the Golden Dawn.

Chapter 3. Thinking in Other Categories

1. Antonio Melechi, *Mindscapes* (West Yorkshire, England: Mono Books, 1998), pp. 21–22.

2. Ibid., p. 20.

3. William James, *Varieties of Religious Experience*, (New York: Collier, 1977), p. 305.

4. P. D. Ouspensky, *Tertium Organum* (New York: Alfred Knopf, 1981), p. 258.

5. As a journalist in a time of experiment and radical behavior, Ouspensky was sure to have known—or at least known of—people who took drugs for less metaphysical reasons; in *Strange Life of Ivan Osokin,* for example, he describes one character preparing his glass of absinthe. Cocaine, morphine, and other substances were popular among the "demonic" crowd of his day; Valery Briussov, the doyen of Russian occult decadence, was several times hospitalized for morphine addiction. As far as we know, Ouspensky's drug of choice was alcohol (vodka, preferably with a salted cucumber), and he didn't develop any addictions until late in life. Like his investigations into dreams, his drug experiments were carried out in a scientific spirit.

6. Ouspensky, *A New Model of the Universe,* p. 277.

7. Ibid., p. 280.

8. From accounts of other drug experiences, Ouspensky's use of the term "hieroglyph" suggests that along with nitrous oxide he more than likely also used hashish. In his essay "The Psychology of Hashish," written around the same time as Ouspensky was conducting his experiments, the magician Aleister Crowley uses "hieroglyph" in an uncannily similar context. Nitrous oxide inhalation is known to produce the sort of metaphysical insights and flood of associations that Ouspensky is at pains to describe, while hashish—which Ouspensky more than likely ate—elicits a dreamy reverie full of striking and highly symbolic imagery.

9. Ouspensky says he was "very young at the time" and "very much depressed" by the death. I at first thought he was speaking about the death of his father or grandfather, but the description of his thoughts at the time suggests that he was somewhat older than he was when their deaths took place. Ouspensky, we know, was a very precocious child, yet the thoughts he recounts still seem to me beyond those of a four-year-old. See *A New Model of the Universe,* pp. 299–300.

10. Reading Ouspensky's account, my first thought was that he was speaking of his friend Sherbakov, but the dates do not seem to tally. I now think he may have been speaking of his sister—especially as the importance of this person's "last years" is repeated several times, and as we know, Ouspensky's sister spent the last years of her life in prison. It is also understandable that although there was clearly little Ouspensky could do, he would still feel a great sense of guilt and responsibility towards her. To feel that we did not do enough for a loved one who has died is a common human trait. For a man with Ouspensky's strong sense of the importance and irreversibility of the past, and his equally strong desire to change it, to know that his sister died at the hands of her captors must have been deeply saddening. A cynic might suggest that Ouspensky's "revelation" that "we are no more responsible for the events in one another's lives than we are responsible for the features of one another's faces" was merely a means of stilling his guilt. Perhaps. I prefer to think that a grief-struck, saddened man gained some relief through recognizing a basic law of life. In Ouspensky's account there is nothing to suggest that he accepted this insight easily; on the contrary, one gets the impression that it took a certain strength to embrace it. See ibid. pp. 300–301.

11. Ouspensky, *Talks with a Devil,* pp. 100–111.

Chapter 4. Tertium Organum

1. Ouspensky, *Tertium Organum,* p. 137.

2. Ouspensky, *Strange Life of Ivan Osokin,* p. 138.

3. For a brief account of Swedenborg's influence on Baudelaire as well as many other poets and writers, see my chapters on him in *The Dedalus Book of the Occult: A Dark Muse* (London: Dedalus, 2003).

4. In his magnum opus *The Ever-Present Origin,* the German philosopher Jean Gebser (1905–1973) argues that mankind has passed through four previous "structures of consciousness" and, since

the beginning of the twentieth century, is in the process of entering a fifth structure that will integrate the previous four. Central to this new consciousness structure is the transcending of the "perspectival" perception characteristic of our current, dissolving "mental-rational" structure. Gebser finds evidence for this shift in many cultural phenomena, particularly the Cubist painting of the early twentieth century. Yet Hinton's notions about hyperspace predate Cubism by more than twenty years. For more on "aperspectival consciousness," see my chapters on Gebser in *A Secret History of Consciousness*.

5. Someone might argue that particle physics, which studies unimaginably small items like quarks, leptons, and so on, is certainly engaged in investigating the "invisible." Yet these and other elementary particles are capable of being observed by the scientific devices physicists employ and hence are visible (measurable) in some way.

6. Michio Kaku, *Hyperspace* (Oxford: Oxford University Press, 1995), pp. 65–67.

7. Ouspensky, *Tertium Organum*, p. 166.

8. Ibid., p. 257.

9. Ibid., p. 138.

10. Ibid., p. 142.

11. Ibid., p. 132.

12. Ibid., p. 133.

13. Ibid.

Chapter 5. The Stray Dog

1. Ouspensky, *Tertium Organum*, p. 193.

2. Ibid., p. 286.

3. Ouspensky's concern with the inadequacies of language puts him in the company of several writers, poets, and philosophers who, in the early part of the twentieth century, faced what they

saw as a "crisis of language." Perhaps the best known of these is the Austrian philosopher Ludwig Wittgenstein, who famously argued that "of that which we cannot speak we must remain silent"—which for Wittgenstein encompassed everything of value. Other thinkers concerned with the growing inability of language to convey the complexity of experience were Karl Kraus, Robert Musil, Hermann Broch, Maurice Maeterlink, and Hugo von Hoffmanstahl, all of whom, to some extent, investigated different aspects of mysticism. For a good introduction to this important period in Western thought, see George Steiner's *Language and Silence* (1970) and *Extraterritorial* (1976).

4.   The Russian avant-garde were not, of course, the only modernists influenced by occult or mystical ideas. Wassily Kandinsky, considered the first abstract painter, was a follower of Rudolf Steiner. Piet Mondrian, known for his geometrical canvases, was a Theosophist. Musicians, too, were tuned into the mystical vibrations. The Theosophical composer Alexandre Scriabin dreamed of a massive "total art work" to be performed in an Indian temple. Along with music, this would include incense and a strange instrument he called a "color organ," a keyboard that would produce colored lights associated with different tones, exemplifying the phenomena of synesthesia. Arnold Schoenberg, the father of atonal music, was a devotee of Emanuel Swedenborg. I have already mentioned Rudolf Steiner's influence on the novelist Andrei Bely. For more on the link between the occult, mysticism, and modern culture, see my *Dedalus Book of the Occult*.

5.   One question that comes to mind is whether the many readers of *Tertium Organum* knew that the central inspiration for the work was Ouspensky's drug experiments. In the first English translation, based on the 1916 second Russian edition, Ouspensky remarks that descriptions of mystical experiences stimulated by "narcotics" would be included in his forthcoming book *The Wisdom of the Gods*—the original title of *A New Model of the Universe*. Yet his reference in *Tertium Organum* to his own participation in the experiments is ambiguous. Also, as any reader with even a limited knowledge of psychoactive substances knows,

neither nitrous oxide nor hashish is a narcotic. *Tertium Organum* is a book with a peculiar publishing history and, like all Ouspensky's works, was subject to several revisions. Subsequent English editions omitted references to both *The Wisdom of the Gods* and the description of drug experiences. Ouspensky may have omitted the reference because he had given up on publishing *The Wisdom of the Gods,* or because he had changed its title, or because he had decided not to emphasize his own participation in the drug experiments. Ouspensky revised the second US edition of *Tertium Organum* in the early 1920s; by then, the anti-drug sensibility that would lead to the draconian Anslinger laws criminalizing natural substances like marijuana was becoming prominent. Ouspensky was always sensitive to the authorities—a leftover from his days under the Tsar and the Bolsheviks—and so it's possible he wanted to lessen any chance of offense.

6. Anna Butkovsky-Hewitt's book *With Gurdjieff in St. Petersburg and Paris* (London: Routledge & Kegan Paul, 1978) was written when she was in her nineties, which may explain the ambiguity about her dating. She has her first meeting with Ouspensky taking place in 1916, but the context of her conversation suggests an earlier date, more than likely 1912. Following James Moore in *Gurdjieff: The Anatomy of a Myth* (Shaftesbury: Element, 1991) and William Patrick Patterson, I accept 1912 as marking her first meeting with Ouspensky.

7. Butkovsky-Hewitt, *With Gurdjieff in St. Petersburg and Paris,* p. 18.

8. Ibid., pp. 18–19.

9. Ouspensky was certainly not alone in holding a romantic vision of India and the East. The idea that the East holds the promise of wisdom unknown in the West has a long tradition, and in Ouspensky's own time figures like Madame Blavatsky and Edward Carpenter made a trip to the East almost a requirement for personal spiritual evolution. Others who ventured eastward were Count Hermann Keyserling, whose *Travel Diary of a Philosopher* (1919) became a bestseller, and the novelist Hermann Hesse, from whose novel *The Journey to the East* derives the phrase.

Ironically, although he did travel to Ceylon and Sumatra in 1911—two years before Ouspensky—Hesse didn't really make it to India, and his accounts of his journey suggest it was not a pleasant experience. See Ralph Freedman's *Hermann Hesse: Pilgrim of Crisis* (1979) for a description of Hesse's failed journey to the East. Like Ouspensky, Hesse discovered that visiting the India of his *imagination* was a more inspiring voyage than his actual sojourn in the Orient; curiously, the two writers followed similar itineraries: both speak of a visit to the holy Temple of the Tooth in Kandy. Unlike in our own era of easy air travel and near-ly instantaneous communication via the Internet, travel in the early part of the twentieth century was a kind of initiatory experience, often combining inconvenience with a certain amount of personal danger, offering a complete break from one's normal routine. To travel from St. Petersburg to India was no simple feat, and this in itself, aside from Ouspensky's vivid observations, would have made him a sought-after authority on the mysterious ways of the East.

10. In contemplating how to proceed in the wake of his nitrous oxide experiments, Ouspensky spoke of employing certain methods involving breathing, fasting, exercises of the attention and imagination, and "above all, of overcoming oneself at moments of passivity or lassitude" (*A New Model of the Universe*, p. 9).

11. Ouspensky, *Talks with a Devil*, p. 131.

Chapter 6. The Incomparable Mr. G.

1. Ouspensky, *A New Model of the Universe*, p. 11.

2. Butkovsky-Hewitt, *With Gurdjieff in St. Petersburg and Paris*, p. 31.

3. Ouspensky, *In Search of the Miraculous*, p. 3.

4. Ibid., p. 5.

5. Ibid., p. 4.

6. Quoted in Maria Carlson, *No Religion Higher than Truth: A History of the Theosophical Movement in Russia 1875–1922* (Princeton: Princeton University Press, 1993), p. 75.

7. Ouspensky, *A New Model of the Universe*, p. 9.

8. Ouspensky, *In Search of the Miraculous*, p. 7.

9. James Webb, *The Harmonious Circle* (New York: G. P. Putnam's Sons, 1980), p. 25.

10. For Gurdjieff and the Great Game, see ibid., pp. 48–73.

11. Strangely, Gurdjieff as Prince Ozay seems to embody the type of "romantic" guru who Ouspensky at first hoped to meet, but after his failed "search," spoke of only ironically. As we will see, at their first meeting, Ouspensky had a "vision" of Gurdjieff as he may have appeared in his guise as the prince.

12. Although, as his career makes clear, Gurdjieff had no problem addressing people, he seems to have operated best in small groups, where his personal force could be felt—and be seen to be felt—more immediately. When, for example, his Prieure in Fontainebleau became successful and drew large numbers of students, Gurdjieff began to have doubts about it. Not long after, he was involved in a near-fatal car crash. Although devotees maintain otherwise, none of his books—except perhaps *Meetings with Remarkable Men*—reach a wide audience or are particularly successful in presenting his ideas. His last years were spent teaching in the intimate setting of a small dining room in his Parisian flat.

13. Ouspensky, *In Search of the Miraculous*, p. 15.

14. Butkovsky-Hewitt, *With Gurdjieff in St. Petersburg and Paris*, p. 31.

Chapter 7. Meeting a Remarkable Man

1. Ouspensky, *In Search of the Miraculous*, p. 7.

2. Anonymous, collected in *Views from the Real World: Early Talks of Gurdjieff* (New York: E. P. Dutton, 1975), pp. 3–4.

3. Ibid., p. 10.

4. What became of Gurdjieff's early Moscow group is unknown. Sergei Mercourov went on to become a highly successful sculptor, famous for his death masks of Tolstoy and Lenin. About Vladimir Pohl I was unable to gain more information.

5. Ouspensky, *In Search of the Miraculous*, p. 14.

6. Ibid., p. 15.

7. Ibid., p. 18.

8. Ibid.

9. Ibid., pp. 18–19.

10. Ibid., p. 20.

Chapter 8. Finding the Miraculous

1. Butkovsky-Hewitt, *With Gurdjieff in St. Petersburg and Paris*, p. 35.

2. Ibid., pp. 35–36.

3. It's curious that Anna should speak of Gurdjieff's eyes in this way. In fact, Gurdjieff's eyes were the first thing most people noticed about him. For example, when J. G. Bennett encountered Gurdjieff in Constantinople in 1920, he remarked that Gurdjieff's eyes "were so different that I wondered if the light had played some trick on me." And when the composer Thomas de Hartmann met Gurdjieff for the first time, in the company of Dr. Stoerneval, he spoke of Gurdjieff as the man with "those eyes." This is curious because, prior to meeting Gurdjieff, Ouspensky spoke sarcastically of "people who, in the presence of (an) Oriental, suddenly feel he is looking right through them, seeing all their feelings, thoughts, and desires" (*In Search of the Miraculous*, p. 7). He goes on to speak of people who, when caught in "the Oriental's" gaze, "have a strange sensation in their legs and cannot move." This was precisely the experience of the journalist Rom Landau when he met Gurdjieff in a New York hotel room in 1935. What Ouspensky originally saw as evidence of charlatanism becomes, for most people who met him, proof of Gurdjieff's power.

4. Butkovsky-Hewitt, *With Gurdjieff in St. Petersburg and Paris*, pp. 35–36.

5. Ibid.

6. Ibid.

7. Years later, at the end of a trip to the United States, on returning a valuable harmonium he had borrowed during his stay, Gurdjieff laughed when A. R. Orage remarked that now it would be even more valuable as a "sacred relic." Orage thought of Gurdjieff as a "solar God," and Gurdjieff himself once remarked that after his death churches would be established for the teaching of his ideas.

8. Mouravieff, *Ouspensky, Gurdjieff, and the Work,* pp. 11–12.

9. Ouspensky, *In Search of the Miraculous,* p. 154.

Chapter 9. You Do Not Remember Yourself

1. Although his followers maintain that Gurdjieff's ideas and system are unique, familiarity with similar notions of other thinkers shows that this is not really the case, at least not to the degree expressed by students of the Fourth Way. In this instance, "personality" and "essence" are, to me at least, very close to C. G. Jung's "persona" and "Self"—although Jung is less scathing about the flaws of personality and maintains that to be effective in the world an individual needs a strong persona, a kind of mask, protecting the true Self from an abrasive environment. "False personality," another of Gurdjieff's terms, can, I believe, be related to Jung's concept of the shadow—all those unsavory aspects of oneself that one would like to ignore. Similarly, Jung shared with Gurdjieff the central belief that unbalanced development is the most common problem of modern humanity. Both of them argued that for an individual to achieve wholeness, all sides of the psyche need to be actualized, not, as is most often the case with modern individuals, merely the logical, rational ego. This belief was also espoused by Rudolf Steiner who, in a different language and with different emphasis, also spoke of man being "asleep" in different parts of his being.

   A full survey of the points of contact between Gurdjieff's and other thinkers' ideas is beyond the scope of this book and would perhaps prove tedious reading. However, some of the main themes of the Fourth Way can be found not only in other esoteric doctrines, which might be expected, but in mainstream sources. For example, while writing this book I chanced to reread Arthur Koestler's classic attack on behaviorism, *The Ghost in the Machine*. Not only does Koestler go into great detail about the various levels or gradations of consciousness, human and otherwise, but his central theme is the need to recognize what he calls a hierarchy of acquired habits—a series of reflexes ranging from conscious volition to automatic response. To take myself as an example, my conscious intention to write this note leads downward from the intuitions I am trying to form into words to my fingers hitting the keys on the keyboard. Between the vague, fleeting intuitions and the end product a whole series of behavior patterns are activated and set in motion, many of which happen automatically. I do not consciously direct my fingers as they hit the keys, although at one time, when I was learning to type, I did. That function has now been taken over by a kind of automatic pilot, which allows me to focus on the ideas I am trying to express. Yet often—and this is where Gurdjieff's ideas come in—through habit and lack of challenge, we give up a great deal of our conscious control and rely almost exclusively on our automatic pilot. When this happens, we can reach a state in which we are very much "asleep" although to all intents and purposes we appear "awake." A break in routine, an unfamiliar setting, or a new, unusual challenge demands from us a new response and cuts off the automatic pilot, forcing us to be "present" and deal with the situation. In a sense, all of Gurdjieff's radical behavior, and the demanding and at times dangerous conditions he created, can be seen as attempts to break the circuit of habit and elicit from his students new and creative patterns of behavior.

I don't believe Koestler had more than a passing familiarity with Gurdjieff, and from his remarks about other "gurus" I would be surprised if he thought him worthy of study. Yet Koestler's notion of the "holon," in which an individual, whether a person, atom, or galaxy, is both an independent unit and a part of a greater whole (also found in *The Ghost in the Machine*) is remarkably similar to Gurdjieff's ideas on scale. In saying this I am not implying that Gurdjieff's ideas are not original, only that some of them can be profitably studied without having to accept some of their more questionable context.

2. Butkovsky-Hewitt, *With Gurdjieff in St. Petersburg and Paris,* p. 69.

3. Beryl Pogson, *Maurice Nicoll: A Portrait* (New York: Fourth Way Books, 1987), p. 102.

4. Thomas de Hartmann, *Our Life with Mr. Gurdjieff* (Middlesex, England: Penguin Books, 1972), p. 6.

5. Ibid., p. 46.

6. Ouspensky, *In Search of the Miraculous,* p. 118.

7. Ibid., p. 117.

8. Ibid., p. 119.

9. Ibid., p. 120.

Chapter 10. "I" and Ouspensky

1. Ouspensky, *In Search of the Miraculous,* p. 255.

2. Ibid., p. 149.

3. Ibid., p. 218.

4. Ibid., p. 144.

5. Ibid., p. 209.

6. Ibid., p. 227.

7. Ibid., p. 203.

8. Ibid., p. 222.

9. Ibid., p. 99.

10. Ibid., p. 204.

11. Ibid., p. 277.

12. Ibid., p. 228.

13. Ibid.

Chapter 11. The Miracle

1. Ouspensky, *A New Model of the Universe,* p. 285.

2. Although Ouspensky does not mention it, this could be a case of "sleep paralysis," the kind of dream he argues is caused by one's physiological state. Ouspensky wants to speak while he is asleep but cannot—a common dream experience. It is unclear in his account whether he was trying to reply to Gurdjieff mentally or vocally. If the former, it is unclear how his paralysis could prevent him from thinking a reply.

3. The necessity of this peculiar emotional state is why, in later years, Ouspensky was adamantly opposed to all attempts to study psychic phenomena scientifically, even when the investigators were believers in the reality of the paranormal. The work of J. B. Rhine, for example, came under severe criticism from Ouspensky for this reason. However, if Ouspensky had taken the trouble to study Rhine's work, instead of summarily dismissing it, he would have seen that Rhine's experiments actually proved him right. Rhine discovered that although initially subjects tested for, say, clairvoyance, showed a higher-than-chance average of correct answers, after a time their accuracy fell off, until it reached average or even below. Rhine discovered that a certain interest and enthusiasm were needed for the phenomena to appear. After hours of testing in dreary laboratory conditions, Rhine's subjects understandably grew bored and their performance suffered. Ouspensky was wrong to maintain that *all* psychic phenomena required the kinds of conditions he had experienced, but he was right that a strong emotional state was necessary for their appearance. He was also right to maintain that the standard scientific environment was the worst possible setting for the miraculous.

4. Years later, Gurdjieff would subject his "second lieutenant," A. R. Orage, to similar treatment, requesting that all the members of Orage's New York group sign an oath not to have anything to do with Orage. In a gesture of total self-effacement— or absurdist wit—Orage cheerfully signed it himself, saying he

would be happy not to have anything to do with Orage. Soon after, he, like Ouspensky, left Gurdjieff.

Chapter 12. Noah's Ark

1. De Hartmann, *Our Life with Mr. Gurdjieff*, p. 9.

2. Ibid., p. 11.

3. Ibid., p. 12.

4. Kasimir Malevich, Vladimir Mayakovsky, Anna Akhmatova, and others from The Stray Dog would come to grief under the new regime. Mayakovsky would commit suicide; Velimir Khlebnikov—who shared with Ouspensky a profound sense of time—would die of starvation; Malevich would sink into obscurity; and Akhmatova would be hounded throughout her career. Many others met similar fates, while some, like Nicolai Berdyaev, went into exile in the West.

5. Ouspensky, *Letters from Russia 1919*, p. 23.

Chapter 13. Super Efforts

1. As in the case of Ouspensky and Sophie, it's unclear whether Gurdjieff and Julia were actually married, although again like the Ouspenskys, she was always considered his wife. Her background is equally unclear; she is referred to both as a lady-in-waiting in the court of Nicholas II and as a prostitute. Although she was devoted to Gurdjieff, as he was to her, he is known to have had several mistresses. Regarding Ouspensky's relation with the formidable Sophie Grigorievna, Gurdjieff allegedly advised Ouspensky against a union. This was perhaps one time when Ouspensky should have heeded his master's suggestion.

2. It was at this point that Gurdjieff developed his ideas about the efficacy of physical work as a means of self-study. It strikes me that this method of compelling his students to clean house, cook, garden, and perform other domestic tasks could be effective only because they had never done these things before. More

than likely, Ouspensky had never cooked for himself—he would either eat out or have a cook. The same was true of the de Hartmanns. Certainly they never cleaned house, and Ouspensky, methodical and orderly in his writing, was known to live amidst disarray.

3. This exercise, or a variation of it, was taught during my time in the work. It was spoken of as "sensing" oneself, and, along with self-remembering, formed the foundation of everything else.

4. De Hartmann, *Our Life with Mr. Gurdjieff*, p. 19.

5. Ibid., p. 65.

6. Ouspensky, *In Search of the Miraculous*, p. 369.

7. Ouspensky, *Letters from Russia 1919*, p. 3.

8. Accounts of this and a second expedition can be found in Thomas and Olga de Hartmann's reports in *Our Life with Mr. Gurdjieff*. Space prevents me from going into detail about either of these adventures, but they are essential for a full understanding of Gurdjieff's "method."

9. Ouspensky, *In Search of the Miraculous*, p. 373.

10. In Gurdjieff's teaching, all processes follow a pattern, which, using musical symbolism, he describes as an "octave." The Law of Seven maintains that a process—whether in nature, a human activity, or a human life—from its beginning, "do," continues for a period, but then reaches an "interval," at which point a "shock" is needed in order for it to carry on to its end. If the requisite shock doesn't appear, the trajectory can be skewed, and it will begin to move in the opposite direction. Gurdjieff's system was aimed at providing a variety of shocks in order to help students complete their different "octaves."

Chapter 14. The Break

1. Ouspensky, *Letters from Russia 1919*, p. 1.

2. Ibid., pp. 2–3.

3. Ibid., p. 3

4. Ibid., p. 6.

5. Mrs. Beaumont later became Bennett's second wife; he abandoned his first wife and child in order to pursue his love of the East. Mrs. Beaumont was considerably older than Bennett, enough to have been his mother. Bennett, however, was not alone in preferring an older woman for a companion. Madame Ouspensky was four years older than her husband, and Rodney Collin, Ouspensky's most devoted student, also had a wife considerably older than himself.

6. J. G. Bennett, *Witness* (Tucson: Omen Press, 1974), p. 53.

7. Ibid., p. 55.

8. Ibid.

9. Ibid.

10. Claude Bragdon, *Merely Players* (New York: Alfred Knopf, 1929), p. 197. Indeed, in his account of this time in *In Search of the Miraculous*, Ouspensky makes no mention of either the success of *Tertium Organum* or his extreme good fortune in receiving the royalties and subsequent other benefits from the book's US and UK publication. He seems, in fact, to disown these to some extent—a sign that although he had escaped from Gurdjieff's immediate influence, the years of repeated acquaintance with his "nothingness" and bruising of his romantic "Peter" side had had a powerful effect.

Chapter 15. London Calling

1. David Garnett, *The Flowers of the Forest* (London: Chatto & Windus, 1955), p. 225.

2. Orage's Nietzschean and Theosophical ideas came together in a short but impressive book, *Consciousness: Animal, Human, Superhuman* (London: Theosophical Publishing House, 1907), originally a series of lectures given at the Leeds Theosophical Society. For a fuller account, see my chapter on Orage in *A Secret History of Consciousness*.

3. Butkovsky-Hewitt, *With Gurdjieff in St. Petersburg and Paris,* pp. 22–23. Having been to the same finishing school as Ouspensky—Gurdjieff's groups—it seems incredible that Anna is surprised at the change in her old flame. Ouspensky's new hard, authoritarian manner is undoubtedly the result of the buffeting he experienced at the hand of his master.

4. Colin Wilson, *The Strange Life of P. D. Ouspensky* (London: Aquarian Press, 1993), pp. 74–75.

5. Landau, *God Is My Adventure,* p. 172.

6. Garnett, *Flowers of the Forest,* p. 226.

7. Paul Selver, *Orage and the New Age Circle* (London: George Allen & Unwin, 1959), p. 72.

8. Stephen Graham, *Part of the Wonderful Scene* (London: Collins, 1964), pp. 252–53.

9. Algernon Blackwood, "Passport to the Next Dimension," *Prediction,* March 1948.

10. Graham, *Part of the Wonderful Scene,* p. 253.

11. For more on Blackwood, see my chapter on him in *The Dedalus Book of the Occult.* Like Ouspensky, Blackwood was fascinated with the mysteries of time; one friend with whom he discussed these matters was the aeronautical engineer J. W. Dunne, author of the very influential *Experiment with Time* (1927), in which Dunne gives an account of his precognitive dreams. Another popular author who would be influenced by Ouspensky, although they never met, was John Buchan, best known for *The Thirty-Nine Steps* (1915). Buchan's novel *The Gap in the Curtain* (1932) presents the first fictional depiction of Ouspensky in the form of Professor August Moe, a Scandinavian scientist who has developed a means of seeing the future. For much of the 1920s and 1930s in London, Ouspensky was a "mystery man" hovering in the background, his presence felt in a number of subtle ways.

12. Claude Bragdon, *The Secret Springs* (London: Andrew Dakers, 1938), p. 320.

13. Bland, *Extracts from Nine Letters,* p. 1.

14. Ibid., p. 5.

15. Ibid., p. 45.

16. Ibid., p. 24.

17. C. S. Nott, *Journey through This World* (London: Routledge & Kegan Paul, 1966), p. 38; Claude Bragdon, *The Secret Springs*, p. 327.

18. Bland, *Extracts from Nine Letters*, p. 54.

19. Bennett, *Witness*, p. 87.

Chapter 16. The Return of Mr. G.

1. For more on this strange affair, see Webb, *The Harmonious Circle*, p. 189.

2. G. I. Gurdjieff, *Life is Real Only Then, When I Am* (New York: Triangle Editions, 1975), p. 25.

3. Ouspensky, *In Search of the Miraculous*, p. 384.

4. Ouspensky's original title, *Fragments of an Unknown Teaching*, was scrapped when he discovered that his friend G. R. S. Mead had already published *Fragments of a Faith Forgotten*. In *A New Model of the Universe* he refers to the book as *Man and the World in Which He Lives—Fragments of an Unknown Teaching* (p. 270), a less than compelling title. Many work purists use *Fragments* when alluding to the book, but it's clear that Ouspensky's publisher did his estate and the book a favor by choosing the more gripping if sensational title—one, in any case, that Ouspensky had himself used for a series of articles during his *Wanderjahren*.

5. Ouspensky, *In Search of the Miraculous*, p. 385.

6. Bennett, *Witness*, p. 122.

7. Webb, *The Harmonious Circle*, p. 363.

Chapter 17. "He Could Go Mad"

1. Pogson, *Maurice Nicoll*, p. 95.

2. Kenneth Walker, *Venture with Ideas* (London: Jonathan Cape, 1951), pp. 24–26.

3. Ibid., p. 40.

4. Ibid., pp. 43–44.

5. Bennett, *Witness*, p. 126. Another possible reason, one that the discreet Ouspensky would not mention, is that he had discovered the truth about the rumors concerning Gurdjieff and his female students.

6. Ibid.

7. Margaret Anderson, *The Unknowable Gurdjieff* (New York: Weiser, 1970), pp. 83–84.

8. Mouravieff, *Ouspensky, Gurdjieff, and the Work*, pp. 11–12.

9. Ibid., p. 16.

10. Bennett, *Witness*, p. 111.

11. Thomas de Hartmann tells another story. At one point he asked Gurdjieff if he had to place complete confidence in him and fulfill unquestioningly all he advised him to do. Gurdjieff replied, "Certainly, on the whole it is so. But if I begin to teach you masturbation, will you listen to me?" (*Our Life with Mr. Gurdjieff*, p. 66). This raises the question of the "double-bind" students find themselves in regarding the dictums of their teacher. By definition the teacher is above the level of the student, and so the student is in no position to judge the teacher's actions. Yet if one is not to be a "round idiot," one is supposed to use common sense and think for oneself, something Gurdjieff warned was a sure road to disaster. If you don't do this you are an idiot; if you do, you exhibit self-will. It's a no-win situation. And if the answer is that the student is supposed to outgrow the need for the teacher, then why, in several instances, does the teacher urge the student to depend on him? It seems the best way to obey your teacher is to disobey him—which suggests that those who rejected Gurdjieff were several steps ahead of the game.

12. Mouravieff, *Ouspensky, Gurdjieff, and the Work*, pp. 20–21.

13. Aside from *Meetings with Remarkable Men,* all of Gurdjieff's writings pose severe obstacles for the reader. The outrageous claims, the jaw-breaking neologisms, and boa-constrictor syntax are enough to put off the average person, and even the most dedicated seekers have a difficult time discovering what Gurdjieff is trying to say, let alone understanding it. No work presents these hurdles more relentlessly than *Beelzebub's Tales to His Grandson,* a 1200-page science-fiction epic made up of the conversation between Beelzebub (one of the names, we remember, of the Devil) and his grandson as they hurtle through the cosmos in the spaceship Karnak. Here Gurdjieff opines freely and at length on everything from the creation of the universe to feminism. Responses to this situation differ widely. Orage remarked that Gurdjieff's writings demand to be read "from the real heart" and that in them he found "a parallel with the Bible." Bennett claimed to have read *Beelzebub's Tales* dozens of times. Claude Bragdon commented that reading Gurdjieff's prose was like "bumping over cobblestones," and Rom Landau remarked that "It gave you in many instances the impression of the work of a man who was no longer sane."

Followers argue that the difficulties are intentional, another example of Gurdjieff not making anything easy for his students. Others remark that he was simply an atrocious writer, while still others, like the psychologist Anthony Storr, suggest that Gurdjieff's prose style displays a tendency towards "schizotypy." While not schizophrenic, schizotypic people display certain behaviors and characteristics associated with the mental disorder. One of these is a penchant for neologism—inventing new words—something Gurdjieff seems quite fond of. Another is a pompous, bombastic style—again a quality familiar to Gurdjieff's readers. Another is a detached, affectless demeanor and a tendency toward megalomania. Gurdjieff's remark to C. S. Nott about his working to achieve a condition in which "nothing from outside could touch [him] internally" suggests the first, while, to give only one example, Gurdjieff's fantastic claims about future projects found in *Herald of Coming Good* suggest the second.

Gurdjieff, of course, is not alone in displaying these traits; anyone of an artistic, poetic, or introverted bent is prone to display some level of schizotypy; but coupled with some of his more outrageous actions, it is difficult for the question of his sanity—for sake of a better word—not to arise. A catalog of Gurdjieff's "crazy" behavior would require a book, but a few instances do reveal, if nothing more, a clear predilection for the bizarre. After his mother's death in 1925, Gurdjieff erected a gravestone that read "Here lies the mother of one who sees himself forced by her death to write the book Les Opiumistes." She was well over eighty and her death was no shock, while the book was never written. Two telegrams sent to Orage in 1930 were signed "Grandson and Unique phenomenal Grandmother" and "Ambassador from Hell." In Paris in 1944, at the death bed of the novelist Luc Dietrich, Gurdjieff produced two oranges and informed him that this was the most important day of his life. The announcement for *Herald of Coming Good* read "First Appeal to Contemporary Humanity" and was priced "From 8 to 108 French Francs." The book was ill-received and was quickly withdrawn and repudiated.

All this, of course, can be understood as part of Gurdjieff's unique method, his "crazy guru" style. But perhaps living in France—for many years in Paris—rubbed off: Gurdjieff was aware of the surrealist climate and so made use of it. Yet, to this writer at least, too many of these explanations are as far-fetched as what they want to explain. I, for one, can make no sense of several of Gurdjieff's remarks, which strike me as in-jokes couched in an exceedingly private language, another schizotypic habit. But then, like Ouspensky, I would no doubt have been exasperated by Gurdjieff's "acting." Added to his often arbitrary behavior, his sudden mood swings from ferocious rage to solicitous concern, and his seeming need to dominate others and unwillingness to accept them on their own terms, his writings suggest, to me at least, a personality radically *unlike* most people's. This, of course, is what attracted many people to him.

Chapter 18. "The System Is Waiting for Workers"

1. Bennett, *Witness*, p. 129.

2. Walker, *Venture with Ideas*, p. 90.

3. Merrily Taylor, ed., *Remembering Peter Demianovich Ouspensky*, Commemorative Brochure (New Haven, Conn.: Yale University Library, 1978).

4. Bennett, *Witness*, p. 154

5. Walker, *Venture with Ideas*, p. 104.

6. Irmis B. Popoff, *Gurdjieff: His Work on Myself with Others for the Work* (Wellingborough, England: Aquarian Press, 1978), pp. 110, 108.

7. Walker, *Venture with Ideas*, p. 106.

8. Taylor, *Remembering Peter Demianovich Ouspensky*, p. 38.

9. Bennett, *Witness*, p. 159.

10. Ibid., p. 163.

11. Landau, *God Is My Adventure*, p. 166.

12. Ibid., p. 174.

13. Ibid., p. 198.

14. Nott, *Journey through This World*, p. 96.

Chapter 19. Nirvana and Strawberry Jam

1. Nott, *Journey through This World*, p. 97.

2. Ibid., p. 98.

3. Ibid., p. 106.

4. Ibid., p. 107.

5. Bennett, *Witness*, p. 176.

6. Robert S. de Ropp, *Warrior's Way* (London: George Allen and Unwin, 1980), p. 99.

7. Taylor, *Remembering Peter Demianovich Ouspensky*, p. 37.

8. De Ropp, *Warrior's Way*, p. 101.

9. Ibid., p. 104.

10. Ibid., p. 109.

11. Ibid., p. 168.

Chapter 20. The Journey to the West

1. De Ropp, *Warrior's Way*, p. 139.

2. Ibid., p. 151.

3. Ibid., p. 152.

4. Bennett, *Witness*, pp. 178–79.

5. Ouspensky, *A New Model of the Universe*, p. 30.

6. Nott, *Journey through This World*, p. 160.

7. Ibid.

8. Ibid.

9. Popoff, *Gurdjieff: His Work on Myself with Others for the Work*, p. 29.

10. Walker, *Venture with Ideas*, p. 115.

11. Popoff, *Gurdjieff: His Work on Myself with Others for the Work*, p. 35.

12. Ibid.

13. Bennett, *Witness*, p. 258.

14. Marie Seton, "The Case of P. D. Ouspensky," *Quest* no. 34, 1962, Bombay, India.

15. Nott, *Journey through This World*, p. 110.

16. De Ropp, *Warrior's Way*, p. 170.

17. Ibid., p. 171.

18. Ibid.

19. Ibid., p. 173.

Chapter 21. The End of the System

1. Popoff, *Gurdjieff: His Work on Myself with Others for the Work*, p. 107.

2. Ibid.

3. Ibid., p. 62.

4. Ibid., p. 111.

5. Ibid., p. 116.

6. Ouspensky, *A New Model of the Universe*, p. 341.

7. Walker, *Venture with Ideas*, p. 128.

8. For a full transcript of these last extraordinary meetings, see P. D. Ouspensky, *A Record of Meetings* (London: Arkana, 1992), pp. 585–642.

9. Rodney Collin, *The Theory of Conscious Harmony* (London: Watkins, 1958), p. 53.

10. Ibid., p. 179.

11. Ibid., p. 39.

12. Ibid., p. 6

13. Ibid., p. 28.

14. Ibid., p. 53.

15. Ibid., p. 157.

16. Ibid., p. 47.

17. Ibid., p. 152.

18. Ibid., p. 64.

19. See Joyce Collin-Smith's letter regarding my article on Ouspensky's biographer James Webb in *Fortean Times* no. 152, September 2001.

20. Collin, *Theory of Conscious Harmony*, p. 152.

21. For much of the material in this section I am indebted to James Webb's chapter on Ouspensky's last days in his masterful *The Harmonious Circle*, pp. 439–60.

22. Taylor, *Remembering Peter Demianovich Ouspensky*, p. 32.

23. Rodney Collin, *The Theory of Eternal Life* (Boulder: Shambhala, 1984), p. 116.

24. Collin, *The Theory of Conscious Harmony*, p. 91.

25. Ibid., p. 176.

Epilogue

1. Walker, *Venture with Ideas*, p. 132.
2. Bennett, *Witness*, p. 219.
3. Ibid., p. 252.
4. Webb, *The Harmonious Circle*, p. 435.

INDEX